Lincoln's Political Ambitions, Slavery, and the Bible

Lincoln's Political Ambitions, Slavery, and the Bible

Edwin D. Freed

PICKWICK *Publications* · Eugene, Oregon

LINCOLN'S POLITICAL AMBITIONS, SLAVERY, AND THE BIBLE

Pickwick Publications
An Imprint of Wipf and Stock Publishers
199 W. 8th Ave., Suite 3
Eugene, OR 97401

www.wipfandstock.com

ISBN 13: 978-1-61097-933-7

Cataloging-in-Publication data:

Freed, Edwin D.

Lincoln's political ambitions, slavery, and the Bible / Edwin D. Freed.

xiv + 190 p. ; 23 cm. — Includes bibliographical references.

ISBN 13: 978-1-61097-933-7

1. Lincoln, Abraham, 1809–1865. 2. Slavery—Emancipation—United States—History—19th century. 3. Bible—Use—History. I. Title.

E456 F74 2012

Manufactured in the U.S.A.

For Ann and Jane

Contents

Acknowledgments

Y EARS AGO WHEN I mentioned to Gabor Boritt, a colleague at Gettysburg College and renowned Civil War historian, that I would like to write a book on Abraham Lincoln and the Bible, both lifelong interests of mine, he warmly encouraged me. He gave me some bibliographical references, which became the basis of a small Lincoln library. However, after I moved to Ohio, and because of his serious illnesses, I discontinued my communications with him, but I remain grateful for his encouragement.

Thanks to members of library staffs, some of whom wanted to remain anonymous, of several institutions who were always prompt and cordial in assisting me. They are The College of Wooster; Oberlin College; Wayne County Public Library; Weidner Library of Harvard; Ashland University; Allegheny College, especially Jane Westerfelt; and Kent State University, especially Cynthia Barton, for providing microfiche from an Ostervald Bible.

Special thanks to Cindy VanHorn of the Lincoln Museum, Fort Wayne, Indiana, for reproductions of pages from the Lincoln Family Bible and other materials. Thanks to Jennifer Jones and Debbie Davendonis of the Abraham Lincoln Birthplace National Park, Hodgenville, Kentucky, for information on the Lincoln Family Bible. It was not there when we visited the site because it was being treated elsewhere for further preservation. And thanks to park personnel for information about Christopher Bush, father of Sarah Bush. Many thanks to Daniel W. Stowell, Director and Editor, Papers of Abraham Lincoln, Abraham Lincoln Presidential Library and Museum, Springfield, Ohio, for graciously responding to my queries.

Hearty thanks to my editor K. C. Hanson and to all others who have helped in any way in the process of transforming my manuscript into a book.

Special thanks to Clark Evans and other staff members of the Library of Congress for information about Lincoln Bibles there.

To my friend Donald Karaiskos, who has a commendable knowledge of American history and of the Bible, I express great appreciation for reading the manuscript and for insightful comments.

I am most grateful to our daughter Jane F. Roberts for help whenever needed, especially in formatting the manuscript for the publisher, and to my wife Ann, who read the manuscript several times, corrected errors, and made helpful suggestions. To them I affectionately dedicate this unique volume.

Preface

SCHOLARS HAVE PUBLISHED MYRIADS of books and articles on numerous subjects concerning Abraham Lincoln, and many include something about his use of the Bible. Such works often begin with Lincoln's humble origins and his learning to read the Bible as a youth and how it influenced his life, faith, and religion. This book is not simply another volume on Lincoln's use of the Bible. In contrast to previous works, it discusses this topic more thoroughly and provides a clearer insight into probable fact rather than popular lore. With my professional background, having earned a PhD from Harvard University in Classics in the special field of biblical studies, having taught that discipline for thirty-six years at Gettysburg College, and having had a lifelong interest in Lincoln, I offer a unique approach to this field of study.

The primary sources for this contribution to Lincoln studies are his own communications and speeches. Specifically, I used *The Collected Works of Abraham Lincoln*, edited by Roy P. Basler and others, which I cite by volume and page numbers (5:65; 6:10–14). Although there are more than 8,000 unclassified documents in the Abraham Lincoln Presidential Library and Museum in Springfield, Illinois, Daniel W. Stowell, Director and Editor of the Papers of Abraham Lincoln, has informed me that they would likely not be useful for this study.

In continuing this project, I came to realize that much of what has been written about Lincoln and the Bible is actually myth. According to Webster, myth is "a popular belief or tradition that has grown up around someone, especially one embodying the ideals and institutions of a society or segment of society." By critically studying *what Lincoln wrote*, instead of concentrating on *what has been written about him*, my conclusions contradict the popular lore that Lincoln relied heavily on, and was significantly influenced by, his knowledge of the Bible. Lincoln's use of the Bible is paradoxical in that his language is replete with biblical vocabulary, but his knowledge is superficial. He did not reveal profound insight, nor did he always carefully quote every passage, contrary to popular beliefs.

The prevalent thinking of scholars is that Lincoln used the so-called Lincoln Family Bible and was seen reading it in the White House. It is more likely that it never got to Washington. I will suggest what Bible he probably read and why and how he really used it.

The book's central thesis is that, along with the Declaration of Independence and the U.S. Constitution, Lincoln used the Bible to win voters to help him achieve his political ambitions, to defend his positions on political issues before and during his presidency, and eventually also to support the emancipation of slaves.

In Lincoln's first political document, Communication to the People of Sangamon County, Illinois, March 9, 1832, he announces his candidacy for county representative in the next General Assembly in the state of Illinois. He also mentions the Bible—scriptures—for the first time. In a society in which more people were becoming familiar with the Bible, Lincoln aptly used it to help him achieve his political ambitions, not to promote biblical faith or religion. In fact, after his election as president, he used the Bible less frequently. In the course of events, motivated by his devotion to the Declaration of Independence and the Constitution and his conscientious effort to abide by the oath taken when he became president, Lincoln gradually changed his attitude toward slavery and concluded that it had to be eliminated and the Union preserved. After being reelected, Lincoln used the Bible in his Second Inaugural Address to further his compelling ambitions, particularly the reconciliation among the states and the restoration of the Union.

After a thorough study of the documents in the first two volumes of Basler's work and other documents in which Lincoln mentions the word Bible, I realized that they and several additional speeches, which may or may not contain biblical references, were sufficient to confirm the thesis of this book. The other documents are the Cooper Union Address, because it enlightens our understanding of his use of the Bible elsewhere; the Gettysburg Address, because it is the most widely known of all his speeches; Reply to Loyal Colored People of Baltimore, because it is overemphasized in support of Lincoln's personal faith and of his use of the Bible; and the second Inaugural Address, because it is regarded as his greatest speech. Additional documents are also considered as they relate to points under discussion. In appendices I deal with several subjects related to our study and present evidence to show that, among other things, the tradition about

Lincoln's regular church attendance and his friendship with the Reverends Smith and Gurley cannot be substantiated.

It also did not take long for me to realize that a lifetime of research would not be long enough to consider all of the works that include something about Lincoln and the Bible, so I limited my study to a number of books on the subject, beginning with those by Sandburg (1926) and ending with that by O. V. Burton (2007). In the bibliography I include numerous other works as a start for anyone who may be interested in continuing this study further. In general, Lincoln scholars accept too many myths about Lincoln and the Bible as facts. By carefully studying *what Lincoln wrote*, I determined that we cannot be sure how he learned to read the Bible, but we do know what Bible he probably read and how he used it.

Some scholars may object to the fact that support for some of my arguments about Lincoln's use of the Bible is based on Lincoln's silence. However, the value of silence for insightful study has long been recognized. The Greek epigrammatic poet Palladas of Alexandria (fourth century AD) said: "Silence is man's chief learning" (*Greek Anthology,* 1:16). Silence is one of the hardest arguments to refute, and it is at least as valid as arguments based primarily on lore that is likely to be fallible from the start.

For the convenience of readers, I cite references in the *The Collected Works of Abraham Lincoln* (hereinafter referred to as *CW*) within the text and books listed in the bibliography by author and page numbers within parentheses. For authors of more than one book, I also include an abbreviated title. Unless stated otherwise, all translations of biblical texts are from the King James Version (KJV, 1611), the one Lincoln used.

1

Getting Back to Lincoln and the Bible

PRIMARY AND SECONDARY SOURCES

BIOGRAPHERS OF THE EARLIEST "lives" of Lincoln often relied primarily on secondary sources that include legends, myths, even fantasies. Although their books may be interesting reading, they were generally based on recollections and reminiscences, whose sources were often fallible, incomplete, inaccurate, and contradictory. Enhanced by admiration for Lincoln, sympathies, convictions, interests, concerns, and even biases of his biographers altered their information in transmission. Some of the things they wrote may be historical, but it is not always easy to distinguish between fact and fantasy.

Early "biographies" and "lives" of Lincoln are often more like eulogies than historical biographies. This is true for the booklet, *The Life of Abraham Lincoln*, published already in 1866 by Josiah Gilbert Holland, writer for the *Springfield Republican*, Springfield, Massachusetts, who portrays Lincoln as the Christian Gentleman. The authors of two books dealing specifically with Lincoln and the Bible stress his dependency on it throughout his career. This is especially true of Samuel Trevena Jackson's *Lincoln's Use of the Bible* (1909), a booklet of thirty pages that is more like a devotional than a biography. This quotation defines it:

> In a log cabin at Nolin's Creek, Hardin County, Kentucky, the boy breathed the first breath of life. Hope's anchor living on a slender string, if we are to measure by the child's home surroundings. But his birthplace possessed a soul; for a home with a good book in it has a soul. This book was the Bible. It mastered his manners, molded his mind, made mighty his manhood, and gave to America the matchless man. In the Bible he found the truth for the ills of men, the secret for the solution of life's perplexing problems,

the boon for the best beaten path, the succor for the suffering, the calmest comforts for the dying, and the faithful friend when foes are near and other friends so far away. (5–6)

The same emphasis, though to a lesser degree, is expressed in Clarence Edward Macartney's little volume, *Lincoln and the Bible* (1949). Scholars often repeat much of the same lore, expressed in modern terms, and that also makes our study more difficult.

LINCOLN AND HIS DOCUMENTS

Although the editors of the *CW* edited the documents, their work does not make the words of Lincoln dubious to a forbidding degree. They have also "tried to work entirely from original manuscripts or photostatic copies of originals . . . in not a few cases facsimiles have been relied upon in the absence of the original." Moreover, the editors "have verified the fact that words have been changed or omitted in numerous facsimiles which have been widely distributed in past years" (1:xi). These observations should caution us about always taking words attributed to Lincoln as invariably his.

In addition to original manuscripts of Lincoln's documents, the editors have included contemporary newspaper accounts when public records were not available. Since most of Lincoln's words from the Bible occur in newspapers, would editors always report what Lincoln said literally without either negative or positive bias with respect to religion or politics?

White (*Greatest Speech*, 70) claims that "Lincoln routinely checked on the transcripts of his speeches, though not to embellish them. His intent in checking a reporter's version was to be sure that the speech was printed precisely the way he had spoken it." However, there is little evidence to support White's view. Lincoln did supervise the preparation of the pamphlet on his address before the Cooper Union on February 27, 1860 (3:522–50), but he did not supervise "the printing of the speech from his manuscript in the New York *Tribune*, February 28, 1860, or in the issues of the *Tribune Tracts* No. 4 which followed" (3:522 n. 1). Lincoln's correspondence with Charles C. Nott, a gifted writer who contributed notes to the Cooper Union speech, confirms Lincoln's supervision of Nott's publication. Lincoln writes: "Of course I would not object to, but would be pleased rather, with a more perfect edition of that speech," and he gives numerous suggestion and improvements and asks to see the proofs if Nott intends to publish a new edition (4:58–59). But, after he received the proofs, Lincoln says that he has "touched them only very lightly," and he has not attempted to compare Nott's notes "with originals, leaving that entirely to you" (4:113).

On June 23, 1858 (2:471), Lincoln wrote to John L. Scripps, editor of the Chicago *Daily Democratic Press,* about the reporting of his "late speech" (presumably the House Divided speech at Springfield, June 16, 1858). Lincoln says that he was "much flattered by the estimate" Scripps put on his speech, but he then adds: "and yet I am much mortified that any part of it should be construed so differently from anything intended by me" (2:471).

Boritt (*Gospel,* 265–72) has shown how words Lincoln spoke in his Gettysburg Address, November 19, 1863 (7:23), were altered in newspaper reports. Here are some examples. "Four score and seven years ago" became "Four score and ten years ago" in the *Chicago Times* and "Ninety years ago" in the *Centralia Sentinel* (Illinois). "Our fathers brought forth, on this continent" became "Our fathers formed a Government" in the *Centralia Sentinel* and "Our fathers established upon this continent" in the *Cincinnati Daily Gazette.* "The world will little note" became "The world will little know" in *The Philadelphia Inquirer,* "The world will little heed" in the *Chicago Times,* and "The world would" in the *Centralia Sentinel* (Illinois).

LINCOLN'S BIBLES

There is universal agreement that the Lincoln Family Bible was the KJV. However, evidence presented here shows that the traditional family Bible was not the one Lincoln used. We also consider three Bibles that were given to him.

Lincoln Family Bible

One of Lincoln's Bibles is given various titles, including "the Thomas Lincoln family Bible" (1:304 n. 1) and "Lincoln's Mother's Bible,"[1] which is usually referred to as the Family Bible. Now on display in the Visitor Center at Abraham Lincoln Birthplace National Historic Site, National Park Service, near Hodgenville, Kentucky, it is sealed in a vacuum show case and may no longer be removed. According to Park Service person-

nel, "The Bible is in Fair Condition, recent conservation work has stabi-
lized the binding, repaired some of the pages, and treated some of the
damage caused by water and mold over the years . . . the cover is made of
leather. The dimensions are 9.6 (L), 6.25 (W), 3.5 (D) all in inches."[2] The
Apocrypha are included between the Old and New Testaments.

According to the Park Service, "The Lincoln Family Bible was in
the possession of the Johnston family, stepchildren of Thomas Lincoln,
until 1893, when it was purchased for exhibition at the Chicago World's
Fair. Several years later the Bible was sold to a private collector of Lincoln
memorabilia. On August 30, 1926, the United States Government purchased the private collection, which included the Lincoln Family Bible."[3]

We may properly call the Bible mentioned The Lincoln Family Bible
because it was saved by the Johnston family and the words Abraham and
Lincoln are on the inside cover. Abraham is written about an inch above
the Lincoln. The two words are written with different pens and in different hands. Before the Abraham there is what appears to be an "e" written
with the same pen as the Lincoln. It may be the last letter of "Abe," the way
he was known among his early friends, so it would have been natural for
him to write "Abe Lincoln." The Abraham was written at another time by
a different person with a different pen.[4]

Lincoln made some entries in the Family Bible, perhaps in 1851
(2:94–95). If he visited his stepmother in 1851, after the death of his
father (Coleman, *Abraham Lincoln*, 133), he probably made the entries
then. Coleman also says that President-elect Lincoln went to visit his
stepmother Sarah Bush Johnston in Coles County, Illinois, on January
31, 1861. According to tradition, the visit lasted most of a day and was a
cordial and emotional one. The Family Bible was still in her possession
at both those times. Who would imagine that Lincoln took it from his
dear stepmother on the latter visit so that he could take it with him to
Washington? The lore about Lincoln being seen reading from that Bible
in the White House is just that—lore.

Because the name of Ostervald and the city of his residence,
Neufchatel, Switzerland, occur on the title page of the Family Bible, it is
also known as the Ostervald Bible and the Neufchatel Bible. The biblical text is a revised translation of the Geneva Bible into French in 1724
by the Reverend J. F. Ostervald (1663–1747), a distinguished Professor
of Divinity and a minister of the Swiss Reform Church in Neufchatel,
Switzerland. After a comparison of many passages in the Geneva Bible, the

Ostervald Bible, and the KJV, I concluded that the revisions of Ostervald pertain mostly to the copious notes, as the statement on the title page implies. The translation is almost entirely that of the KJV of 1611.

Abraham Lincoln's Bible

A Bible given this name in 1:304 is in the Library of Congress, Washington, D. C.[5] On the title page it is called *The Comprehensive Bible*, first published in London in 1826. Entries in it begin with November 4, 1842. It is the KJV and, conceivably, it could be a Bible Lincoln sometimes used, but it would have to be a London edition because the American edition was not printed until 1847, the year Lincoln first went to Washington as a congressman. However, the Bible discussed next may be the one he used most often and which could more appropriately be called "Lincoln's Bible."

Oxford Bible Given by Lucy Speed

On the back of a photograph Lincoln gave to Mrs. Lucy G. Speed, October 3, 1861 (4:546), mother of Joshua F. Speed, Lincoln's good friend, he wrote: "For Mrs. Lucy G. Speed, from whose pious hand I accepted the present of an Oxford Bible twenty years ago. A. Lincoln." Lincoln had visited Joshua Speed's family in Kentucky in August and September 1841, during his period of depression after he broke off his engagement to Mary Todd in January 1841. Lincoln refers to the Bible Mrs. Speed gave him when he wrote to Mary Speed, half sister of Joshua Speed, on September 27, 1841 (1:259–61): "Tell your mother that I have not got her 'present' with me; but I intend to read it regularly when I return home" (1:261). Lincoln's words that he would read it regularly imply that he was not in the habit of reading a Bible, perhaps because he did not own one. Why would Mrs. Speed give him a Bible if he already had one?

Lucy's Oxford Bible may have been one published in 1838, of which I have a copy, or in 1839. It is plausible that the Bible Lincoln used was a copy of either one. Is it not plausible also to think that by 1841 Lucy Speed had just gotten a copy of one of the editions mentioned and presented it to Lincoln? Copies of those Bibles are in some libraries and in the hands of some dealers in second-hand books, so they were not among the rarest books in the time of Lincoln.

Bible Used at Lincoln's First Inaugural

At the first inauguration of Lincoln on March 4, 1861, the Bible used for the ceremony was an 1853 edition of the Oxford Bible. Its dimensions are 5-3/4 inches long, 3-3/4 inches wide, and 1-3/5 inches thick. With a velvet cover that is somewhat worn, it is in the Rare Book and Special Collections Division of the Library of Congress, to which it was donated either by the Robert Todd Lincoln family or the Johnston family about 1937.[6] How it happened that an Oxford Bible was used at the inauguration ceremony is not known, and it is also not known what happened to the Bible Lucy Speed gave Lincoln. But is it not possible that one of those Bibles was the one he may have been seen reading in the White House? Since there is no substantive evidence that the Lincoln Family Bible ever got to Washington, the notion that it was not used at the first inauguration because it was still in luggage that had not yet arrived in time for the ceremony is mere imagination.

HOW AND WHEN LINCOLN ACQUIRED HIS KNOWLEDGE OF THE BIBLE

Lincoln scholars continue to echo the all-embracing statement of Sandburg in 1925, in whole or in part: "Lincoln read the Bible closely, knew it from cover to cover, was familiar with its stories and its poetry, quoted from it in his talks to juries, in political campaigns, in his speeches, and in his letters" (*Prairie Years*, 1:415).

As late as 2007, the tradition that Lincoln learned his Bible early has been transmitted by Burton (114): "From an early age Lincoln knew his Bible and later deployed biblical lessons in the stories he told and the speeches he gave." If the first part of that sentence is true, Lincoln must have learned it from either of his mothers or in school. What follows reflects on the statements of Sandburg, Burton, and others.

From His Mothers

According to Benjamin Thomas (6) and others, whenever Nancy Hanks Lincoln "signed a legal document she made her mark." She died on October 5, 1818, when Lincoln was not yet ten years old. If she was illiterate, as is most likely, all the traditions about Lincoln learning about the Bible from his mother are not true. Lincoln's father Thomas was barely literate, if at all, so it is unlikely that Lincoln learned to read from his family.

There is no evidence in the *CW*, nor does Wolf give any, to support his statements (35–36): "Lincoln is said to have told a friend, 'My mother was a ready reader and read the Bible to me habitually.'" Wolf does say, though: "Some Lincoln scholars maintain, however, that Nancy Hanks was illiterate." But Wolf continues: "He learned by heart some of the biblical texts which his mother sang as she worked at chores in the cabin. One of the campaign biographies [unknown to me] for which Lincoln furnished material describes mother, son, and daughter taking turns reading the Scriptures on the Sabbath." And Wolf assumes that the "Scriptures" were "the battered old Bible from which Lincoln was seen reading in the White House." Lincoln does not mention the scriptures, the Sabbath, or the Bible in any of his autobiographies in the *CW*. Wolf's words "Lincoln is said to have told" are hardly a good basis for historical fact.

A repeated tradition is that Dennis Hanks, Lincoln's cousin and boyhood companion, said "a family Bible was not purchased until 1819, when Abraham was ten years old" (Trueblood, 50–51, from Sandburg), perhaps because the family was too poor. According to one tradition, Sarah Bush Lincoln brought some books, including her family Bible, with her when she moved in with the Thomas Lincoln family in early December 1819. Perhaps this was the Bible Hanks had in mind. According to Donald (30 and notes, 605), quoting from Mrs. Thomas Lincoln saying to William H. Herndon, Sept. 8, 1865: "Abraham read it [her family Bible] at times . . . 'though not as much as said: he preferred more congenial books—suitable for his age.'" Mrs. Lincoln says nothing about her teaching him to read it or any of the other books suitable for his age, perhaps some she brought with her. We should compare her modest statements with the self-glorifying words of Dennis Hanks about teaching Lincoln to write discussed below.

The statement "though not as much as said" indicates that already in only five months after Lincoln's death his reading of the Bible was exaggerated. Mrs. Lincoln's words also indicate that the Bible was not the only book in the Lincoln household and that Lincoln had not mastered it as a youth. The quoted words also anticipate evidence from our study that Lincoln displays more in-depth knowledge of Euclid and Shakespeare than of the Bible, and that when he had a choice between Shakespeare and the Bible, he chose Shakespeare (all discussed later).

According to Donald (33), Lincoln was fourteen years old when his father and step-mother joined the Pigeon Baptist Church. His stepmother is to have said: "Abe had no particular religion—didn't think of these question[s] at that time, if he ever did. That difference appears to have led to the sharpest words he ever received from his father." According to his stepmother, Lincoln would hear the sermons and then sometimes parody the preacher's words. Lincoln's actions offended his father and, "'as one of the children recalled,' would come and make him quit—send him to work" (Donald, 33 and notes, 605–6). Such things, if true, would only intensify Lincoln's dislike for his father and would not be conducive to his acquiring an in-depth knowledge of the Bible at a young age.

Donald suggests, "Possibly young Lincoln knew how to read a little before he entered Crawford's school" (28–30 and notes, 605). And Donald accepts the tradition that Dennis Hanks taught Lincoln to write: "I taught Abe to write with a buzzards [sic] quill which I killed with a rifle and having made a pen—put Abe's hand in mind [sic] and moving his fingers by my hand to give him the idea of how to write." Donald also says that Sarah Bush Lincoln was illiterate. If true, it seems unlikely that she could be a critical judge of Lincoln's reading: "He must understand every thing—even to the smallest thing—minutely and exactly," fancy words for an illiterate person. However, if Sarah Bush Lincoln was illiterate, why, then, were there a number of books in her household that she took with her to the Lincoln home?

There *may be* an answer to that question. According to the National Park Service (see note 2), Sarah Bush was part of a flourishing family whose father, Christopher Bush, was "an industrious man." Perhaps he or someone else in the family had gone to school and learned to read. If so, that would explain why Sarah Bush Lincoln took some books with her to the Lincoln household.

When reading what Dennis Hanks and other family members are to "have said," we must remember that Dennis Hanks "was only marginally literate himself" (Donald, 28), as is clear from his language, including grammar and spelling. Moreover, Hanks spoke as early as June 13, 1865, only two months after Lincoln died, hardly enough time for a man of his ability to speak with careful forethought. Quickly thinking, Hanks became more interested in self-glorification than in historical truth.

In School

Our knowledge of exactly what Lincoln learned about the Bible in school is as uncertain as some other aspects of his young life. According to a tradition handed on by Trueblood (50) and others, Lincoln is to have said to Senator John B. Henderson that in school: "We had no reading books or grammars, and all our reading was done from the Bible." In his autobiography for John L. Scripps, Lincoln wrote that he attended schools other than Crawford's, but he gives no information about learning to read the Bible there. In the same autobiography, Lincoln also wrote that he "studied and nearly mastered the Six-books of Euclid, since he was a member of Congress" (4:62). Does Lincoln's "since he was a member of Congress" (1846–1849) mean from the time he went to Congress or after he finished his term? At any rate, he was an adult before he studied Euclid. Herndon reports that "On the circuit . . . he studied Euclid until he could with ease demonstrate all the propositions in the six books" (Wilson and Davis, 194).

Perhaps some observations will provide insight into our present discussion and throw light on the discussion in the chapters that follow. If the things mentioned about Lincoln's learning to know the Bible at an early age are true, it is surprising that he says nothing on the subject in his autobiographies in the *CW*, especially since he talks about his lack of formal education. On about June 15?, 1858 (2:459), Lincoln wrote an autobiography of seven lines, for inclusion in the *Dictionary of Congress*, 1859. The second line is "Education defective."

Lincoln also prepared an autobiography for Jesse W. Fell, December 20, 1859 (3:511–12). Fell was a friend and newspaper man who supported Lincoln's campaign for the presidency. In his cover letter to Fell, Lincoln calls it "a little sketch. . . . There is not much of it, for the reason, I suppose, that there is not much of me. . . . If anything be made out of it, I wish it to be modest." Of his mother he says only that she "was of a family of the name of Hanks." Of his time in Indiana where he grew up, Lincoln writes:

> It was a wild region, with many bears and other wild animals still in the woods. . . . There were some schools, so called; but no qualification was ever required of a teacher, beyond 'readin, written, and cipherin, to the Rule of Three. If a straggler supposed to understand latin [*sic*], happened to sojourn in the neighborhood, he was looked upon as a wizard." Lincoln continues: "There was absolutely nothing to excite ambition for education. Of course

> when I came of age I did not know much. Still somehow, I could read, write, and cipher to the Rule of Three; but that was all. I have not been to school since. The little advance I now have upon this store of education, I have picked up from time to time under the pressure of necessity. (3:511)

Perhaps Lincoln was just being modest, but if the Bible was his main reading, we should think he might have mentioned it, especially since he used language from it during his campaigns.

After Lincoln was nominated for president at the Republican Convention on May 18, 1860, he composed a much longer autobiography (4:60–67) for John L. Scripps, of the *Chicago Press and Tribune*, who had requested it. Concerning his education, Lincoln wrote: "What he has in the way of education, he has picked up. After he was twentythree [*sic*], and had separated from his father, he studied English grammar, imperfectly of course, but so as to speak and write as well as he now does . . . He regrets his want of education, and does what he can to supply the want" (4:62).

In none of the autobiographies does Lincoln even hint that he read or knew the Bible well. That he was very familiar with the language of the KJV is not disputable. However, evidence that follows indicates that his knowledge of the Bible was not deep, extensive, or profound and that he was not careful to quote every word exactly.

DEPTH OF LINCOLN'S KNOWLEDGE OF THE BIBLE

Traditions related to those of Lincoln's learning to read the Bible are those about the depth of his knowledge of it and its tremendous effect on him. White (*Greatest Speech*, 110 and 218 n. 21) accepts the tradition that "Lincoln 'fixed in his memory' whole chapters from the New Testament . . . from Isaiah and the Psalms. A favorite Lincoln practice was to 'correct a mis-quotation of Scripture,' quickly responding with 'the chapter and verse where it could be found.'"

According to another bit of lore, after Lincoln wrote a will that was witnessed and signed for a dying woman, "she asked him to read a few verses out of the Bible. A copy of the Scriptures was produced, but Lincoln did not open it. Instead, he recited from memory the Twenty-third Psalm and the opening verses of the fifteenth chapter of John" (Trueblood, 50–51; from Sandburg, *Prairie Years* 1:416).

On May 21, 1848 (1:472–73), Lincoln wrote to John M. Peck, widely known Baptist preacher in St. Clair County, Illinois, to express his disappointment with Peck's trying to justify the origin of the Mexican War. At the end of his letter, Lincoln asks: "Is the precept 'Whatsoever ye would that men should do to you, do ye even so to them' obsolete?" Similarly, in the first debate with Stephen A. Douglas on August 21, 1858 (3:1–37), Lincoln refers to his house divided quotation as "the maxim which was put forth by the Saviour" (3:17). In light of the lore that Lincoln was fond of quoting chapter and verse, would it not have been more impressive for him to do so here than to use the designations "the precept" and "the maxim," especially before a Baptist preacher? In his Second Inaugural Address, March 4, 1865 (8:332–33), Lincoln quotes two passages from the Bible verbatim, one of them from the Psalms, allegedly one of his favorite biblical books, but he does not give references for either quotation.

In the last debate with Douglas, October 15, 1858 (3:283–325), Lincoln responds to Douglas's implication that he wants to get his seat in the Senate. He admits that "there are office seekers amongst us." Then he was flustered when he appealed to the Bible by saying: 'The Bible says somewhere that we are desperately selfish. I think we would have discovered that fact without the Bible." Not a very profound statement. But after Lincoln says that he does not claim to be less selfish than the average person and that he does claim that he is "not more selfish than Judge Douglas," he gets roars of laughter and applause (3:310). Lincoln gives no biblical reference, and the word selfish does not occur in the KJV. At almost fifty years of age, Lincoln was on the defensive with respect to his political ambition, and his reply displays a lack of in-depth knowledge of the Bible. Apparently, just the reference to it was enough to delight his audience, some of whom probably knew as little of the Bible in depth as Lincoln did. These observations are enough for us to rethink the statements of White (*Eloquent President*, 307–8) that presidential candidates were often to be seen with a Bible or quoting from it. Lincoln would welcome public debate on the use of the Bible and religion in public speech. "He [Lincoln] spoke a great deal about the use of the Bible. His use of the Bible was always informed and inclusive." There is no evidence in the *CW* to support such claims—quite the contrary.

If "presidential candidates were often to be seen with a Bible or quoting from it," and if Lincoln welcomed the use of the Bible in public speech, it is hard to understand why he never produced a Bible, especially in his debates with Douglas, to support his arguments, is it not? If he had done so, Lincoln might have met his match with Douglas, whose knowledge of the Bible may have been as deep as his. And he certainly would not have become flustered when confronted by Douglas and resorted to saying that the Bible says somewhere. He would have been even more flustered if he had a Bible and tried to find the passage.

Except in his First Lecture on Discoveries and Inventions, April 6, 1858 (2:437–42), when he obviously used a Bible, Lincoln does not give Bible references. Although he mentions Solomon, Job, and Isaiah by name, he does not give chapter and verse for any book associated with those men (2:437, 438, 442). In his Speech to the Springfield Scott Club, August 14, 1852 (2:135–57), Lincoln mentions Jeremiah incidentally (2:144). He never mentions the name of Jesus or of a gospel writer. With respect to the human lifespan, he mentions the "Psalmist's limit" (Ps 90:10) without a reference (8:118).

In contrast to the lack of references from the Bible, Lincoln displays a surprising knowledge of Euclid. Recall his words "*readin, written*, and *cipherin*, to the Rule of Three" in the autobiography written for Jesse Fell. In his rejoinder to Judge Douglas in their fourth debate, September 18, 1858 (3:145–201), Lincoln cites Euclid three times. He accuses Douglas of calling Lyman Trumbull a liar. Then he says to his audience: "If you have ever studied geometry, you remember that by a course of reasoning Euclid proves that all the angles in a triangle are equal to two right angles. Euclid has shown you how to work it out" (3:186).

In a letter to Henry L. Pierce, businessman and politician in Boston, April 6, 1859 (3:74–76), who had invited Lincoln to attend a celebration of the birth of Thomas Jefferson, Lincoln pays tribute to Jefferson by saying, that it is "no child's play to save the principles of Jefferson from total overthrow in this nation. One would start with great confidence that he could convince any sane child that the simpler propositions of Euclid are true; but, nevertheless, he would fail, utterly, with one who should deny the definitions and axioms. The principles of Jefferson are the definitions and axioms of free society" (3:375).

In a speech at Columbus, September 16, 1859 (3:400–425), Lincoln argues against the position of Douglas on the principle of popular sovereignty as "the right of one man to make a slave of another, without any right in that other, or anyone else, to object." If Douglas can "dem-

onstrate it as Euclid demonstrated propositions—there is no objection"
(3:416–17).

Lincoln says nothing about the Bible or any part of it comparable
to what he writes about Shakespeare and his plays to James H. Hackett,
August 17, 1863 (6:392–93). Lincoln thanks the famous Shakespearean
actor and critic for a copy of his book on several of Shakespeare's plays
and criticisms. He says that Hackett's presentation of Falstaff was the first
he saw, and the best compliment he can pay is that he is "very anxious to
see it again," and then he says:

> Some of Shakespeare's plays I have never read; while others I
> have gone over perhaps as frequently as any other unprofessional
> reader. Among the latter are Lear, Richard Third, Henry Eighth,
> Hamlet, and especially Macbeth. I think nothing equals Macbeth.
> It is wonderful. Unlike you gentlemen of the profession, I think
> the soliloquy in Hamlet commencing 'O, my offence is rank' sur-
> passes that commencing To be, or not to be.' But pardon this small
> attempt at criticism. I should like to hear you pronounce the open-
> ing speech of Richard the Third. (6:392)

The sources of the quotations from Shakespeare are given, and the quotations are exact.

For centuries, devoted readers of the KJV have memorized some of
its language and even become mesmerized by it. From my experience
in teaching groups of Sunday school teachers and other devoted church
members, I know people who read the KJV and can quote its language,
but if asked a question about the context from which it comes, they often
do not know the answer. The same thing was true for Lincoln, evident
especially in his befuddled response to Douglas. With few exceptions,
Lincoln's biblical quotations are not exact, and his allusions sometimes
are of uncertain origin. His use of the Bible is paradoxical in that he
shows extensive use of its language, but he shows no depth or profundity
of knowledge of it, including the contexts of the language he uses. And
sometimes if a context were known to him or to his hearers or readers,
it would be irrelevant and even damaging to his cause, a special example
of which is his exact quotation from the Psalms in his Second Inaugural
Address (discussed later).

LINCOLN'S READING THE BIBLE

Scholars still transmit traditions about persons seeing Lincoln reading the Bible in the White House. According to some lore,[7] "a lady staying at the White House" says that it was Lincoln's "custom when waiting for lunch to take his mother's old worn-out Bible and lie on the lounge and read." According to White (*Greatest Speech*, 110–11 and 218 n. 22), "Julia Taft Bayne, who turned sixteen on the day of Lincoln's first inauguration," saw "Lincoln's big leather-covered Bible" on a table and "had 'a distinct recollection' that 'quite often,' after the midday meal, Lincoln would sit sprawled out in his big chair in his large stocking feet reading the Bible."

Traditions changed bit by bit in transmission. Compare "mother's old worn-out Bible" with "Lincoln's big leather-covered Bible" and "when waiting for lunch" with "after the midday meal" and "lie on the lounge and read" and "sprawled out in his big chair in his large stocking feet reading the Bible." If we consider the lore about Lincoln's reading the Bible under many different circumstances and bodily positions, the single exception seems to be reading while standing on his head!

Another tradition about Lincoln being seen in the White House reading the Bible is reported by Donald (503 and 670 n.). When a friend reported in detail to Lincoln about the non-unified Republicans and small number that attended the nominating convention in Cleveland on May 31, 1864, Lincoln was amused. Then, says Donald, "He quietly picked up the Bible, which customarily lay on his desk, and read a passage from 1 Samuel: 'And every one that was in distress, and everyone that was in debt, and everyone that was discontented, gathered themselves unto him; and he became a captain over them: and there were with him about four hundred men'" (1 Sam 22:2). Except for the one speech mentioned, Lincoln never gives chapter and verse for biblical passages cited, even for ones not well known. During his campaigns, he might have impressed his audiences more if he had cited the Bible by book, chapter, and verse. Since he never did, it is doubtful, therefore, that he could turn to the precise chapter and verse for such an obscure and unfamiliar passage as the one in First Samuel. Incidentally, the words about Lincoln picking up the Bible that customarily was on his desk would seem more likely for a small Oxford Bible than for the large family Bible.

Lincoln was interested in every person acquiring an education. In his Communication to the People of Sangamon County, March 9, 1832

(1:5–9), he wrote that it is the most important subject people can be engaged in: "That every man may receive at least, a moderate education, and thereby be enabled to read the histories of his own and other countries, by which he may duly appreciate the value of our free institutions, appears to be an object of vital importance, even on this account alone, to say nothing of the advantages and satisfaction to be derived from all being able to read the scriptures and other works, both of a religious and moral nature, for themselves" (1:8).

At twenty-three years of age, did Lincoln's words about the scriptures imply that he had no in-depth knowledge of the Bible? Consider Herndon's remarks about him and his reading the Bible. "Among the books he read were the Bible, 'Aesop's Fables,' 'Robinson Crusoe,' Bunyan's 'Pilgrim's Progress,' a 'History of the United States,' and Weems' 'Life of Washington' . . . He kept the Bible and 'Aesop's Fables' always within reach, and read them over and over again" (Wilson and Davis, 37, 40). Compare those remarks with some Herndon made later: "Beyond a limited acquaintance with Shakespeare, Byron, and Burns, Mr. Lincoln, comparatively speaking, had no knowledge of literature. He was familiar with the Bible. . . . He never in his life sat down and read a book through, and yet he could readily quote any number of passages from the few volumes whose pages he had hastily scanned" (Wilson and Davis, 200). "No one can put his finger on any great book written in the last or present century that he read thoroughly. When young he read the Bible, and when of age he read Shakespeare; but, though he often quoted from both, he never read either one through" (Wilson and Davis, 354). Recall what Lincoln wrote to the literary critic about reading Shakespeare.

The statement that Lincoln always kept the Bible within reach suggests that it was smaller than the family Bible. Compare Herndon's statement that Lincoln did not read things through with that of Donald (30–31) that Lincoln read Aesop's Fables "so many times that he could write it out from memory." And compare those statements with the reported words of Lincoln's school teacher, Mentor Graham of Salem, that "'the young Lincoln read principally the Bible'" (White, *Greatest Speech*, 109 and 218 n. 18). That idea had been intimated by Wolf (35): "The Bible was probably the only book this frontier family owned." This statement contradicts one repeated by Donald that Sarah Bush Lincoln brought some books with her to the Lincoln household.

Traditions about Lincoln reading the Bible go from the sublime to the ridiculous, even humorous. While Senator John B. Henderson of Missouri was visiting Lincoln, he complained to the senator that Charles Sumner and Henry Wilson of Massachusetts and Congressman Thaddeus Stevens of Pennsylvania were constantly pressuring him to issue an emancipation proclamation. When he looked out the window and saw those three men coming toward the White House, Lincoln turned and told Henderson a story about a boy in a school he attended in Indiana where the Bible was read out loud by the pupils. Sandburg (*War Years*, 1:566):

> One day we were standing up reading the account of the three Hebrew children in the fiery furnace. A little tow-headed fellow who stood beside me had the verse with the unpronounceable names. He mangled up Shadrach and Meshach woefully and finally went to pieces on Abednego. For this the boy took a licking that made him cry. Then the class reading went on again, each boy in turn till the same tow-headed boy was reached again. As he looked in the Bible and saw the verse he was to read, he let out a pitiful yell. The school master asked what was the matter. The boy, pointing to the next verse, cried out, "Look there! Look! there comes them same damn three fellers again."

Lincoln would hardly have had time to say all that before the fellows knocked on the door.

William E. Barton (*Lincoln and His Books*, 10) had mentioned the same story. Among other differences from Sandburg's version is that Burton did not mention "damn" before "three fellers." The fact that in the biblical story of Daniel and the lions' den in Dan 3:12–30 the three persons are Jewish men, not children, is sufficient evidence for rejecting the Lincoln story as myth, as it is in Daniel.

White (*Greatest Speech*, 188) stresses how Lincoln "had been fascinated by newspapers his whole life." He read them in the post office where he worked before he passed them out to subscribers. He hung out "at the newspaper shop," took subscriptions from others, and wrote letters to editors and, as White says, Herndon "reported that what Lincoln chiefly read was newspapers." This contradicts Mentor Graham's statement to Herndon, mentioned by White (*Greatest Speech*, 109 and 218 n. 18) that "the young Lincoln read principally the Bible."

Recall that when Lincoln was president he wrote a letter to Hackett (1863), the Shakespearian actor and critic, that he had frequently gone over several plays of Shakespeare. There is an account of Colonel LeGrand B. Cannon of Fort Monroe telling that Lincoln said to him, "I suppose you have neither a Bible nor a copy of Shakespeare here? Cannon replied that he had a Bible and that the General [Wool] had Shakespeare. When the President asked if he would lend it to him, he was given the Shakespeare. The next day after reading for two hours alone, he read to the General "from *Macbeth*, *Lear*, and finally, *King John* (Wilson and Davis, 376 and 453 n. 18). When reading for his own pleasure, Lincoln chose Shakespeare over the Bible. He had a greater interest in and a greater depth of knowledge of Shakespeare than of the Bible.

Many admirers of Lincoln may not be aware of other diverse traditions about him and the Bible. According to Donald (514), "Often, when he could spare the time from his duties, he sought an answer to his questions in the well-thumbed pages of the Bible, reading most often the Old Testament prophets and the Psalms." Others think that the New Testament was Lincoln's favorite. A lot more careful study of the Lincoln documents is necessary to determine his favorite biblical books, because there are many times when it is impossible to be certain which of several he may have had in mind.

Donald (514) says that Lincoln "found comfort and reassurance in the Bible. He was not a member of any Christian church . . . he drew from the Scriptures such solace that he was prepared to forget his earlier religious doubts." Donald's view is quoted with approval by Packard (202) with added sympathetic detail. Although not a regular churchgoer, Lincoln "found solace in the Bible and, one hopes, justification for what he was required to preside over daily, which is to say slaughter and misery and heartbreak," in which he believed God shared his goals. Lincoln's greatest heartbreak surely came with the death of his sons, yet there is not the slightest indication in the *CW* that he found comfort for his suffering in the Bible. Nor does he mention such an experience in any of his personal letters of condolence to grieving persons.

According to William Lee Miller (49), "One cannot read much from Lincoln's own hand without becoming aware of his knowledge of the Bible. Whatever we make of young Lincoln's contrariness with respect to the doctrines and beliefs of churchgoers in the villages in which he lived, there cannot be much doubt that he read and reread and came to know a good deal of the Bible." Miller's first sentence would be true if we phrased the last part as "know a great deal of the language of the Bible." And as the statement is, it does not coincide with Herndon's report that Lincoln rarely read a book through. The question is the depth or extent of Lincoln's knowledge. That is not a question, though, for Lucas E. Morel (21 and 330 n. 8). "From his Lyceum Address to his 1865 Second Inaugural Address, Lincoln quoted or alluded to the Bible with a depth with a familiarity and profundity that rivaled the preachers of his day." Morel (23) quotes from Lincoln on his "reverence for the laws" and his exhortation that it should be expressed in the current institutions and be "preached from the pulpit." It may be carrying profundity a bit too far, though, in saying that Lincoln "imitates Moses," who exhorted the Israelites to meditate continually on the commandments and then quotes Deut 6:6–7 as evidence.

Morel also says: "Lincoln clearly uses 'the pulpit' to symbolize the influence of the church, while he includes the legislature and judiciary to represent the general influence of government" (24). Lincoln was always grateful for the support of the churches, but he was careful not to side with or offend any one denomination, and he followed a strict policy of not interfering with the churches. However, Lincoln rarely, if ever, thought of the *church* as a universal institution (Appendix 1).

The most unlikely view that reads too much (Christian) religion into Lincoln's use of the Bible is that of Thurow (11; see also 7): "The Biblical cadences of the language, the theme of birth, death, and rebirth, the overtones in the dedication of the nation to equality. . . . suggest the dedication of a child to God in baptism." The facts that there is nothing specific about child baptism in the Bible and that there is no substantial evidence that Lincoln or any member of his family, including his wife, a faithful church member, was ever baptized cast doubt on that view.

LINCOLN, POLITICAL PERSONAGE
WITH A MORAL SENSITIVITY

We have learned that in his communication to the people of Sangamon County Lincoln said that at least a moderate education would enable people "to read the scriptures and other works, both of a religious and moral nature." Toward the end of that handbill Lincoln affirmed his political ambition, with moral implications. He has spoken as he thought, perhaps wrong in any or all things he said, "but holding it a sound maxim, that it is better to be only sometimes right, than at all times wrong." When he discovers that his opinions are wrong, he will renounce them. According to Lincoln, "Every man is said to have his peculiar ambition. Whether it be true or not, I can say for one that I have no other so great as that of being truly esteemed of my fellow men by rendering myself worthy of their esteem." That ambition "is yet to be developed," and he is young and unknown to many. He has no prestige or wealth to recommend him. If elected, he will make every effort to compensate, and if the voters decide to keep him in the background, he has "been too familiar with disappointments to be very much chagrined" (1:8–9).

According to a Fragment on Stephen A. Douglas, December 1856? (3:382–83), at one point in his political quest, Lincoln felt that his "race of ambition has been a failure—a flat failure," compared with that of Senator Douglas, whose quest "has been one of splendid success" (2:383). Later, in a Fragment: Notes for Speeches, c. August 21, 1858 (2:547–53), while campaigning against Douglas for the U. S. Senate in 1858, Lincoln wrote a little defensively about his ambition: "I claim no extraordinary exemption from personal ambition . . . But I protest I have not entered upon this hard contest solely, or even chiefly, for a mere personal object" (2:548).

The words "personal ambition" and those mentioned earlier about "being truly esteemed" of his fellow men and "worthy of their esteem" are clues to understanding Lincoln's use of the Bible. He often adapted material from the Bible in order to win that esteem and to help him achieve his political goals. It was expedient to do that, in order to appeal to the people in his audiences who were Bible-reading Christians. At the same time, any personal religious faith, including belief in a personal deity, Lincoln may have had cannot be separated from his personal ambition for political success. That ambition was the primary context and the reason for his use of the Bible, and that ambition led him to the highest office in the land.

As Lincoln's political ambition intensified, so did his moral sensitivity. This is apparent in many of his documents, but perhaps it is most evident in his Lyceum Address (1:108–15), in the Temperance Address (1:271–79), and in his Cooper Union Speech (3:522–50). Slavery was wrong because it violated a basic principle of liberty set forth in the Declaration of Independence, "all men are created equal." Black persons, who by the sweat of their faces have to earn the bread of white men, are not equal. Lincoln found support for that view in Gen 3:19, the punishment for Adam's disobedience of the Lord—"In the sweat of thy face shalt thou eat bread." This is an exact quotation that Lincoln uses the same way in 1:411 and 7:368; but in the latter he puts the emphasis on *thy* face to apply it to the men to whom he was speaking.

Near the end of the war, two ladies from Tennessee asked Lincoln to free their husbands from prison. One of them stressed how religious her husband was. Lincoln freed the men, and then he told the woman to tell her husband that he is not a judge of religion, but he thinks, "The religion that sets men to rebel and fight against their government, because, as they think, that government does not sufficiently help *some* men to eat their bread on the sweat of *other* men's faces, is not the sort of religion upon which people can get to heaven" (8:155). In the Second Inaugural Address, in the context of his ambition for restoring the Union and not blaming either South or North for the war, Lincoln uses the quotation from Gen 3:19 loosely and effectively by saying, "It may seem strange that any men should dare to ask a just God's assistance in wringing their bread from the sweat of other men's faces" (8:333).

The saying from Genesis, which he does not quote exactly every time, and the loose citation of Jesus saying that "a house divided against itself cannot stand" (Mark 3:15) are the two basic biblical texts Lincoln used to buttress his thought that originated from the documents of the founding fathers. Both biblical texts would be known by the Bible readers in his audiences. He applied the first to the institution of slavery and the second to the disregard for the U.S. Constitution and the dissolution of the Union threatened by that institution. The Declaration and the Constitution were the foundation and support for his political faith, including the belief that slavery was immoral.

Lincoln was confronting people with different views on slavery. Slaves found comfort and hope in the Bible, and advocates for and against the possession of slaves used it to defend their views. As we shall learn in the chapters that follow, Lincoln used the Bible, sometimes in dubious ways, but aptly, in his quest for political success and as a main weapon in the battle against slavery.

2

Hewn from the Solid Quarry of Sober Reason

IN THE NINETEENTH CENTURY education made great strides in the United States, and the number of public schools increased. One reason for this was to enable people to read the Bible (Scriptures). Although literacy rates are not given in census reports for 1850 and 1860, they were still low, especially in the rural areas of Pennsylvania, Ohio, and Illinois, since there were few public schools in those regions until after Lincoln's time. Literacy was probably higher among men than among women. We may assume that most persons learned about the content of the Bible in their churches, from public forums, and from literate friends. However, how many people in Lincoln's audiences were Bible-reading is uncertain.

If we are aware of those things, it is not surprising how few allusions to and quotations from the Bible there are in Lincoln's documents. Although he mentions the word Bible a number of times, he rarely uses the designations "scripture" and "scriptures." In reply to the "Loyal Colored People of Baltimore," who presented a Bible to him, he refers to it as "this Great Book," "the best gift of God," and "the Great Book of God" (7:542; discussion in chapter 8).

In contrast to the Bible, Lincoln stresses the Declaration of Independence, the Constitution, law, and government. The Bible was not uppermost in his mind, and he did not use it to convert his hearers to "biblical religion," but to enhance his political career. After his election as president, Lincoln used the Bible fewer times. In his first inaugural address there may be one slight allusion to it, but in his second one, biblical vocabulary, allusions, and quotations are more numerous than in any speech of comparable length. Why? In the first inaugural speech his ultimate political ambition of becoming president was fulfilled. However, in his second inaugural address, Lincoln uses the Bible to win support of the people of both North and South for his new goals of healing, reconciliation, and reconstruction of the Union after the Civil War.

After his communication to the people of Sangamon County, Illinois, Lincoln served four months as a captain in the Black Hawk War, was defeated in an election to the Illinois State Legislature, served as store keeper and postmaster, and began to study law. In August 1834, he was elected to the Illinois House of Representatives, and he was reelected in August 1836. He received a law license a month later. In the Legislature, Lincoln joined a colleague in a protest against slavery.

On January 11, 1837, Lincoln delivered a speech in the Illinois Legislature concerning a state bank (1:61–69). The speech, his longest thus far, was awkward and poorly organized. But in spite of its literary shortcomings, it enhanced his esteem in the state legislature and in the newspapers, which, in turn, helped to influence voters to support his political ambitions. The speech includes several allusions to the Bible, and it is also one of the most informative in showing how he used it.

Lincoln voiced his objection to a resolution by Usher F. Linder, a Democrat, to investigate the management of the state bank. Lincoln argues that an investigation would do no good because it would only harm those who should not be harmed. Concerning the committee to be appointed to make an investigation of the constitutionality of the bank, Lincoln asks: "Are they to be clothed with power to send for persons and papers, for this object?" (1:63).

The words clothed with power reflect reported words of the resurrected Jesus to his disciples advising them to stay in the city of Jerusalem until they are "endued with power from on high" (Luke 24:49). The Greek word *enduo*, translated as endued in Luke, and its equivalent in the Hebrew Scriptures, are usually rendered as "clothed with." Literally it means "put on clothes" or "clothe oneself," and used metaphorically it means acquire some quality. Here are some examples of its use in the Bible with respect to the Lord, humans, and things in nature. "The Lord . . . is clothed with majesty . . . with strength" (Ps 93:1); "clothed with linen" (Ezek 9:2), "with shame" (Job 8:22), "with righteousness" (Ps 132:19), and "with humility" (1 Pet 5:5); and "pastures are clothed with flocks" (Ps 65:11).

It is puzzling that Lincoln's "clothed" is a more precise translation of the Greek *enduo* than "endued" of the KJV. Clothed became the translation of *enduo* in versions used in America, beginning with the *American Standard Version* of 1901. So how did Lincoln get the word clothed? He did not get it from the Lincoln Family Bible, because "endued" is the reading of the Geneva Bible, the KJV, and the Neufchatel Bible. In his translation of the Bible into French, Ostervald uses "clothed" (*revetus*) in Luke 24:49, but in the Neufchatel he retains "endued," apparently from the KJV. It is unlikely that Lincoln was familiar with the French translation, although it dates back to about 1794.

These observations raise the question of whether Lincoln knew some Greek. According to a tradition handed on by Carl Sandburg and others, Jesse W. Fell gave him a copy of the sermons of the heterodox preacher William Ellery Channing, about which Sandburg writes: "[Lincoln] put it in his little library where it kept company with 'Exercises in the Syntax of the Greek Language,' by Rev. William Nielson. . . . On page 34 was a sentence reading in Greek, 'Ye have loved me, and have believed that I came forth from God,' with the words 'from God' crossed with a pen and the words 'from nature' scribbled in Lincoln's handwriting" (*Prairie Years*, 1:415).

There is a copy of the work Sandburg mentions (for correct spelling of author's name and title of book see bibliography) in the Weidner Memorial Library of Harvard University. In that edition there is a passage in English from John 16:27 on p. 34 that includes the words "from God." According to Rufus Rockwell Wilson (50), the book on the Greek syntax is one of the books Lincoln read. The book in the Harvard library is dated 1842, but Lincoln's *clothed* is from his speech in the Illinois Legislature on January 11, 1837. There are, however, editions of Neilson's work as early as 1825. That work includes passages from a conglomeration of ancient texts, including some from the Bible, but I could not find Luke 24:49, even in an earlier edition.

Lincoln applied the words clothed with power to the authority of the committee to investigate the State Bank of Illinois. Perhaps his Bible-reading hearers understood the implication of divine influence, but why did Lincoln leave out the words from on high that imply such influence? Interestingly, the omission coincides with the crossing out of the words from God in the textbook on Greek syntax and with his statement to Mary Speed that he does not doubt that the Bible is "the best cure for the 'Blues' could one but take it according to the truth" (1:261).

Like others of his time, Lincoln used the phrase "clothed with power" in the sense of acquiring a quality. In notes for speeches at Columbus and Cincinnati, Ohio, September 16, 1849 (1:425–36), Lincoln discusses Douglas's view about popular sovereignty, the responsibility of Congress

for the situation, and the effects it would have on the spread of slavery. "If individuals choose to plant it, the people can not prevent them,
for they are not yet clothed with popular sovereignty" (3:428). For the
phrase on the lips of others, see "Gentlemen clothed with full power"
(7:451, Annotation), "one clothed with the highest responsibilities"
(8:189, Annotation), and "clothed with the full power to pardon" (8:211,
Annotation).

For two reasons, the most likely explanation for Lincoln's "clothed
with power" is that he used the current phrase, probably not derived from
the Bible. The word "power" is used in the current phrases, but not in
the biblical ones. The suggestion also explains Lincoln's omission of the
words "from on high" with reference to the deity, an idea he implies in
his phrases "before High Heaven" (1:178) and "the Most High" (5:498),
which are biblical (e.g., Num 24:16; Ps 50:14; Acts 7:48).

In April 1837, Lincoln moved to Springfield, Illinois, where he joined
John T. Stuart as a law partner, and Stuart became a friend and foe in the
political arena. On January 27, 1838 (1:108–15), Lincoln delivered an address before the Young Men's Lyceum of Springfield. Such lyceums were
established at various places in the country, and the one at Springfield was
organized in 1833 by a group of men, including some of Lincoln's friends.
Members generally had some formal education, and they were concerned
with their further learning and with the development of public schools.
Much of their education came through listening to debates and lectures
on current subjects. Members were interested in rhetorical skills, cultural
development, and religious life.

Greatly concerned about the recent mob riots in New England,
Louisiana, Mississippi, Illinois, and elsewhere, Lincoln chose "The Perpetuation of Our Political Institutions" as the subject of the speech, one
of his most significant. The riots were a blight on society and must be
controlled by the institution of law and order.

The Lyceum Address is sometimes taken as a sort of biography of
Lincoln's ambitious quest for fame, "unconsciously describing himself,"
or, in Herndon's words, "a little engine that knew no rest" (Donald, 81 and
612 notes). Fornieri (*Political Faith*, 106) tempers "the sinister interpretation" that Herndon's "little engine" signified that "Lincoln's motivation to
reenter politics was driven by an insatiable will to power." Fornieri men-

tions Lincoln's desire for the esteem of his fellowmen and his speech at Lewistown, Illinois, August 17, 1858 (2:544–47), from which he quotes Lincoln: "While pretending no indifference to earthly honors, I *do claim* to be actuated in this contest [with Stephen A. Douglas for the U.S. Senate] by something higher than an anxiety for office" (2:547). These comments indicate that Lincoln's Lyceum speech has become an excellent forum for discussions, analyses, and hypotheses not only with respect to the speech, but also for Lincoln's personality, life, and thought.[8]

Whatever else the Lyceum speech may reveal about Lincoln's quest for political office, it provides the first significant insight into how he used biblical language oblivious of its context and, therefore, often not relevant to the context of his speech. Lincoln uses the word 'Bible' for the first time when he says that he hopes the scenes of the revolution "will be read of, and recounted [in history], so long as the bible shall be read." He uses biblical phrases, some of which I mention, and a literal quotation, which I study carefully in light of what he says in the address and crucial statements elsewhere.

Lincoln begins with "In the great journal of things happening under the sun" (1:108). The last three words are favorites of the writer of Ecclesiastes. The closest parallels to Lincoln's words are "all things that are done under the sun" (Eccl 9:3) and "any thing that is done under the sun" (Eccl 9:6; see also 1:14; 2:17; 4:3; 8:9, 17). Lincoln says that it is our task to preserve the political institutions of liberty and equal rights "to the latest generation" (1:108; see also 4:194; 5:537). He speaks about dangers that threaten the political institutions and remarks: "If destruction be our lot, we must ourselves be its author and finisher" (1:109). The last three words are used in Heb 12:2, where the writer applies them to Jesus as "the author and finisher of our faith." According to Heb 5:9, Jesus is "the author of eternal salvation unto all them that obey him." In both passages the end is made possible by the sufferings of Jesus on the cross. If the words of Lincoln come from Hebrews, he used them oblivious of their context or meaning. Moreover, he never mentions Jesus by name, to say nothing about faith in him, as stated in the passage from Hebrews.

Turning to specific incidents of riots in Mississippi, Lincoln says that hangings by mobs and other criminal violations of the law are becoming more frequent. Throughout the address, Lincoln thinks of sound morality as equally important with general intelligence and reverence for the constitution and laws. He says, "Those who have ever set their faces against violations of law in every shape" become victims of mob violence (1:111). The phrase "set the face against" is used in the Bible for emphasizing opposition to something. For example, the Hebrew deity warns against eating food with blood in it: "I will even set my face against that soul that eateth blood" (Lev 17:10). In the same way, God will set his face against any Israelites who sacrifice their children to a pagan deity (Lev 20:3; see also Jer 21:10; 44:11; Ezek 14:8; 15:7; 25:2). Lincoln speaks about the ravages of mob violence continuing until the walls for the defense of persons and property "are trodden down, and disregarded . . . destroyed" (1:111; see also 5:344). He uses the phrase "trodden down" also in a letter to Cuthbert Bullitt, July 28, 1862 (5:344–46), in which he asks why the majority of persons opposed to the Secession Ordinance of Louisiana "stand passive and allow themselves to be trodden down by a minority" (5:344). The contexts of the biblical accounts indicate that Lincoln had only phrases from them in mind. Any attempt to discover more than that is to read too much into what he says in order to stress his in-depth knowledge of the Bible. None of the biblical contexts fits with the subject of the perpetuation of American political institutions.

In Isaiah's parable of the Lord's vineyard, symbolic of his people, cared for carefully by the Lord, the prophet says that the vineyard will be destroyed because of their sinfulness. The Lord will "break down the wall thereof, and it shall be trodden down" (Isa 5:5; see also Deut 1:36; Isa 25:10; Luke 21:24). It is plausible that Lincoln might have had language from this parable in mind when he composed his address, because it was probably one of the better known passages in the long book of Isaiah. If so, he adapts it to the context of his speech.

The basic principles of "civil and religious liberty . . . *were* a fortress of strength," but the walls are being leveled. "They *were* a forest of giant oaks," but the hurricane has swept over them, leaving a mere trunk here and there, to be no more after other storms. "They *were* the pillars of the temple of liberty; and now, that they have crumbled away, that temple must fall, unless we, their descendants, supply their places with other pillars, hewn from the solid quarry of sober reason" (1:114–15). After Lincoln states that the pillars of liberty will fall unless others are "hewn from the solid quarry of sober reason," he continues by saying that passion, now the cause of the riots, has helped us in the past, but can no longer do so, and will be our future enemy. "Reason, cold, calculating, unimpassioned reason, must furnish all the materials for our future support and defence.

Let those [materials] be molded into *general intelligence, [sound] morality* and, in particular, *a reverence for the constitution and laws."*

Immediately after Lincoln's words about intelligence, morality, and laws quoted above and followed with only a semicolon, he continues:

> and, that we improved to the last; that we remained free to the last; that we revered his name to the last; [tha]t, during his long sleep, we permitted no hostile foot to pass over or desecrate [his] resting place; shall be that which to le[arn the last] trump shall awaken our Wash[ington.
>
> Upon these] let the proud fabric of freedom r[est, as the] rock of its basis; and as truly as has been said of the only greater institution, *"the gates of hell shall not prevail against it."* (1:115)

The language is incoherent and vague, and it must have seemed that way also to Lincoln's hearers and readers. Those familiar with the Bible might know that some of his phrases are allusions to it, and they would recognize the quotation in italics. However, the allusions raise questions about Lincoln's use of the Bible and even about several of his own words. Some expressions are unclear, apocalyptic/eschatological, and in the Bible they refer to the end of the world and the resurrection of the dead.

"The last trump" are words of Paul in his discussion of the resurrection of the dead: "In a moment, in the twinkling of an eye, at the last trump: for the trumpet shall sound, and the dead shall be raised" (1 Cor 15:52; see also 1 Thess 4:16). The metaphors of sleeping and awaking are probably taken from Paul's vivid apocalyptic language in describing the return of the Lord Jesus in 1 Thess 4:13–17. The passage is too long to quote, but here are some pertinent phrases: "concerning them which are asleep," "shall not prevent them which are asleep," and "with the trumpet of God" (see also Matt 24:31).

Words Lincoln used four years later in his Temperance Address before the Springfield Washington Temperance Society, February 22, 1842 (1:271–79; discussed separately) throw light on a possible meaning of our present text. In that address Lincoln strongly supported the efforts of the Temperance Society to subvert the demon intemperance, and he used "the trump" figuratively in proclaiming the signs of victory for their efforts. That demon keeps families "prostrate in the chains of moral death. To all the living every where we cry, 'come sound the moral resurrection trump'" (1:278). Those words enlighten our present discussion of Lincoln's sound morality, with the other virtues he mentions, as the "last trump" that "shall awaken our Washington."

In his discussion of the Lyceum Address, Fornieri (*Political Faith*, 92 and 186 n. 1), deals only with the quotation from Matt 16:18 about the gates of Hell. Let's consider it carefully. The words "the rock of its basis" seemingly allude to Jesus' words to Peter as the rock foundation of the church: "Thou art Peter, and upon this rock I will build my church." The words *"the gates of hell shall not prevail against it"* are a literal quotation of Matt 16:18. According to Matthew, the "it" in the words quoted is "my [Jesus'] church." Lincoln's words "the only greater institution" appear to be an allusion to the church in Matthew, which only the Bible-reading persons in the audience might understand. But why did Lincoln not use the word "church"? Suggested answers come later. About the quotation from Matthew, Fornieri (*Political Faith*, 98) writes: "It was an example of evocative biblical rhetoric used to reinforce the central Whig teaching of the speech: the maintenance of the rule of law to ensure the Union's perpetuity." It "clearly subordinated the secular realm to the spiritual realm when describing the church as a 'greater institution' than the state." What follows casts doubt on such an emphasis.

The words "Upon these" hark back to the antecedents, intelligence, morality, and reverence for the constitution and laws that are the rock as the basis of the proud fabric of freedom. The words "our Washington," immediately before that, and the rock, an allusion to Peter as the foundation of the church in Matthew, and Lincoln's rock as the basis of freedom make what follows hard to understand. The "it" at the end of the quotation refers to freedom, not the institution of the church. The words "only greater institution" are completely incidental to "the proud fabric of freedom." This interpretation coincides with the theme of the whole address.

A perplexing question remains: Why would Lincoln bring in George Washington's name without having mentioned it earlier? Would his hearers have understood it, even though he had referred to the Revolution? The usual answer is that Lincoln had great admiration for George Washington, probably as the result of reading the well-known book, *The Life of George Washington* by M. L. Weems (1806). For a discussion see Fornieri (*Political Faith*, 92–106, 166).

Would people in Lincoln's audience know that he had read Weems's book and that he was greatly influenced by it? Considering the things we have mentioned, there are reasons for not taking the "our Washington" as George Washington, in spite of arguments to the contrary. Up to this point in the *CW*, Lincoln has not referred to the man Washington. On the other hand, there are some important references to the city of Washington and persons serving in the government there.

With his mind on higher political goals, Lincoln became more vocal and critical of opponents and of the government in Washington. According to the *Sangamo Journal*, July 11, 1836 (1:49–50), Lincoln is to have said at a political rally in Springfield: "In these degenerate days it seems to be the fashion of the day for all parties to admire even the frailties of the [Jackson] administration. The Van Buren men, particularly, are even taking shelter like ghosts under the rotten bones and tombstones of the dead acts of the administration" (1:50). In his speech in the Illinois Legislature concerning the state bank, Lincoln remarked: "Some gentleman [Usher F. Linder, a Democrat] at Washington city has been upon the very eve of deciding our bank unconstitutional" and probably would have succeeded "had not some one of the Bank officers placed his hand upon his mouth, and begged him to withhold it" (1:62; see also 1:63). Lincoln says that the movement concerning the bank "is exclusively the work of politicians; a set of men who have interests aside from the interests of the people, and who, to say the most of them, are, taken as a mass, at least one long step removed from honest men" (1:65–66).

In the Lyceum address, Lincoln speaks critically of the mobs and the current government:

> [Mobs have become] absolutely unrestrained. Having ever regarded Government as their deadliest bane, they make a jubilee of the suspension of its operations; and pray for nothing so much, as its total annihilation. While, on the other hand, good men, men who love tranquility, who desire to abide by the laws, and enjoy their benefits, who would gladly spill their blood in the defence of their country; seeing their property destroyed; their families insulted, and their lives endangered; their persons injured; and seeing nothing in prospect that forebodes a change for the better; become tired of, and disgusted with, a Government that offers them no protection. (1:111)

Later in his speech on the Sub-Treasury in the Illinois State Legislature (see below), Lincoln says that an evil spirit is reigning in Washington, where under President Van Buren, "the great volcano . . . is belching forth the lava of political corruption . . . sweeping with frightful velocity . . . to leave unscathed no green spot or living thing, while on its bosom are riding like demons on the waves of Hell, the imps of that evil spirit, and fiendishly taunting all those who dare resist its destroying course" (1:178). This metaphor harks back to the gates of Hell in the Lyceum address.

In light of the ineptness of Lincoln's literary style and logic in the use of "his name," "his long sleep," and "his resting place," the switch to "*our* Washington" as the person makes no sense. The most likely answer is to understand the words not as the person, but as the government in the city of Washington. Assuming that to be true, we return to the last two paragraphs of the address. Recall that the subject of the address is "The Perpetuation of *our Political Institutions*" (my italics) and that "the noblest cause" is "that of establishing and maintaining civil and religious liberty" (1:115). The exhortation "Let those [materials] be" applies not only to the virtues of general intelligence, sound morality, and a reverence for the constitution and laws, but also to the "that" clauses that follow, beginning with "that we improved to the last." Accordingly, the "his" in the exhortations may be understood metaphorically as reason personified, as in the book of Proverbs, especially Prov 8:1—9:12, where wisdom is sometimes personified as feminine.

The basis for this interpretation is that Lincoln was not very gender conscious, and evidence supports the argument for his personification of reason as masculine. In the beginning of his speech to the Temperance Society in Springfield, February 22, 1842 (1:271–79), he says that the cause of temperance is "suddenly transformed from a cold abstract theory, to a living, breathing, active, and powerful chieftain [a masculine figure], going forth" (1:271). Near the end of that speech, Lincoln exults over the "day, when, all appetites will be controlled, all passions subdued, all matters subjected, *mind*, all conquering *mind*, shall live and move the monarch of the world. Glorious consummation! Hail fall of Fury! Reign of Reason, all hail!" (1:279). Mind is personified.

Lincoln also uses metaphor later in his first and second lectures on discoveries and inventions. In the first lecture he begins: "All creation is a mine, and every man, a miner . . . the mine was unopened, and the miner stood *naked*" (2:437). Lincoln begins the second lecture: "We have all heard of Young America. He is the most *current* youth of the age." Then Lincoln speaks of Young America as "he," "himself," and "him" (3:357). Here he refers to America as masculine to fit the occasion of an all-male audience. Later, in his eulogy on Henry Clay, July 6, 1852 (2:121–32), he refers to America in the feminine. Clay "was called upon to legislate for America, and direct her policy" (2:123). In his reply to Governor Edwin

D. Morgan at Albany, NY, February 18, 1861 (4:224–25), Lincoln says that if he is correct, "The great Empire State at this time contains a greater population than did the United States of America at the time she achieved her national independence" (4:225).

The most interesting example of Lincoln's gender indifference is his description of the ant in a Fragment on Slavery, July 1, 1854? (2:222): "The ant, who has toiled and dragged a crumb to his nest, will furiously defend the fruit of his labor, against whatever robber assails him." Lincoln was aware of the popular proverb, "Go to the ant, thou sluggard, consider her ways and be wise" (Prov 6:6), because he refers to it later in his first lecture on discoveries and inventions (2:437). These examples show that Lincoln was not very gender conscious.

In light of these observations, I suggest that we understand Lincoln's thought in the Lyceum address as follows. Passion can no longer help us in preserving our political institutions. Reason must provide the virtues of general intelligence, sound morality, and reverence for the constitution and laws, so that by practicing them it may be said that we have improved to the last, remained free to the last, revered reason to the last, that during its long disuse we permitted no foe to desecrate it so that it shall be the moral call to awaken our Government in Washington to perpetuate our political institutions. These things put the "our Washington" in focus. The pronoun "our" before it refers to current, not past, time—that of George Washington. Molded by reason, not passion, the three virtues are the last moral trump for awakening the city of Washington.

Now let us return to the last three lines of the Lyceum address, where Lincoln again uses an exhortation: "Upon these let the proud fabric of freedom rest, as the rock of its basis" (1:115). "These" are the three virtues molded by reason that are the rock as the basis of the freedom Government brings, against which the gates of hell shall not prevail, that is, provided new pillars to support it have been "hewn from the solid quarry of sober reason" (1:115). Here the metaphor "the gates of hell" anticipates the corrupt government in Washington "riding like demons on the wavers of Hell" in the speech on the sub-treasury.

Lincoln has been speaking extemporaneously. I suspect that at the last moment he became fully aware of the religious members of his audience, perhaps in a church building. He inserted the "only greater institution" (implying the church) and the biblical quotation to appeal to his audience. This would be similar to his insertion of "under God" in his Gettysburg Address (see the magisterial work on that address by Boritt). The difference is, though, that we have no other copies of the Lyceum speech where the presumed inserted words are missing. If my interpretation is correct, it helps to explain the incoherence of Lincoln's last remarks. The biblical quotation has nothing to do with the church as a greater institution that "subordinated the secular realm to the spiritual realm," as Fornieri and others contend.

The view I am proposing is later confirmed by President-elect Lincoln in a speech before Governor Morton of Indiana and some citizens of Indianapolis, when he stopped on his way to Washington on February 11, 1861 (4:193–94). Then he uses the quotation from Matt 16:18 again. When the people rise in masses "in behalf of the Union and the liberties of their country, truly may it be said, 'The gates of hell shall not prevail against them'" (4:194). There is no difficulty here in understanding Lincoln's change to "them" for "it" of the quotation from Matthew to support his political views. And the church never entered Lincoln's mind, to say nothing about it as a greater institution that puts the spiritual realm above the secular realm. And if there is a "realm" that is superior, it is the moral virtues established by sober reason that bring freedom.

The quotation from Matt 15:16 in the Lyceum Address, then, is expressive of political, not religious, faith. Earlier in that speech, in response to the riots, Lincoln had laid the foundation for his political faith based on the Declaration of Independence and the Constitution. He uses the hortatory style: "Let every American, every lover of liberty, every well wisher to his posterity, swear by the blood of the Revolution, never to violate in the least particular, the laws of the country . . . As the patriots of seventy-six did to support the Declaration of Independence, so to the support of the Constitution and Laws, let every American pledge his life, his property, and his sacred honor" (1:112).

3

Chained Like So Many Fish upon a Trot-line

B Y DECEMBER 1839, THE campaign for the presidential election of 1840 was in full swing. Lincoln had become ever more vocal in the Illinois Legislature, and he was elected to a fourth and final term in August 1840. During those years most of his documents are correspondence with personal and political friends and speeches in the legislature, and in most of them there is little evidence of influence from the Bible, even on his language. His immediate political goal was achieved.

In November 1840, William Henry Harrison, a Whig, was elected president. He died shortly afterward, and his term was completed by John Tyler, a Whig and Democrat (1841–1845).

The Democrats had proposed a plan for a sub-treasury for keeping public money controlled by the government. The Whigs, supported by Lincoln, favored a national bank. However, after President Jackson's dealings with the national bank, Lincoln strongly supported a state bank of Illinois, especially a branch in Springfield. In a speech in the State House of Representatives, December 26, 1839 (1:159–79), on the Sub-Treasury, Lincoln argued that such a treasury, proposed by the Democrats, would have ill effects on the economy. He accused the administrations of Andrew Jackson (1829–1837) and Martin Van Buren (1837–1841) of spending more money in the last ten years than in all the previous years of American government (1:172).

Lincoln managed to get himself appointed to a committee for investigating the treasury question. He says that no matter how members of an investigative committee are chosen, there will be some dishonest men, as "the experience of the whole world, in all by-gone times, proves this true" (1:167). Alluding to those appointed to investigate the Sub-Treasury, Lincoln says, "The Saviour of the world chose twelve disciples, and even one of that small number, selected by superhuman wisdom, turned out a traitor and a devil. And, it may not be improper here to add, that Judas carried the bag—was the Sub-Treasurer of the Saviour and his disciples" (1:167).

The tradition that Jesus had twelve special disciples is established in the four gospels (Matt 10:1–5; 11:1; Mark 3:13–14; 4:10; 6:7; 9:35; 10:32; Luke 6:13–14; 8:1; 9:1; John 6:67–71) and in Acts 6:6 and 1 Cor 15:5. The exact phrase "The Saviour of the world" occurs in John 4:42 and in 1 John 4:14. See also "God, who is the Saviour of all men" (1 Tim 4:10). Although Lincoln uses "Saviour of the world" only here, he uses "Saviour" or "Savior" also in 2:442, 501, 511; 3:17; 7:368, 542. In every instance he merely mentions the name without any intimations of a personal religious faith. Is merely mentioning a common designation for Jesus enough to assume Lincoln's personal faith in him? That is unlikely. To have the Savior on one's side would impress the members of his audience. Or was he just being facetious?

Judas as the betrayer of Jesus was also well known (Matt 26:14, 46–50; Mark 14:10, 43–46; Luke 22:3, 47–48; John 6:71; Acts 1:16, 25). Lincoln's words "chose twelve disciples," though not exact, are from Luke 6:13: "He [Jesus] called unto him his disciples: and of them he chose twelve" or John 6:70: "Have not I chosen you twelve, and one of you is a devil?" (see also John 15:16). Lincoln's words "a traitor and a devil," which never occur together in the gospels, are also from Luke, who concludes his list of the disciples' names with "Judas Iscariot, which also was the traitor" (Luke 6:16). According to Luke 22:3–4, "Then entered Satan into Judas," and he talked with authorities about "how he might betray him unto them." John's version is: "The devil having now put into the heart of Judas . . . to betray him . . . Satan entered into him" (John 13:2, 27). The difference between the accounts of Luke and John shows Lincoln's recollection of Luke, where both 'traitor' and 'betray' are mentioned, although not in the same passage.

The words "Judas carried the bag" allude to John 12:3–6, where Judas complains because the expensive ointment Mary used to anoint Jesus' feet was not sold and the money given to the poor. The author of John adds: "This he said, not that he cared for the poor; but because he was a thief, and had the bag, and bare what was put therein" (see also John 13:29).

We might wonder if Lincoln was aware of John's words that Judas was a thief and if he does not mention that in order to avoid falsely accusing anyone. Although Lincoln would not want to make a false accusation,

I doubt that he remembered that Judas was called a thief because of the following observation. According to John 12:6, Judas "had the bag, and bare what was put therein." Lincoln emphasizes the one who carried the bag, not what was in it. And his modernization of the KJV by using "carried" instead of "bare" indicates that he was not at all concerned with repeating exactly words of the Bible.

After calling off his wedding to Mary Todd, Lincoln became severely depressed, and the fact that his good friend Joshua Speed moved to Kentucky did not help matters. Encouraged by Speed, Lincoln visited the Speed homestead. Still depressed after his visit with Speed and his family and the familiar surroundings in Kentucky, Lincoln started home. After he got home, he wrote to Miss Mary Speed, September 27, 1841 (1:259–61), half-sister of Joshua Speed, about his sight on the boat on the way back to Springfield. He saw a gentleman who "had purchased twelve negroes in different parts of Kentucky and was taking them to a farm in the South. They were chained six and six together . . . precisely like so many fish upon a trot-line." In that condition they were separated from their homes and family members.

That observation did not help his depression and led him to say to Mary Speed: "How true it is that 'God tempers the wind to the shorn lamb,' [a line from Robert Browning, *Pippa Passes*], or in other words, that He renders the worst of human conditions tolerable, while He permits the best, to be nothing better than tolerable" (1:260). After some reminiscing with Mary, Lincoln writes about the "present" (Oxford Bible) her mother gave him. He says, "I doubt not that it is really, as she says, the best cure for the 'Blues' could one but take it according to the truth" (1:261). The source and meaning of Lincoln's words according to the truth are puzzling, but they may reflect biblical language. The phrase occurs in slightly different ways in Gal 2:14 and Rom 2:2. In Gal 2:14 Paul rebukes his adversaries because "they walked not uprightly according to the truth of the gospel." In Rom 2:2 Paul says, "The judgment of God is according to truth against them [Jew and pagan] which commit such things," that is, immorality. Lincoln's phrase about the truth may or may not be biblical, but he probably meant to say, "if we take it as the truth." Nevertheless, the statement indicates doubt about the Bible as a source of comfort, contrary to the view of Donald mentioned in the introduction of this work.

In a handbill replying to charges of infidelity, July 31, 1846 (1:382–83), Lincoln says something different about the Bible. After admitting that he is not a member of any Christian church, he says: "I have never denied the truth of the Scriptures" (1:382). In the heat of his political campaign for election as a representative in the U.S. House of Representatives, those words could not have been more apt, although, as with many politicians, Lincoln's words differ from what he had said before.

Speed came back to Springfield with Lincoln. When he was getting ready to return to Kentucky, where he planned to marry Fanny Henning, Lincoln wrote him a letter, January 3?, 1842 (1:265–66). He wants Speed to know how deeply he feels "for the success of the enterprise you are engaged in." Lincoln puts his feelings in writing because he can express them better than orally "in case (which God forbid)" he should need any further aid. The words "God forbid," used only here by Lincoln, occur often in the Bible (e.g., Gen 44:7, 17; Josh 22:29; 24:16; 1 Sam 12:23; Gal 6:14), and they may be only a trite phrase of Lincoln's time, as they are in ours. He says that Speed will have concerns between now and the time of his marriage. One cause for that is the lack of business and "conversation of friends," which would divert his thought that sometimes might turn "the sweetest idea" to the "bitterness of death" (1:265). Lincoln's last three words, used only here, occur exactly in 1 Sam 15:32.

In the context of 1 Samuel, Agag, an Amalekite king, was spared from death by Saul, who had been commanded by Samuel to kill all the Amalekites. Summoned by Samuel, Agag said, "Surely the bitterness of death is past." But he was mistaken, because Samuel "hewed Agag in pieces before the Lord" (1 Sam 15:33). If the context of the passage in 1 Samuel were known to Speed, which of course it wasn't, it would have been devastating to the groom-to-be, would it not? And if Lincoln had known the context of the words, he would not have used them.

In a letter to Speed, February 13, 1842 (1:269–70), just before his marriage to Fanny, Lincoln wrote: "I hope with tolerable confidence, that this letter is a plaster for a place that is no longer sore. God grant it may be so" (1:270). Lincoln uses the words "God grant" only here and in a speech in the U. S. House of Representatives on the war with Mexico, January 12, 1848 (1:442). Lincoln's words are closest to Job 6:8: "Oh . . . that God would grant me the thing that I long for!" (see also 1 Sam 1:17; Ps 85:7;

Acts 4:29; 2 Tim 1:18). Perhaps for Lincoln, as often for others, the words were only a trite saying.

Despite whatever past regrets Lincoln had had about his love affair with Mary Todd, he was showing signs of love for her again. When invited to speak before a temperance society in Springfield, he was happy to accept the invitation. The coming event was well publicized in the local paper, and he delivered a Temperance Address before the Springfield Washington Society, February 22, 1842 (1:271–79). The event took place in the Second Presbyterian Church. Although not a church attendant, Lincoln was glad to speak in churches because such occasions enhanced his political career. In the early 1800s, temperance societies were organized in a number of states. Eventually, many members became zealous advocates of prohibition, with whom Lincoln disagreed, as we know from his comments in the speech. Members were also concerned with religion and with morality in general.

Lincoln begins his address to the society by personalizing the cause of temperance "from a cold abstract theory, to a living, breathing, active, and powerful chieftain, going forth 'conquering and to conquer.'" The words quoted by Lincoln are from Rev 6:2, where a white horse and his rider with a bow "went forth conquering, and to conquer." By changing the "went forth" to "going forth," Lincoln applied the quotation to the context of his speech. He continues in some of his most rhetorical language: "The citadels of his great adversary [the demon alcoholism] are daily being stormed and dismantled; his temples and his altars, where the rites of his idolatrous worship have long been performed, and where human sacrifices have long been wont to be made, are daily desecrated and deserted. The trump of the conqueror's fame is sounding from hill to hill, from sea to sea, and from land to land, and calling millions to his standard at a blast" (1:271).

Many passages in the Old Testament warn the Israelites against idolatry and child sacrifice, and reform movements against those practices may provide the background for Lincoln's metaphorical language. During the religious reformation of King Josiah of Judah (621 BC), "the idolatrous priests" in the temple were removed and their places for worship and sacrifices destroyed, as were pagan altars where sacrifices were made to pagan gods (2 Kgs 23:5–20; 2 Chron 14:3–5; 34:4–7; see also Exod 34:13; Deut 7:4–5; Hos 10:2; Zech 6:4–13).

Earlier we learned that some of Lincoln's words about the trumpet reflect biblical language, and they do here. Perhaps he was most influenced by Jer 4:19–21, where, as in his speech, a trumpet sounding, war, and a standard are mentioned together: "the sound of the trumpet, the alarm of war . . . How long shall I see the standard, and hear the sound of the trumpet?" In the New Testament the trumpet signals the apocalyptic end of the world (e.g., Matt 24:29–31; Rev 8:1—10:11).

Lincoln's words "bursts the fetters that have bound him" (the alcoholic; 1:272) reflect the language of either the healing of "a man with an unclean spirit" (Mark 5:1–15), "two possessed with devils, coming out of the tombs" (Matt 8:28–33), or "a certain man, which had devils . . . ware no clothes" (Luke 8:27–36). The words about the fetters that bound the man are an allusion to Mark 5:4: "bound with fetters and chains, and the chains had been plucked asunder by him, and the fetters broken." Luke's version is "bound with chains and in fetters, and he brake the bonds." The exact quotation, "clothed, and in his right mind," is from Mark 5:15 or Luke 8:35.

The words "one, who has long been known as a victim of intemperance" and "appears before his neighbors" are accommodations to the situation at hand. Lincoln's "neighbors" replaces the indefinite "they' in Mark 5:15–17 and Luke 8:35, although the words of Jesus to the man, "Go home to thy friends" (Mar k 5:19) and "return to thine own house" (Luke 8:39) imply neighbors.

These biblical stories are an excellent example of how traditions about Jesus changed from one storyteller to another, precisely the way traditions were changed by persons reporting stories of and about Lincoln. And the way Lincoln uses these miracle stories indicates that he was familiar with phrases from them without knowing any one of them with precision and depth.

Throughout the rest of his speech Lincoln stresses morality as the means of persuasion that leads to the road of reason. The recovering alcoholic must make "a most powerful moral effort," and "he needs every moral support and influence . . . every moral prop." Some persons underestimate the power of moral influence, but "surely no Christian will adhere to this objection." Lincoln's mentioning the word Christian, without any implication of faith on his part, was a good ear-catcher for his audience in a Presbyterian church.

Looking forward to a great triumph for temperance, and with a great rhetorical flourish, Lincoln speaks: "Happy day, when, all appetites controlled, all passions subdued, all matters subjected, *mind*, all conquering *mind*, shall live and move the monarch of the world. Glorious consummation! Hail fall of Fury! Reign of Reason, all hail!" (1:279).

On the way toward that happy day and the conclusion of his address, Lincoln inserts precise and imprecise phrases from the Bible. Most, if not all, could be eliminated without detracting from the thought and language of the speech. That is why I discontinued discussing them until now.

Lincoln says that the Washingtonians do not consign "the habitual drunkard to hopeless ruin." They believe in a present and future good for all living now and in the future. "As applying to *their* cause, *they* deny the doctrine of unpardonable sin. As in Christianity . . . *they* teach that 'While the lamp holds out to burn/The vilest sinner may return'" (1:276). Instead of referring to a passage from the New Testament, Lincoln quotes from Isaac Watts.[9] The doctrine of the unpardonable sin was well known in Lincoln's time. John Bunyan (1628–1688) had dealt favorably with it in his *The Doctrine of Law and Grace Unfolded* (1659), and Jonathan Edwards (1703–1758) strongly defended it in several works, especially in his *The Salvation of All Men Strictly Examined: and the endless punishment of those who die.* The emphatic *they* and *their*, instead of *our*, indicate that, as usual, Lincoln sets himself apart from Christian beliefs. That explains his use of "no Christian" earlier.

The basis of the belief in the unpardonable sin is Mark 3:28-30, where Jesus is to have said that all sins and blasphemies will be forgiven, "but he that shall blaspheme against the Holy Ghost [Spirit] hath never forgiveness, but is in danger of eternal damnation" (see also Matt 12:31–32; Luke 12:10). Here the "unpardonable sin" is blasphemy against the Holy Spirit, and only Mark adds the comment that "because they said, 'He hath an unclean spirit.'" This limits guilt to blasphemy against the Holy Spirit, because his critics accused Jesus of having an unclean spirit (see Mark 3:22: "He hath Beelzebub"). Lincoln was not aware of that statement, and most Christians today are not aware of it, either, when they talk about the unpardonable sin. Jesus' words about a kingdom divided against itself are part of the same context.

Lincoln praises the Washingtonians because they forgive even the vilest sinner. However, he shows no understanding whatsoever of the context in the gospel of Mark from which the ideas originated. Indeed, his words "As in Christianity" and the quotation from Isaac Watts may indicate that he got the idea of the "unpardonable sin" from some source other than the Bible. However, the phrases that follow may echo biblical language. For "the chief of sinners" see 1 Tim 1:15:"sinners; of whom I am chief," and for "the chief apostles" see 2 Cor 12:11: "the very chiefest apostles." The contexts of these two passages, though, are far different from that of the unpardonable sin.

"Drunken devils are cast out by ones, by sevens, and by legions; and the unfortunate victims, like the poor possessed, who was redeemed from his long and lonely wanderings, in the tombs, are publishing to the ends of the earth, how great things have been done for them" (1:276). Again, Lincoln's language shows influence from the three miracle stories mentioned. Being in tombs is mentioned in the three accounts (Matt 8:28; Mark 5:2–5; Luke 8:27). In Mark 5:9 and in Luke 8:30 the name of the man is Legion. In Mark 5:15 the man is referred to as one who "had the legion." For "ones" see Matt 9:32; 12:22; Luke 11:14; for "seven" see Matt 12:45; Mark 16:9; Luke 8:2; 11:26; Acts 19:14-16.

Lincoln's words "to the ends of the earth," which he uses only here (1:276), are an exaggeration based on a vague recollection of Luke 8:34–37 (see also Matt 8:33–34; Mark 5:14–20). The words quoted occur often in the Old Testament but only in Acts 13:47 in the New Testament. See, for example, "a noise shall come even to the ends of the earth" (Jer 25:31). According to Acts 13:47, Paul and Barnabas had been sent "to be a light of the Gentiles, that thou shouldest be for salvation unto the ends of the earth" (see also Deut 33:17; Isa 40:28; Job 28:34; Zech 9:10). Lincoln's words are clever linguistic adaptations from the gospel stories, but again they show neither precision nor depth of knowledge.

According to Lincoln, whether all intoxicating beverages should be banished is not *now* an open question, because "Three-fourths of mankind confess the affirmative with their *tongues*, and . . . all the rest acknowledge it in their *hearts*" (1:276–77). Lincoln may be influenced by several biblical passages. The combination of tongue and heart occurs in Ps 45:1; Prov 10:20; 16:1; Isa 32:4; Jer 9:8; Acts 2:26; and Jas 1:26. Do Lincoln's *italics* on the two nouns indicate that he was influenced by the combination of the words in the Bible, or were they for emphasis? Perhaps he was most influenced by Isaiah: "This people draw near me with their mouth, and with their lips do honour me, but have removed their heart far from me" (Isa 29:13), loosely quoted by Jesus in Matt 15:8 and Mark

7:6. See also "If thou shalt confess with thy mouth the Lord Jesus, and shalt believe in thine heart . . . with the heart man believeth. . . . and with the mouth confession is made" (Rom 10:9-10) and "every tongue shall confess" (Rom 14:11; see also Phil 2:11). The plural tongues does not occur in any of those passages. The words "in their hearts" occur often in the Bible. Although "acknowledge it in their hearts" does not occur there, the following are close: "say in their hearts" (Ps 35:25; 74:8; Zech 12:5), "reasoning in their hearts" (Mark 2:5), "thinking in their hearts" (Mark 2:8), and "wandering in their hearts" (Luke 3:15). Lincoln's language is imprecise and the source of his words uncertain.

The drinker should reject every thought of "backsliding" (1:277), a word frequently used by Jeremiah and Hosea of the backsliding of Israel (e.g., Jer 3:6–22; 8:5; 31:22; 49:4; Hos 4:16; 11:7; 14:4). Lincoln's "wallowing in the mire," with quotation marks, is from 2 Pet 2:22, where the author says that the person who turns from a former state of righteousness is like "the sow that was washed [returns] to her wallowing in the mire." Lincoln is saying that no one will beckon back the former drinker to his former miserable state of "wallowing in the mire" (1:277). Lincoln reverses the ideas in the maxim by putting the miserable state first, a clever manipulation to fit the circumstances. The origin of the words in 2 Pet 2:22 is the widely known pagan *Story of Ahikar* 8:18: "My son, thou hast been to me like the swine that has been to the baths, and when it saw a muddy ditch, went down and wallowed in it." In none of the sources that may have influenced Lincoln is there any hint of the subjects of temperance, alcoholism, or alcoholics.

According to Lincoln, no Christian will adhere to the objection of non-drunkards who do not want to reveal themselves as being thought drunkards by joining "a reformed drunkard's society." Then he switches to the plural: "If they [Christians] believe, as they profess, that Omnipotence condescended to take on himself the form of sinful man" and died "an ignominious death for their sakes" they should not object to the reformation of a drunkard "for the temporal, and perhaps eternal salvation" for one "of their own fellow creatures" (1:277–78). The biblical view that human beings are sinful is well known. Peter confesses before Christ: "I am a sinful man" (Luke 5:8; see also Luke 24:7). See also "the likeness of sinful flesh" (Rom 8:3). Again, the pronouns Lincoln uses set him apart from Christians who believe.

Omnipotence is not a biblical word, and omnipotent occurs only in Rev 19:6: "Alleluia: for the Lord God omnipotent reigneth." Lincoln applies the designation to Jesus, for which there is no evidence in the New Testament. Lincoln's words about Omnipotence taking the form of man are an allusion to Phil 2:5–8, where Paul transmits part of an early Christian creed or hymn, which in the Greek text is set off in poetic form. According to Paul, Christ Jesus did not take advantage of his being equal with God, but took the form of a slave in human form. "And being found in fashion as a man, he humbled himself, and became obedient unto death, even the death of the cross." The belief that Christ died for the sin of mankind became a cardinal doctrine of Christianity.

Significantly, Lincoln uses the designation "Christ" for Jesus only once, and it is in a historical statement, not in a religious one (2:10). Again, his words "no Christian . . . death for their sakes . . . they will not . . . their own fellow creatures" are far from including himself, so they give no insight into Lincoln's religious faith.

According to Lincoln, "The demon of intemperance" has caused many to fall "a sacrifice to his rapacity. He ever seems to have gone forth like the Egyptian angel of death, commissioned to slay if not the first, the fairest born of every family" (1:278). The words allude to the story of the Israelites in bondage and the death of some Egyptians and animals in the last plague (Exod 11:1–9; 12:29–34). However, the source of Lincoln's words is not so obvious. Here are some passages that may have entered his mind: "All the first born in the land of Egypt shall die, from the first born of Pharaoh . . . even unto the firstborn of the maidservant that is behind the mill" (Exod 11:5) and "shall smite all the firstborn in the land of Egypt, both man and beast" (Exod 12:12; see also 12:29). His allusion to such passages leaves what he says incorrect. The plagues did not affect Israelite families.

There is no record of an Egyptian angel of death, and an angel and death are never linked together in any of the plague stories, where the Lord himself is the subject of the action. For example, the Lord says, "When I see the blood, I will pass over you, and the plague shall not be upon you to destroy you, when I smite the land of Egypt" (Exod 12:13–14; see also Exod 11:7–8; Num 3:13). This is one of the best examples of Lincoln's careless use of the Bible and disproves the myths of his profound and inclusive knowledge of the Bible and his wanting to quote every word just right.

In defense of temperance, Lincoln calls for a trump "to sound the moral resurrection" (1:278). Here the trumpet sounding the coming of the physical resurrection alluded to earlier now becomes a call for moral action by people to "rise and stand up, an exceeding great army—'Come from the four winds, O breath! and breathe upon these slain, that they may live.'" (1:278). Rise and stand up are used together in synonymous parallelism in Ps 94:16: "Who will rise up for me against the evildoers? or who will stand up for me against the workers of iniquity?" In what follows, Lincoln shows a more careful use of the Bible. An exceeding great army is an exact phrase from Ezek 37:10, and the quotation after the dash is an exact quotation from Ezek 37:9, except for the exclamation point after "O breath" instead of a comma. Lincoln reverses the order of quotations, perhaps because he remembered the phrase about the army and checked it out. The break with a dash before the second quotation may indicate that it was an after thought to stress his position on temperance to appeal especially to Bible-readers in his audience. In Ezekiel, the lines are applied to the fallen of Israel who will be restored to life. Lincoln applies the quotations to the restoration of alcoholics, which is more apt than most of his biblical references.

Lincoln uses "the four winds" again in his speech on "a house divided" (2:468), where in each instance it means "from all directions." The origin of the phrase may be Jer 49:36, where the Lord says that he will "bring the four winds from the four quarters of heaven" to scatter the people of Elam (see also Dan 7:2; 8:8; 11:4; Zech 2:6; Matt 24:31; Mark 13:27; Rev 7:1).

According to Lincoln, the political revolution of 1776 brought political freedom for mankind, although at the cost of great suffering. Similarly, there are blessings that come with the victory of the alcoholic after a series of evils caused by alcoholism. For example, "a viler slavery manumitted," "more disease healed," "no widows weeping," and "the universal song of gladness" (1:278–79). For "widows weeping," see Acts 9:39: "Widows stood by him [Peter] weeping." See also "Rachel weeping for her children" (Jer 31:15). For "song of gladness," see Isa 30:29: "Ye shall have a song . . . and gladness of heart" (see also Prov 15:13). For Lincoln's "Glorious consummation," which he uses also in 2:132, 482, see "even until the consummation" in Dan 9:27. It is impossible to determine how much Lincoln's language was influenced by any of these passages.

About Lincoln's temperance address, Wolf (59 and 62) says: "The speech shows such an intimate acquaintance with biblical language and incidents that, had its authorship been unknown, scholars would probably have assigned it to one professionally trained in the field of biblical study." Not really. One needed only a moral sense of compassion and forgiveness, coupled with a fantastic memory for words and phrases from the Bible, not professional training in biblical studies.

Wolf continues: "While its perspective was a deep Christian compassion for one's fellow man, it rubbed many church members the wrong way. They just did not like having their virtue over against the drunkard explained away as 'absence of appetite' rather than commended as 'mental or moral superiority.' In this temperance address the analysis is biblically oriented, the program of action deeply Christian in context, but the motivation still remains rationalistic." Our study shows that Wolf's statements need rethinking.

Having served four terms in the Illinois State Legislature, Lincoln was looking forward to higher political goals. Before an audience of Christians in the Second Presbyterian Church in Springfield, he became the sagacious politician who preached a conglomeration of biblical language and texts, the contexts of which are unrelated to the subjects of temperance, alcoholism, and alcoholics. With respect to "deep Christian compassion" and "the program of action deeply Christian in context," morally sensitive persons who were not Christians would agree with Lincoln's methods of dealing with alcoholics.

If Lincoln had in mind the Christian doctrine of the Incarnation (Wolf, 61), he was completely oblivious of the contexts of it origins in Phil 2:5–8 and in John 1:14. As the personal pronouns indicate, Lincoln immediately set himself apart from believing in that Christian doctrine. Indeed, his words are a back-handed criticism of it. Lincoln appeals for moral support and reason in approaching the subject of alcoholism, not theology.

It is true that "Lincoln's political popularity suffered in a subsequent election partly, as he believed, because of his speech" (Wolf, 59). However, that only indicates that what happened was contrary to what Lincoln had expected, perhaps because of all his references to the Bible made in a church. His "Christian" political adversaries were not impressed as the result of his language, including that from the Bible.

While campaigning for representative in the U. S. House of Representatives, Lincoln wrote a handbill replying to charges of infidelity, July 31, 1846 (1:382). He denies that he is "an open scoffer at Christianity." He says that he is not sure he could "be brought to support a man for office, whom I knew to be an open enemy of, and scoffer at, religion." Without saying anything about Christianity, he states his concern for morality: "I do not think any man has the right to insult the feelings, and injure the morals, of the community in which he may live. If, then, I was guilty of such conduct, I should blame no man who should condemn me for it; but I do blame those, whoever they may be, who falsely put such a charge in circulation against me" (1:382).

Recall that in the temperance address he set himself apart from Christian doctrine. After his election to the U.S. House, he wrote to Allen N. Ford, August 11, 1846 (1:383–84), editor of the *Illinois Gazette*, about the report of his infidelity. Lincoln says that a man should not make any charge against a fellowman, "without *knowing* it to be true." Lincoln stresses morality: "I believe it is an established maxim in morals that he who makes an assertion without knowing whether it is true or false, is guilty of falsehood; and the accidental truth of the assertion, does not justify or excuse him. This maxim ought to be particularly held in view, when we contemplate an attack upon the reputation of our neighbor" (1:284). How fitting it would have been for one supposedly interested in biblical religion to quote one of the apt passages in the Bible about man's relationship with his fellowmen.

This chapter leaves us with some differences of opinions about Lincoln's use of the Bible, and there are still more to come.

4

We Are Not to Do Evil That God May Come

Lincoln and Speed exchange several letters about their love lives, the first from Lincoln, February 25, 1842 (1:280). Lincoln had been immensely concerned about Speed for the last ten hours, but he is relieved to learn that the news is better than expected. He feared lest the situation between Speed and Fanny had gotten worse, and Lincoln assures him that as his nerves get steady, things will get better. Speed is afraid that the Elysium about which he dreamed will never be realized, to which Lincoln replies that if it is not it will not be the fault of the one who is now his wife. It would be ridiculous to think that anyone should be unhappy with Fanny. His father used to say that "'if you make a bad bargain, *hug* it the tighter.'" If Speed's bargain could possibly be called a bad one, it "is certainly the most *pleasant* one for applying that maxim to."

Lincoln wrote a second letter to Speed on the same day (1:281) in which he acknowledges a letter from Speed announcing that Miss Fanny and he "are no more twain, but one flesh." Now he is afraid the two will be so devoted to one another that they will forget about him. He tells Speed how much happiness he wishes for them, regrets that Speed will not return to Illinois, understands that Speed's obligations are to Fanny, who desires to remain with relatives and friends, and asks him to "give her a double reciprocation of all the love she sent" him.

The words about one flesh allude to the Lord God's creation of Adam from the rib of Eve: "A man shall leave his father and his mother, and shall cleave unto his wife: and they shall be one flesh" (Gen 2:22–24). The words quoted are a euphemism for something Speed said about the couple's sexual relations and are an exact quotation from Matt 19:5 or Mark 10:8. There the words are part of Jesus' response to a question the Pharisees had asked him about divorce. Jesus' reply includes an allusion to Gen 3:22–24 in words appropriate to the context: "They are no more twain, but one flesh." It is interesting that Lincoln says nothing to Speed about cleaving to his wife, present in both biblical texts. Was he possibly uncertain about the two remaining together because of differences between them?

In another letter to Speed, March 27, 1842 (1:282–83), Lincoln expresses his pleasure on hearing that Speed's happiness with his marriage far exceeded expectations. That is all he needs to know. "I say, enough, dear Lord" (1:282). Elijah, brooding about the idolatry of his people, says, "It is enough; now, O Lord, take away my life" (1 Kgs 19:4). Lincoln was reassured about Speed, whereas Elijah had given up hope for his people. As with the biblical language Lincoln used earlier, he is oblivious of the context of 1 Kgs 19:4, and he is not concerned with getting the language exactly right. A superb memory of biblical language served his purpose.

Lincoln now has more pleasure than the sum of all he has enjoyed since the day he broke his engagement with Mary Todd. He is brooding over that experience and feels that she is still unhappy. However, after she returned from a party trip to Jacksonville, he learned that she enjoyed the trip and says, "God be praised for that" (1:282). Although the Bible was far from Lincoln's mind, he may have been influenced by its language, in which praising God (Lord) is a repeated refrain, especially in the Old Testament. Of many examples, see "I will sing praise to the Lord God of Israel" (Judg 5:3; see also 1 Chr 16:4; 2 Chr 20:19); "Praise ye the Lord" (Ps 113:1; 150:1); "Give God the praise" (John 9:24; see also Heb 13:15); and "Praise the Lord, all ye Gentiles" (Rom 15.11; see also Rev 19:5). Lincoln's phrase does not coincide with any of the passages, and it sounds as though he was at an evangelistic meeting. Indeed, his words may have been part of the religious language of the time and therefore not directly from the Bible. Lincoln has written what Speed wanted to hear, and his words are self-assurance as he contemplates again a marriage to Mary Todd.

In yet another letter to Speed, July 4, 1842 (1:288–90), Lincoln says that Speed makes "a kind of acknowledgement" to him for his happy marriage, and he believes that God made him "one of the instruments" in getting Speed and Fanny together and that God "fore-ordained" their union. "Whatever he designs, he will do for *me* yet," with respect to his relationship with Mary Todd. Then Lincoln says, "'Stand *still* and see the salvation of the Lord' is my text just now." The text, within quotation marks in Lincoln's words, is a verbatim quotation of Exod 14:13 (1:289).

In that passage, the Israelites, finding the Egyptians in hot pursuit, complain to Moses that it would have been better for them had they remained in Egypt. Moses replies with the quotation, which is preceded with words of assurance: "Fear ye not." The point of the miracle of the parting of the waters that follows is that by it the Lord will bring honor upon himself at the expense of Pharaoh, and thereby the Egyptians shall know that the Lord is the God of the Israelites (Exod 14:17–18). Lincoln's mind is really on what God is doing for Speed and for him, not in God bringing honor to himself. Biblical language is enough to comfort a man temporarily sick over love.

Subsequent letters to Speed raise doubt about Lincoln's sense of providence or personal salvation. In the first one, October 5, 1842 (1:302–3), Lincoln says nothing about God's design in his relationship with Mary Todd. He asks Speed a very personal question, which only a true friend would understand: "Are you now, in *feeling* as well as *judgment*, glad you are married as you are?" And then he requests Speed: "Please answer it quickly as I feel impatient to know" (1:303). This was only a month before Lincoln and Mary were married. In a letter, July 18, 1843 (1:305–6), nine months after they were married, Lincoln writes to Speed: "Mary is very well and continues her old sentiments of friendship for you. How the marriage life goes with us I will tell you when I see you here" (1:306).

Were Lincoln's feelings so personal that he did not want to mention them in a letter? Or were they the sentiments of a man who was still uncertain about the providential design for his life yet to come and that he would wait to see the salvation of the Lord? If so, the quotation of Exod 14:13 can hardly be taken as evidence for it. There is nothing in the context to indicate a personal salvation from the deity for the individual, as in Luke 19:9, for example: "Today is salvation come to this house." Moreover, in Exod 14:13 the Hebrew word translated as "salvation" in the KJV is better translated as "deliverance" as in modern versions, for similar events in Israelite history. The biblical quotation from Exodus came into Lincoln's mind at a time of anxiety without any forethought or afterthought.

Wolf (55–68) devotes a whole chapter to the subject inspired by the quotation from Exod 14:13 about seeing the salvation of the Lord. Fornieri (*Political Faith*, 36–38, 58–60, 172) and others use the series of Lincoln's letters to Speed to argue for Lincoln's biblical faith already in his early life. But this raises a significant question. Recall that on September 27, 1841, Lincoln wrote to Mary Speed: "I doubt not that it [the Bible] is really, as she [Speed's mother Lucy] says, the best cure for the 'Blues' could one take it according to the truth" (1:261). About five months later Lincoln wrote the first of his series of letters to Speed. In that short time, did Lincoln come to such profound biblical faith? I suspect that many other love-smitten persons have felt similar emotions about their relationships. Lincoln expresses such religious emotions elsewhere only in his letter to John D. Johnston, January 12, 1851 (2:96–97). In his letters to Speed, as in that letter, he "comforts too much."

Lincoln became deeply involved in politics at the national level. Supporters of Lincoln, who called themselves Liberty men instead of abolitionists, intended to help unify the Whigs in the next election. In a letter to Williamson Durley, October 3, 1845 (1:347–48), about the election in Putnam County, Illinois, Lincoln writes: "If the whig abolitionists of New York had voted with us last fall, Mr. Clay would now be president, whig principles in the ascendent, and Texas not annexed." Their reasoning was, "'We are not to do *evil* that *good* may come.'" According to Lincoln, that position is doubtless correct, but did it apply? If their votes could have helped to prevent the spread of slavery, "would it not have been *good* and not *evil*? . . . By the *fruit* the tree is to be known. An *evil* tree cannot bring forth *good* fruit." If the election of Henry Clay would have helped to prevent the spread of slavery, "could the act of electing have been *evil?*" (1:347). The words "We are not to do *evil* that *good* may come" may be an adaptation from Rom 3:8, where Paul says that it was being slanderously said by some persons, "Let us do evil that good may come," that is, so they could continue to sin and be saved by grace (Rom 6:1–2). Lincoln calls the words "a general proposition," again a way of referring to something in the Bible without being specific about its source or author or implication of any sacred authority (Appendix 4).

The words about the tree and its fruit are loosely quoted from Matt 7:15–20, a saying of Jesus about false prophets: "Ye shall know them by their fruits . . . every good tree bringeth forth good fruit; but a corrupt tree bringeth forth evil fruit. A good tree cannot bring forth evil fruit, neither can a corrupt tree bring forth good fruit . . . Wherefore by their fruits ye shall know them." Lincoln changes the order of some phrases, and he uses "evil" all through instead of "corrupt" sometimes as in Matthew. Without a thought of preciseness or of the original context, Lincoln has taken a widely known saying of Jesus, originally spoken about the behavior of false prophets, and adapted it to suit his political feelings about Whigs.

In 1841, after four terms as representative in the Illinois State Legislature, Lincoln could not seek that office again. He lost in a campaign for election as representative to the U.S. House of Representatives in 1843, and Clay lost the presidential election to James K. Polk (1845–1849), a Democrat. However, both events brought Lincoln general recognition as a viable political prospect of the Whig Party. He was elected to the U.S. House of Representatives in August 1846 from the Seventh Congressional District of Illinois.

The charge of infidelity continued to haunt Lincoln, and he bemoans that fact in his letter to Allen N. Ford mentioned earlier. He informs Ford that Peter Cartwright, famous Methodist preacher, circuit rider, and Democratic opponent in the race for election to Congress, "was whispering the charge of infidelity against" him in Jacksonville and other neighborhoods. As late as September 1860, the tradition of Lincoln's infidelity was kept alive by John Hill, son of Samuel Hill, a former friend of Lincoln from New Salem. He accused Lincoln in a pamphlet on "Opposing principles of Henry Clay, and Abraham Lincoln" (4:104–8). Hill's accusation raises a question. If Lincoln had become accustomed to attending church regularly, as tradition has it, and if he had been so Christian-oriented, as some traditions avow, how likely is it that there would still be a charge of infidelity in the last months of 1860? A similar question arises with respect to the Temperance Address, with its "deep Christian compassion," and an approach that is "the deep Christian one of the incarnational principle," all part of the "program of action deeply Christian in context" (Wolf, 59–62). These questions relate to our understanding of the difficult texts in the Lyceum Address, especially the church as "the only greater institution."

Among the fragments of Lincoln documents during the period in Springfield is one titled Fragment of a Tariff Discussion, December 1,

1847? (1:407–16), an issue on which he sometimes vacillated. His chief concern was that persons should have a fair return on the money earned by their labor. He sums up his principle with a verbatim quotation from Gen 3:19: "In the sweat of thy face shalt thou eat bread" (1:411). This is one of the few times he mentions the context of a quotation, which he introduces with the words, "In the early days of the world, the Almighty said to the first of our race." Does this mean Lincoln had the Bible in front of him and wanted to get the words exactly right in supporting his argument that slavery was immoral because slave owners took the money earned by the fruit of slaves' labor? The fact that in what follows Lincoln used "labour" and "laboured" of the *KJV* instead of "labor" and "labored" suggests that he used the text. Even if he used the Genesis text, it has nothing to do with slavery or politics, much less with tariffs. Rather, the Lord punishes Adam because he listened to his wife instead of obeying the Lord.

Among other things, Lincoln was responding to an increase of tariffs on iron and manufacturing, for which he would favor a moderate protective tariff if it could be free of political differences and uncertainties. "It has so happened in all ages of the world, that *some* have laboured, and *others* have, without labour, enjoyed a large proportion of the fruits" (1:412). This is an allusion to Gen 3:19 about God's words to Adam mentioned earlier. The fact that slaves were laboring by the sweat of their faces to produce fruits while their owners received most of the fruits of their labors continued to trouble Lincoln. He uses the passage again in a reply to three Baptist preachers (7:368), in a story for Noah Brooks, a newspaper reporter (8:155), and in his Second Inaugural Address (8:333).

Lincoln could not find much fault with the administration of President Polk, but in Congress he criticized him on the War with Mexico.[10] He suspects that President Polk feels greatly in the wrong by going to war with Mexico and that he feels its blood, "like the blood of Abel, is crying to Heaven against him" (1:439), an allusion to the story of Cain killing his brother Abel (Gen 4:2–11). The Lord says to Cain, "What hast thou done? the voice of thy brother's blood crieth unto me from the ground" (Gen 4:10). Lincoln uses the metonym Heaven for the Lord in Genesis, and "unto me from the ground" in Genesis becomes "against him," that is, Polk. Lincoln has adapted a passage from the Bible to fit the context of his argument. The writers of Matthew and Luke used the story about Abel in speaking about Jesus prophesying about future punishment to come on the scribes and Pharisees, beginning "from the blood of Abel" (Luke 11:51; see also Matt 23:35). The statement about the blood of Abel is used more appropriately in the gospel context than it is in the Lincoln context.

It is doubtful that Lincoln thought the situation of Polk closely paralleled that of the Cain and Abel story. It is easy to read too much into Lincoln's thoughts about the Bible and how he used it. Fornieri (*Political Faith*, 48) comments that "Lincoln's appeal to the story of Cain and Abel . . . illustrated the importance of a leader's accountability to God and the people. Cain's evasion of fraternal responsibility ('Am I my brother's keeper?') parallels Polk's evasion of political responsibility. In addition to allegorical symbolism, Lincoln used biblical language in an evocative sense to persuade his listeners of Polk's guilt . . . Cain's ruthless fratricide of Abel pricked the moral conscience of the nation. The images of 'the blood of this war, like the blood of Abel,' were intended . . . to arouse righteous indignation against Polk." If Lincoln thought of the story in that way, I think it unlikely that his hearers drew those parallels. The last sentence of Fornieri is certainly true, and perhaps that may be all Lincoln had in mind. However, in the Genesis narrative only the Lord is indignant toward Cain; the people are not.

According to Gen 4:13–15, the Lord violates his own commandment of "death for death" (Exod 21:12) by putting a mark on Cain so that no one would kill him (Gen 4:13–15). Then Cain went into a land where he built a city, without a hint of indignation by anyone, and he had descendants and prospered (Gen 4:17–24). Lincoln's words about Abel give no indication that he was aware of any of these things in the context of the story. This observation weakens the importance of Lincoln's words, "The Almighty *will* not, be evaded" (1:439), which Fornieri uses as the introduction to his argument. Lincoln had used those words earlier in connection with the question of how the Mexican War began, without reference to the Cain and Abel story. Lincoln does not mention Cain, as does Fornieri, but his guilt would be assumed by most of his hearers. Although the Lord said to Cain that if he does not do well, "sin lieth at the door" (Gen 4:7), that was before the murder, and the writer of Genesis does not mention sin again until Gen 18:20 in an entirely different context. According to Lincoln, it is "the blood of this war, like the blood of Abel, is crying to Heaven against him" that makes Polk conscious of being in the wrong. That is the point Lincoln wanted to make, not punishment, but his readers probably believed that the mark placed on Cain was a punishment.

The note in the *CW* 1:439, is important. After the words just quoted, it reads: "At this point Lincoln emended as follows: "that he ordered General Taylor into the midst of a peaceful Mexican settlement, purposely to bring on a war; that originally . . ." For Lincoln, the admission of guilt on the part of Polk for starting the Mexican War, not punishment for it, is a crucial point.

In the U.S. House of Representatives Lincoln's political interests and ambitions were considerably heightened. He continued to attack President Polk over the Mexican War, for which he was strongly opposed by the Democrats and even some Whig friends. Among the latter was the well-known Baptist minister John Mason Peck, who spoke at a celebration of victory at Buena Vista. Lincoln wrote to Peck, May 21, 1848 (1:172–3), and quotes him as saying that in "view of *all* the facts . . . the Government of the United States committed no aggression on Mexico." Lincoln mentions facts that Peck had "kept out of view." He asks Peck if he would feel the same way if some nation did the same thing "against the humblest of our people." He knows Peck would not and asks, "Is the precept 'Whatsoever ye would that men should do to you, do ye even so to them' obsolete?—of no force?—of no application?" (1:473). The quotation is exact form a saying of Jesus in Matt 7:12, a part of the Sermon on the Mount. Luke's version differs: "As ye would that men should do to you, do ye also to them likewise" (Luke 6:31). Again, Lincoln uses the word precept instead of citing chapter and verse (Appendix 4). The quotation is exact because it fits the Lincoln context. He uses the same passage in his communication with George B. Ide and other Baptist preachers (7:368). There, as we shall see, he changes the quotation to suit his immediate argument with the preachers.

As a delegate to the Whig National Convention in Philadelphia in June 1848, Lincoln was influential in the nomination of Zachary Taylor, distinguished general in the Mexican War, for president. He writes to William H. Herndon, June 12, 1848 (1:476–77), who had enlisted in the War with

Mexico, to express his jubilation at the nomination of Taylor. His nomin -ation turned "the war thunder against" the Democrats so that the war for them is now "the gallows of Haman" that they built for the Whigs, but "on which they are doomed to be hanged themselves" (1:477). Haman, an officer of the Persian King Ahasuerus (Xerxes I, 485–465 BC), married the Jewess Esther. Haman prepared a gallows for the Jew Mordecai, who refused to do obeisance to him. Queen Esther intervened, and Haman died on the gallows prepared for Mordecai (Esth 7:9–10). Lincoln takes the incident in Esther and uses it facetiously in applying it to those persons in Illinois who were still opposing Taylor, the Republican presidential nominee.

Speaking in the U.S. House of Representatives on the Presidential Question, July 27, 1848 (1:501–16, Lincoln supports Taylor for president. He argues that he, not Lewis Cass, the Democratic candidate, would trust the judgment of the people better in making decisions. Taylor had stated that on issues such as tariffs, internal improvements, and a national bank: "the will of the people, as expressed through their representatives in congress, ought to be respected and carried out by the executive" (1:503). According to Lincoln, people ask: "If you are elected, shall we have a national bank?" Taylor answers: "*Your* will, gentlemen, not *mine*" (1:504). Was Lincoln influenced in what he says by Jesus' words in Gethsemane: "Not as I will, but as thou wilt" (Matt 26:39; Mark 14:36; Luke 22:42)? If so, he reversed the phrases to put the emphasis on the people.

After castigating the Democrat Lewis Cass, Lincoln says that he and Van Buren "are the same 'manner of men'" (1:512). The quoted phrase is biblical, as is "manner of *man*," which Lincoln never uses. Gideon, commander of an Israelite army, asks two of his enemies about persons whom they had killed: "What manner of men were they whom ye slew?" (Judg 8:18; see also Rom 6:19; 1 Cor 15:32; Gal 3:15; 1 Thess 1:5).

Sometime in the fall of 1848, perhaps after speaking at Worcester, Boston, and other cities in Massachusetts, Lincoln visited Niagara Falls. An extant fragment, September 25–30, 1848 (2:10–11), about that visit appears to be a meditation on his experience. Like other visitors, Lincoln was amazed at the wonder of it all, especially the capacity of water flowing through it and how the geologist and philosopher might think about it. Lincoln says the geologist will eventually demonstrate that this world is at least fourteen thousand years old" (2:10). This is a contradiction with a biblical view of creation that Lincoln later takes literally in his first lecture on discoveries and inventions. There he dates events in Genesis according to Bishop Ussher's view of the creation occurring in 4004 BC, so Lincoln's fourteen thousand years ago from 1848 would be about 12,152 BC. James Ussher (1581–1656) was an Archbishop in Ireland, Vice Chancellor of Trinity College in Dublin, churchman, and scholar. He set the first day of creation on Sunday, October 23, 4004 BC. Adam and Eve were driven from the Garden on Monday, November 10, 4004 BC, and the ark settled on Mount Ararat on May 5, 2348 BC. Obviously, Lincoln was not thinking of the Bible when he wrote about his Niagara experience, so he did not try to reconcile the age of Niagara with the time of creation according to Ussher's dating.

The few letters Lincoln wrote to family members usually dealt with some problem. John Johnston, his stepbrother, had written a letter for Thomas Lincoln, Lincoln's father, about his financial problems. In his response to the two men, December 24, 1848 (2:15–17), Lincoln "cheerfully" sends his father twenty dollars to save his land from sale, but he is not cheerful about what he says to Johnston. Johnston has asked for seventy or eighty dollars for which he would almost give his place in heaven. Lincoln responds that Johnston must value his place there very cheaply and that he could probably get the money if he worked for four or five months. If he follows Lincoln's advice, he "will find it worth more than eight times eighty dollars" (2:16). The use of a number with "times" and another number is biblical: "seven times seven years" (Lev 25:8), "ten thousand times ten thousand" (Dan 7:10; Rev 5:11), "seventy times seven" (Matt 18:22). A variation is the use of "score" with numbers, for example, "The days of our years are threescore years and ten" (Ps 90:10; see also 2 Chr 36:21; Josh 14:10; Luke 2:37). Recall "Four score and seven years ago" in Lincoln's Gettysburg Address.

After Lincoln finished his term in Congress, March 4, 1849, he was dejected about possibilities for his political party. Some Whigs had criticized his work, and his stand on the War with Mexico had made him unpopular. A hiatus in his political ambition resulted in little significant use of the Bible. His Eulogy on Zachary Taylor, July 25, 1850 (2:83–90), which he delivered on a day's notice at the invitation of some citizens of Chicago, renewed his interest in politics. The eulogy is a perfunctory narrative of events in Taylor's life, especially his military service and his personal character, with a profound rhetorical exclamation at the end of the first part: "And now the din of battle nears the fort and sweeps obliquely by; a gleam of hope flies through the half imprisoned few; they fly to the wall; every eye is strained—it is—it is—the stars and stripes are still aloft! Anon the anxious brethren meet; and while hand strikes hand, the heavens are rent with a loud, long, glorious, gushing cry of victory! victory!! victory!!!" (2:85).

Lincoln doubts that all the wisdom and patriotism of Taylor will have died with him, but they must be "sustained by the confidence and devotion of the people." He fears that "the one *great* question of the day, is not now so likely to be partially acquiesced in by the different sections of the Union, as it would have been, could Gen. Taylor have been spared to us. Yet, under all circumstances, trusting to our Maker, and through his wisdom and beneficence, to the great body of our people, we will not despair, nor despond" (2:89). The idea of God as Maker goes back to the belief that God created man in his own image (Gen 1:26–27; 2:7, 20–22), and it became a universal theme in the Bible, where Maker is used as a title for the deity innumerable times in the Old Testament and in Heb 11:10. With Lincoln's trusting the Maker, see, for example, Ps 2:12: "Blessed are all they that put their trust in him" (the Lord; see also Ps 4:5; 52:8); and "trusting in the Lord" (Ps 12:7). In the Bible, wisdom is associated with God, for example: "the wisdom of God" (Luke 11:49; 1 Cor 1:21, 24); and "the manifold wisdom of God" (Eph 3:10). In one or more of these passages, the subject may be Jesus, not God. However, Maker as a name for the deity and wisdom are never used together in the Bible. For Lincoln, Maker was just one of the plethora of names for the deity that would impress his special audience.

Of Taylor, Lincoln laments: "The conqueror at last is conquered. The fruits of his labor, his name, his memory and example are all that is left us—his example, verifying the great truth, that 'he that humbleth himself, shall be exalted'" (2:89–90). This saying of Jesus, one easy to remember, is preserved in three different contexts in Matt 23:12 and in Luke 14:11

and 18:14. Matthew 23:12 reads: "He that shall humble himself shall be exalted." Luke 14:11 and 18:14 read: "He that humbleth himself shall be exalted," which Lincoln quotes verbatim. According to Matthew, Jesus denounces the scribes and Pharisees for the superficialities in their religion. In Luke 14:11 the context is a banquet in which the invited guests are not to sit in the highest seats but seek the lowest ones. And in Luke 18:14 the context is the self-righteous Pharisee and the lowly publican (tax collector) at prayer, who prays simply: "God be merciful to me a sinner." In each instance those who follow Jesus' instruction will be exalted. Although the context of Lincoln is far different from any of the gospels, the quotation applied to Taylor would be comforting to Mrs. Taylor, her daughter, and others present. Lincoln elaborates the quotation by saying that it is "teaching, that to serve one's country with a singleness of purpose, gives assurance of that country's gratitude, secures its best honors, and makes 'a dying bed, soft as downy pillows are'" (2:90). Oblivious of the context of either biblical passage, Lincoln quotes it from memory to complete his emphasis on Taylor's service to the country, the theme of the eulogy.

Lincoln concludes the eulogy by calling attention to the universality of human mortality, and in doing so he might have been influenced by the Bible. See, for example, "The time drew nigh that Israel (Jacob) must die" (Gen 47:29; see also Deut 4:22; 31:14; 1 Sam 14:43). However, it is interesting that he does not quote from the Bible to offer hope by referring to the Maker as he had earlier in the eulogy and as he does later in writing about his dying father. Rather, he quotes the first line and selected stanzas from the poem "Mortality" by William Knox, Scottish poet (1789–1825).

Although Taylor's views on religion are uncertain, his mysterious wife Margaret was a devoted Episcopalian. As with his words later to the family of his dying father, Lincoln spoke precisely what they and others would be comforted to hear. Thinking of them, Lincoln chooses biblical texts at random that they would be glad to hear, with little thought of the contexts. Therefore, they cannot be used as evidence for his personal faith.

Thomas Lincoln had become critically ill and was near death. Lincoln writes his "brother," John D. Johnston, January 12, 1851 (2:96–97), that he wants every effort made to see that his dying father is comfortable. "Tell him to remember to call upon, and confide in, our great, and good, and merciful Maker; who will not turn away from him in any extremity" (2:97). According to 2 Chr 30:9, messengers from the "good" king Hezekiah told the Israelites to return to God: "The Lord your God is gracious and merciful, and will not turn away his face from you" (see also Jer 32:40; Deut 4:31; Neh 9:31). A psalmist sings: "For thou, Lord, art good . . . and plenteous in mercy unto all them that call upon thee" (Ps 86:5; Ps 103:8; 116:1–8). The idea of the Lord hiding his face from is prominent in the Old Testament, especially in the Psalms and in Isaiah. For examples see Ps 13:1: "How long wilt thou hide thy face from me?"; and Ps 102:2: "Hide not thy face from me" (see also Pss 51:9; 69:17; Isa 64:7; Jer 33:5; Ezek 39:23; Mic 3:4).

Lincoln writes that the Maker "notes the fall of a sparrow, and numbers the hairs of our heads; and He will not forget the dying man, who puts his trust in Him" (2:97). The first part of the quotation is an allusion to Matt 10:29–31 or Luke 12:6–7, for which the KJV of Matt 10:29–31 is confusing: "Are not two sparrows sold for a farthing? and one of them shall not fall on the ground without your Father. But the very hairs of your head are all numbered." Luke's version, although different, is clear: "Are not five sparrows sold for two farthings, and not one of them is forgotten before God? But even the very hairs of your head are all numbered." Lincoln's words about the dying man not being forgotten indicate influence from Luke's version. The phrase "to put trust in," including trust in the Lord (God), occurs frequently in the Old Testament, especially in Psalms, for example, "Put your trust in the Lord" (Ps 4:5); and "O God . . . in thee do I put my trust" (Ps 16:1; see also Pss 11:1; 25:20; 31:1; Jer 39:18; 1 Chr 5:20; Heb 2:13). The words of Lincoln, "who puts his trust in Him," are closest to Prov 30:5: "Every word of God is pure . . . he is a shield unto them that put their trust in him." Again, Lincoln uses biblical language and ideas to fit the occasion, this time to soothe the family of the dying man.

Lincoln asks Johnston to tell his father that "if we could meet now, it is doubtful whether it would not be more painful than pleasant." Nevertheless, he assures Johnston "that if it be his lot to go now, he will soon have a joyous [meeting] with many loved ones gone before; and where [the rest] of us, through the help of God, hope ere-long [to join] them" (2:97; words in brackets taken from Nicolay and Hay). The words "help of God" occur in the Bible only in Acts 26:22, where Paul tells King Agrippa (Agrippa I, Roman procurator of Palestine, AD 41–44) that he has been able to continue his preaching to the Gentiles up to the present, having "obtained the help of God." The phrase "the help of God" was undoubtedly used often then as it is now, with little depth of feeling.

Wolf (81) maintains that Lincoln's words to his stepbrother John Johnston are the clearest expression . . . of Lincoln's view of personal immortality." According to Donald (153), Lincoln's words about the merciful Maker, the fall of a sparrow, and the hairs of the head are "in unconvincing and strained language, really addressed to his backwoods relatives who thought in the clichés of the Primitive Baptists . . . Unable to simulate a grief that he did not feel or an affection that he did not bear, Lincoln did not attend his father's funeral." Benjamin P. Thomas (134) had made a similar assessment of Lincoln's words: "The letter of reassurance that he [Lincoln] sent during the old man's last illness has an unconvincing tone." For a moderating view see Fornieri, *Political Fatih*, 52–54.

How much weight should we put on Lincoln's words to John Johnston for determining his own personal faith? Are they more than words of comfort for a dying man, and/or do they provide an insight into Lincoln's views on personal immortality? They are words his family would hope to hear from an estranged family member. Lincoln's relationship with his father was never good, and there is nothing that indicates Lincoln's love for him. Lincoln's words about a meeting being more painful than pleasant are not those of grief or sorrow but a reminder of lingering ill feelings.

There is more evidence for doubting that Lincoln's words to his dying father indicate the depth of his religious faith. An associate of Lincoln in the legal profession, Colonel William McCullough, was killed in battle near Coffeeville, Mississippi, on December 5, 1862. Lincoln wrote a letter of consolation to his young daughter Fanny, December 23, 1862 (6:16–17), and the depth of Lincoln's sincerity in this short note is unmistakable:

> It is with deep grief that I learn of the death of your kind and brave Father; and, especially, that it is affecting your young heart beyond what is common in such cases. In this sad world of ours, sorrow comes to all; and, to the young, it comes with bitterest agony, because it takes them unawares. The older have learned to ever expect it. I am anxious to afford some alleviation of your present distress. Perfect relief is not possible, except with time. You can not now realize that you will ever feel better. Is not this so? And yet it is a mistake. You are sure to be happy again. To know this, which is certainly true, will make you some less miserable now. I have had experience enough to know what I say; and you need only to believe it, to feel better at once. The memory of your dear Father,

instead of an agony, will yet be a sad sweet feeling in your heart, of a purer, and holier sort than you have known before. (6:16–17)

A letter similar to the one Lincoln wrote to Miss McCullough is one to Mrs. Lydia Bixby written about two years later, November 24, 1864 (8:116–17). He says he has learned that she is "the mother of five sons [number disputed] who have died gloriously on the field of battle." Lincoln continues:

> I feel how weak and fruitless must be any words of mine which should attempt to beguile you from the grief of a loss so overwhelming. But I cannot refrain from tendering to you the consolation that may be found in the thanks of the Republic they died to save.
>
> I pray that our Heavenly Father may assuage the anguish of your bereavement, and leave you only the cherished memory of the loved and lost, and the solemn pride that must be yours, to have laid so costly a sacrifice upon the altar of Freedom. (8:116–17)

Here the words "our Heavenly Father" as a designation for the deity would be comforting to a woman of faith who had lost sons in battle. Lincoln had used the same designation earlier in replying to his Quaker friend Eliza P. Gurney (5:476). See also the letter of consolation to Ephraim D. and Phoebe Ellsworth upon the death of their son who was killed in battle (4:385–86).

In contrast to his letter to John Johnston, in his Eulogy on Henry Clay, July 6, 1852 (2:121–32), Lincoln's tone is sincere. He shared Clay's views on the fundamental issues of slavery and the Union, and he mentions the Bible effectively in supporting his position. Lincoln calls Clay "the champion of a civilized world," who, like others in the dark days "in the history of all nations," has fallen (2:122). The words "all nations" occur numerous times in the Bible, of which the following are the most relevant: "Thy God hath divided unto all nations under the whole heaven" (Deut 4:19); "God will set thee on high above all nations of the earth" (Deut 28:1; see also Ps 86:9); and "the gospel must first be preached among all nations" (Mark 13:10). "All nations" is really a synonymous expression for "all tongues and kindreds and people" used a few lines earlier in the eulogy. Later Lincoln uses "all nations, and tongues, and kindreds" (7:259), also meaning all peoples and languages. His words in the eulogy are free quotations of Rev 7:9; 11:9; and 13:7, and perhaps he was also influenced by Isa 66:18 and Gen 10:20, 31 (see also Acts 2:3–11).

Like Clay, Lincoln was opposed to slavery on principle, but it could not "be at *once* eradicated, without producing a greater evil, even to the cause of human liberty itself" (2:130). Both Lincoln and Clay agreed that African Americans should be colonized in Africa. Like Clay, Lincoln was opposed to the spread of slavery in places where it did not exist, but he resented the opinion of the abolitionists that it should be abolished immediately. "Those who would shiver into fragments the Union of these States; tear to tatters its now venerated constitution; and even burn the last copy of the Bible, rather than slavery should continue a single hour," have been execrated. The opinions and influence of Clay are against them (2:130).

Lincoln becomes emotional in expressing his view of returning slaves to Africa. He asks: "May it not be one of the great designs of the Ruler of the universe, (whose ways are often inscrutable by short-sighted mortals,) thus to transform an original crime, into a single blessing to that most unfortunate portion of the globe? . . . May it indeed be realized!" (2:132). After Lincoln had used the words all nations and synonymous phrases (2:22), it was most thoughtful of him to use the designation Ruler of the universe for the deity (Appendix 3).

Although Lincoln's title 'Ruler of the universe' does not occur in the Bible, ideas behind it do. "The Lord most high is terrible; he is a great King over all the earth" (Ps 47:2; see also Ps 83:18). From his throne in heaven the Lord's "kingdom ruleth over all" (Ps 103:19; see also Job 36:26–33). For Lincoln's "whose ways are often inscrutable by short-sighted mortals" (2:132), see God does great "things past finding out" (Job 9:10). Paul writes: "O the depth of the riches both of the wisdom and knowledge of God! How unsearchable are his judgments, and his ways past finding out!" (Rom 11:33; see also Ps 109:6). "Canst thou by searching find out God? canst thou find out the Almighty unto perfection?" (Job 11:7; see also Job 26:14).

Lincoln draws an analogy between slavery in the states and that of the Israelites in Egypt (2:132) who served for four hundred years, the plagues on the Egyptians (Exod 7:14—13:16), and the drowning of their hosts in the sea (Exod 14:15–31; 15:4; Ps 136:15). "May like disasters never befall us!" (2:132). The impreciseness of Lincoln's language makes it difficult to determine the specific biblical passages that most influenced him. In Exod 14:4, 17, 24, 28, and in 15:4, the word is not Lincoln's "hosts" but "host" and Lincoln's "more than four hundred years" may be from "four hundred and thirty years" in Exod 12:40–41. According to Acts 7:6, in Stephen's speech against the conduct of the Jews, the number is four hundred years. According to Gen 15:12–13, while Abram was in "a deep sleep" the Lord said to him: "Know of a surety that thy seed shall be a stranger in a land that is not theirs, and shall serve them; and they shall afflict them four hundred years."

Lincoln says that the country could not be all it came to be without such a man that the times demanded and given by the providence of God. Lincoln's final sentence is at the same time an exhortation and a declaration of faith: "Let us strive to deserve, as far as mortals may, the continued care of Divine Providence, trusting that, in future national emergencies, He will not fail to provide us the instruments of safety and security" (2:132).

Lincoln's audience for the eulogy on Clay was mostly Bible-reading Christians. Since Clay was an Episcopalian and the Bible was a part of his family, it is interesting that there is not a single allusion to or quotation from it about the afterlife and resurrection in Lincoln's eulogy. This is in strong contrast to his words in his letter to John Johnston that his father would soon have a meeting with loved ones gone "and where [the rest] of us, through the help of God, hope ere-long [to join] them" (2:97). As usual, Lincoln uses a conglomeration of biblical words and phrases oblivious of their contexts, but effective for the consolation of his audience.

5

He Would Have Construed Away the Difficulty

AFTER HIS ELECTION TO the U. S. Senate in 1847, Stephen A. Douglas won national prominence as a Democrat. Zachary Taylor (1849–1850) died in office in July 1850, a few months after he was elected, and Millard Fillmore (1850–1853), his successor, was not re-elected. With the Whig Party in decline, Winfield Scott was soundly defeated by the Democrat Franklin Pierce (1853–1857) in November 1852.

At home in Springfield after his congressional term, March 4, 1849, for a while Lincoln devoted more time to law than to politics, and it seemed as though his political career was ended. There is no significant influence from the Bible in the documents of that period. At the National Convention in 1852, the Whigs again chose a military hero, General Winfield Scott, who served with distinction in the Mexican War, as their nominee for president. That nomination and the fact that Lincoln's name had been mentioned as a candidate for governor kindled only a slight interest in politics. However, when Tompkins Bush was invited to speak at the Scott Club in Springfield and had to be excused because of a serious illness, Lincoln volunteered to speak, August 14, 1852 (2:135–57). The speech is a reply to one Stephen A. Douglas had made in Richmond, Virginia, on July 9, 1852.

Before the Scott Club, Lincoln is eloquently political and sarcastic. According to him, Douglas had spoken about the dangers of electing a military man as president in saying that by Providence the country was saved from the military administration (under Taylor), which implied that the election of Scott would be a second such election (2:136). Although not an avid supporter of Scott, Lincoln defends him strongly. Scott had said in his acceptance of the nomination for president that he accepted it "with the resolutions annexed." According to Lincoln, Douglas accused Scott of duplicity of language in trying to appease factions of both North and South. Lincoln characterized Douglas's words as a "wonderful acumen . . . on the construction of language!!!" Douglas has taken Scott's word "with" as "equivalent to the word 'notwithstanding,' and also to the phrases 'although I defy' and 'although I spit upon.' Verily these are wonderful substitutes for the word 'with'" (2:140–41).

If the builders of the tower of Babel (Gen 11:1–9) had gotten into difficulty about language and had appealed to Douglas, "he would, at once, have construed away the difficulty," and they could have finished the structure "upon the truly democratic platform on which they were building." Lincoln suggests that at a leisurely moment the members of his audience amuse themselves by taking some sentences and substituting "notwithstanding" for "with" and see how it affects the sentence. For example, "And Enoch walked *with* God; and he was not, for God took him" (2:141). Except for Lincoln's variation in punctuation, this is verbatim of Gen 5:24, which all Bible readers would know, as they would also the Babel story (see also Heb 11:5). Lincoln does not mention a biblical reference for either story. As with the Bible readers in his audience, he knew about the unusual character Enoch. So he looked up the passage without paying attention to the punctuation and without knowing either passage in depth. It is also significant that the context of neither passage fits the Lincoln context. And his words, "upon the truly democratic platform on which they were building," are sheer political buffoonery.

Lincoln quotes Judge Douglas as saying that in his acceptance speech Scott had said that no Democrat would serve in his administration but that "abolition whigs" could do so with no hindrance. Then, says Lincoln, the Judge "falls into a strain of wailing pathos which Jeremiah in his last days might envy, for the old soldier democrats to be turned out of office by Gen. Scott" (2:144). Because Jeremiah's messages contained a lot of lamentations over his people, he became known as "the weeping (wailing) prophet." However, he wept for the fate of his people not only in his last days. Here are two examples: "Oh that my head were waters, and mine eyes a fountain of tears, that I might weep day and night for the slain of the daughter of my people," perhaps with the fall of Jerusalem (Jer 9:1). In Jer 9:10 the prophet laments the sins of the people of Jerusalem: "For the mountains will I take up a weeping and wailing, and for the habitations . . . a lamentation" (see also Jer 9:11–20; 3:21).

In commenting on the Judge's remark that the death of General Taylor was the result of Providence, Lincoln says that he was elected by the people, "and, as is appointed to all men once to do, he died" (2:150). The words "appointed to die" occur in Ps 79:11, where the psalmist prays God to use the greatness of his power to "preserve . . . those that are appointed to die." It may seem that for both Lincoln and the psalmist the word "appointed" means "destined" or "predestined." However, that is not true for the psalmist whose Hebrew word is translated in the KJV as "appointed." It means "doomed" (New Revised Standard Version, 1989) or "condemned" (New Jerusalem Bible, 1999). The psalmist laments the destruction caused by foreign invaders, and he feels the appalling distress of the nation. Prisoners condemned to die were the objects of his plea to God. If Lincoln had the language of the psalmist in mind, he was completely unaware of the context, which would have been most inappropriate.

Perhaps Lincoln was influenced by Num 16:29: "If these men die the common death of all men . . ." The words are spoken by Moses to the Israelites concerning the rebellion of Korah and several other men against him during the desert wanderings. If the rebels die the common death, then the people will know that the Lord did not send Moses to lead them. The men were buried alive and sent to the underworld. This confirmed the leadership of Moses and Aaron. Whether or not Lincoln had this passage in mind, who knows, but I doubt it. If he had it in mind, it would also have been unfitting.

After his speech before the Springfield Scott Club, Lincoln did not deliver an important speech until the one at Bloomington, Illinois, about two years later. Between the two speeches there are only two documents in which I have detected biblical language. The first is in a Fragment on Government, July 1, 1854? (2:221–22). Lincoln raises some questions about governments, which are expensive, may be badly administered, onerous, and even oppressive. "Why, then, should we have government? Why not each individual take to himself the whole fruit of his labor, without having any of it taxed away, in services, corn, or money?" (2:221). With "the whole fruit of his labor" see also 2:222, 493; 3:475, and the words of Paul: "the fruit of my labour" (Phil 1:22). Paul is in prison, perhaps at the point of death, so he meditates on whether living or dying would be better: "For me to live is Christ, and to die is gain. But if I live in the flesh, this is the fruit of my labour" (Phil 1:21–22). Lincoln was oblivious of the context of Paul's words, if indeed he was influenced by them at all.

The second document is a Fragment on Slavery, July 1, 1854? (2:222). A lacuna at the beginning is followed by "Made so plain by our good Father in Heaven, that all *feel* and *understand* it, even down to brutes and creeping insects." Lincoln uses Father in Heaven elsewhere in the following ways: "your Father in Heaven" (2:501, twice), "the Father in Heaven" (2:501), and "our Father in Heaven" (7:535). All those phrases reflect biblical language: "Our Father which art in heaven" (Matt 6:9; Luke 11:2), "your Father which is in heaven" (Matt 5:16, 45, 48; 6:1; 7:11; 18:14; 23:9), and "my Father which is in heaven" (Matt 7:21; 10:32–33; 12:50; 16:17; 16:10, 19). These designations are another example of how Lincoln used various phrases for titles or attributes of the deity and adapted them to particular situations (Appendix 3), in this case for some speech that is not entirely extant.

The words "brutes and creeping insects" reflect the story of creation, especially Gen 1:26, 30. For a psalmist, "Beasts, and all cattle; creeping things, and flying fowl" are among all things that are to praise God (Ps 148:10; see also Lev 5:2; 11:23, 29, 42; 1 Kgs 4:33; Ezek 8:10; 38:20; Hos 2:18; Acts 10:12; 11:6; Rom 1:23). Lincoln would have been thinking of "brutes" in the sense "of or relating to beasts" (2:222). However, in all of those passages neither brutes nor creeping insects occur, so again Lincoln did not get the biblical language exactly right.

Lincoln continues by saying: "The ant, who has toiled and dragged a crumb to his nest, will furiously defend the fruit of his labor, against whatever robber assails him." With respect to the ant, Lincoln may have been most influenced by his observations of nature. However, he could have had in mind: "Go to the ant, thou sluggard; consider her ways, and be wise" (Prov 6:6; see also Prov 30:25). However, there the ant is "her," whereas Lincoln has "his" and "him." We have learned that Lincoln was not very gender conscious. Thinking of the ant as almost human, Lincoln uses the words metaphorically: "The most dumb and stupid slave that ever toiled for a master, does certainly *know* that he is wronged." Although volumes have been written "to prove slavery a very good thing, we never hear of the man who wishes to take the good of it, *by being a slave himself*" (2:222).

By mid-1854, Lincoln had entered the national political arena at full speed. He delivered a series of speeches not only to campaign for the state legislature, but also to oppose the Kansas-Nebraska Bill that became law on May 30, 1854. It repealed the Missouri Compromise of 1820 that forbade slavery from spreading to territories where it did not exist by now making it possible to do so. Never wavering from his position that slavery should not spread, Lincoln now campaigned bitterly to prevent it. And on that issue Lincoln and Douglas became even more antagonistic toward each other.

In the early 1850s, some Protestants became upset with the many non-English speaking foreigners who had immigrated to America to help build the railroads. The protestors formed an American Party that became known as the "Know Nothings," who got that name from the fact that when someone asked them a question about the party they would say, "I know nothing." Intolerant, prejudiced, and secretive, the party was responsible for riots in a number of cities. Douglas was opposed to the party. Lincoln was rather ambivalent toward the Know Nothings, but he knew that he and his party could use any help they might give. Moreover, some of his friends had joined the party, and he did not want to lose their support. Lincoln delivered speeches in several cities, but I have detected no biblical language in some of them. The first in which I do so is in a second speech at Bloomington, Illinois, September 26, 1854 (2:234–40).

Lincoln says that the buying and selling of slaves from the Georgia Pen, "within sight of the National Capitol, began to grow offensive in the nostrils of all good men" (2:237). According to Amos, the Lord sent "the pestilence" like that in Egypt upon his people, so bad that it caused "the stink of your camps to come up unto your nostrils" (Amos 4:10). If Lincoln and his audience had been aware of the Amos passage and its context, it would have offended slave owners of both North and South.

When Lincoln speaks at Bloomington (2:239) and elsewhere of slaves being held in bondage (2:362, 364, 539; 3:89), he was influenced by the story of the Hebrews/Israelites as slaves in bondage in Egypt (Exod 1:1—13:16), a repeated theme in the Old Testament. See especially Exod

6:5, where the Lord says to Moses that he heard the groaning of the Israelites, "whom the Egyptians keep in bondage."

In their rivalry on the campaign trail, Douglas spoke at the Illinois State Fair in Springfield on October 3, 1854. After that speech Lincoln announced that he would reply later and did so on October 4, 1854 (2:240–47). His speech, repeated about the same way later at Peoria, Illinois, contains biblical language that may not be readily recognizable. According to Lincoln, the founders of the Nation intended the eventual end of slavery. He gives reasons why the legislation of the Kansas-Nebraska Bill "had become 'canonized in the hearts of the people'—it was supposed that 'no ruthless hand' would ever be ruthless enough to disturb it" (2:243). Lincoln's words "the hearts of the people" here and in his speech at Quincy, Illinois, November 1, 1854 (2:285), occur exactly in Josh 7:5. In that context, the Israelites were being punished for a violation of a ban by defeat at the city of Ai so severely that "the hearts of the people melted." See also "the heart of the people" (Josh 14:8), "the heart of this people" (1 Kgs 12:27; Isa 6:10; Acts 28:27), "the hearts of many people" (Ezek 32:9), and "the heart of thy people" (1 Chr 29:18; see also Isa 7:2). The phrase occurred in enough various forms for Lincoln to get it exactly right, irrespective of any context.

On October 16, 1854, Judge Douglas spoke at Peoria, Illinois, and he did not stop for over three hours, until after five o'clock. He announced that, by agreement, Mr. Lincoln would answer him. Lincoln took the platform and said he did not wish to speak now, since to do so would go beyond eight o'clock. At his suggestion, the audience left and returned at seven o'clock, when Lincoln delivered essentially the same speech (2:247–83) as the one at Springfield. A notable difference, though, is that Lincoln reveals language from the Bible more often and in a way that would be more obvious to his listeners.

Lincoln is not yet prepared to say that slaves should be freed and made political and social equals with whites, and if he did think so, the majority of whites would not. He says that whether that opinion "accords with justice and sound judgment, is not the sole question, if indeed, it is any part of it. A universal feeling . . . can not be safely disregarded. We can not, then, make them equals" (2:256). The words "justice" and "judgment" were a part of judicial language, and Lincoln uses both of them many times. He repeats what he says here in his first debate with Stephen A. Douglas (3:16), the only other place he speaks the same way.

The words "justice" and "judgment" occur often in the Old Testament, sometimes in that order (Gen 18:19; see also Ps 89:14; Prov 1:3; 21:3), but the order is mostly judgment and justice (e.g., 2 Sam 8:15; 1 Kgs 10:9; 2 Chron 9:8; Job 36:17; 37:23; Ps 119:121; Eccl 5:8; Isa 56:1; Jer 22:15; Ezek 45:9). What makes Lincoln's usage different is the added qualifying word "sound," a combination that does not occur in the Bible. Lincoln explains what he means by saying that gradual emancipation might be used, "but for their tardiness in this, I will not undertake to judge our brethren of the south" (2:256).

With respect to the spread of slavery into free territories after the Missouri Compromise, Lincoln says: "Sufficient unto the day is the evil thereof" (2:260; used only here), an exact quotation from Jesus' words to his disciples in the Sermon on the Mount concerning their not being anxious about days ahead (Matt 6:34). That would be a saying easy to remember, again without awareness of its context.

In opposition to Douglas, on the rights and equality of Negroes as human beings and the doctrine of self-government and the sense of justice (2:265–6), Lincoln says:

> The doctrine of self government is right—absolutely and eternally right—but it has no just application, as here attempted. Or perhaps I should rather say that whether it has such just application depends upon whether a negro is *not* or *is* a man . . . When the white man governs himself that is self-government; but when he governs himself, and also governs *another* man, that is *more* than self-government—that is despotism. If the negro is a *man*, why then my ancient faith teaches me that 'all men are created equal'; and that there can be no moral right in connection with one man's making a slave of another.

In accusing Douglas of misrepresenting his view about governing Negroes, Lincoln says: "No man is good enough to govern another man, *without that other's consent.* I say this is the leading principle—the sheet anchor of American republicanism." In this context of self-government, the equality of man, and morality, Lincoln quotes the Declaration with respect to all men being created equal: "We hold these truths to be self evident: that all men are created equal; that they are endowed by their Creator with certain inalienable rights; that among these are life, liberty and the pursuit of happiness" (2:266).

Here Lincoln uses "Creator" for the first time. Therefore, I believe that he got that designation for the deity from the Declaration of Independence, not the Bible. "All men are created equal" became a repeated slogan in his campaign against slavery. His use of the designation elsewhere is consistent with this. "Creator" occurs in similar contexts in speeches at Chicago (2:489), Carlinville (3:80), Paris (3:91), and Edwardsville (3:94). In his speech at Lewistown, Lincoln says that the Declaration was the fathers' "lofty, and wise, and noble understanding of the justice of the Creator to His creatures . . . to *all* His creatures, to the whole great family of man" (2:546). He mentions the Creator in his second lecture on discoveries and inventions (3:359), where he wonders if speech as a mode of communication was an invention of man or the direct gift of the Creator. His uncertainty leaves the biblical Creator as secondary to the invention itself.

Although writers of the Bible believed that God created the world, compared with Maker and Almighty, the designation Creator is rarely used (Eccl 12:1; Isa 40:28; 43:15; Rom 1:25; 1 Pet 4:19), and Lincoln never alludes to one of those passages. That observation and the fact that Lincoln uses Creator almost exclusively in political contexts attest to the Declaration as its prevailing influence on his thought.

Lincoln's "My ancient faith" becomes "our ancient faith," in order to indicate that the principle of the consent of the governed is totally violated in the master's government of the slave without his consent and by rules different from those set for himself. Lincoln is "not now combating the argument of NECESSITY, arising from the fact that the blacks are already amongst us," but he is "combating what is set up as MORAL argument for allowing them to be taken where they have never yet been—arguing against the EXTENSION of a bad thing, which where it already exists, we must of necessity, manage as we best can" (2:266).

For Lincoln's "the great Behemoth of danger" (2:270), see Job 40:15, where the Lord says to Job: "Behold now behemoth, which I made with thee." Behemoth was a mythological figure that originally meant "beasts" or "cattle"; in Canaanite literature it was taken as the hippopotamus or a dangerous beast like Leviathan. As described in Job 40:15–24, Behemoth is a most dangerous creature, whose tail is like a cedar, his bones like bars of iron, and he drinks up a river (see also Job 41; Pss 74:14; 104:26; Isa 27:1). Aware of the dangers of Behemoth, Lincoln applies the figure to the extension of slavery and its strong grip on the nation. He asks if it should be trusted to the hands of weak rulers. I wonder, though, if Lincoln's hearers comprehended the severity of slavery extension as Lincoln meant to indicate by his use of those mythological figures.

Lincoln says that he is done with the argument of self-government, where the people of a territory could decide to have or not to have slavery: "Go, sacred thing! Go in peace" (2:270; see also 4:436). "Go in peace" is used thirteen times in the Bible, mostly as a farewell benediction (e.g., Exod 4:18; Judg 18:6; 1 Sam 20:42; 2 Kgs 5:19; Mark 5:34; Luke 7:50; Acts 16:36). "Repeal the Missouri Compromise—repeal all compromises—repeal the declaration of independence—repeal all past history, you still can not repeal human nature. It still will be the abundance of man's heart, that slavery extension is wrong; and out of the abundance of his heart, his mouth will continue to speak" (2:271).

The words of Lincoln about speaking out of the abundance of his heart, which he uses only here, are a free citation of Matt 12:34 and are among Jesus' replies to the accusations against him by the Pharisees, of which the saying about a house divided is also a part. Lincoln uses language from that larger context several times elsewhere. In the quotation from Matt 12:34, Jesus speaks against the hypocrisy of the Pharisees and asks how they can speak good things when they are evil: "For out of the abundance of the heart the mouth speaketh." Mark lacks the saying, but Luke 6:45 reads: "For of the abundance of the heart his mouth speaketh." By putting the good and evil persons before the words that are quoted by Lincoln, Luke applies the quotation more directly to the good person bringing from his heart good things, and the evil person producing evil things, as good and evil trees bear respective fruit. It is difficult to tell which passage influenced Lincoln more, although his use of "his" before mouth, with Luke, instead of "the" in Matthew makes the quotation apply directly to the person who thinks the spread of slavery is wrong. Lincoln recalls biblical language and adapts it to support his moral/political arguments against Douglas that slavery is morally wrong.

For the supporters of the Nebraska Bill, it is "a small matter" in establishing a principle of "planting slavery wherever in the wide world" in the future whenever opposition cannot prevent it (2:273). In general, Lincoln uses the phrase "a small matter" in contexts of the spread of slavery into free territories. He uses it that way in speeches at Carlinville (3:77) and Indianapolis (3:469; see also 2:327; 7:66). At Carlinville, after Lincoln has said the fuss about Blacks is taken as a small matter, he says: "The North alone is not to blame—for churches and families divided upon this question—is it then a little thing?" (3:77). In the Bible "a small matter" is used in several ways. According to Gen 30:15, Leah says to her sister Rachel: "Is it a small matter that thou hast taken my husband?" The Israelites are to take great matters to Moses for judgment, "but every small matter they shall judge" (Exod 18:22, 26). Ezekiel condemns the evils of his people, including the sacrificing of their children to images. He asks allegorically: "Is this of thy whoredoms a small matter?" (Ezek 16:20). Perhaps Lincoln was influenced by one or more of the passages, perhaps not.

According to Lincoln, the principles of all men created equal and the spread of slavery by the sacred right of self-government "are as opposite as God and mammon; and whoever holds to the one, must despise the other" (2:275). Lincoln uses God and mammon only here, but he uses mammon later in a speech at Springfield (2:404). Mammon is an Aramaic word which means "wealth" or "riches." According to Matt 6:24, Jesus says; "No man can serve two masters: for either he will hate the one, and love the other; or else he will hold to the one, and despise the other. Ye cannot serve God and mammon." Luke 16:13 reads "no servant" instead of "no man." By placing God and mammon first and by inserting "must" Lincoln emphasizes his point. Once again, oblivious of the context, the important thing for him is using biblical language to support his cause.

Senator John Pettit of Indiana was in favor of the Nebraska Bill, which would have organized Nebraska without reference to slavery and would, therefore, not make it a free territory. Pettit called the statement of equality in the Declaration "a self-evident lie." Lincoln says that if Pettit had made that remark in "Independence Hall seventy-eight years ago, the very door-keeper would have throttled the man, and thrust him into the street" (2:275). Lincoln repeats his words in a more dramatic way later in a speech at Chicago (2:283–84): "The door-keeper would have taken him by the throat and stopped his rascally breath awhile, and then have hurled him into the street." Taking by the throat echoes the words of one servant to a fellow servant in Matt 18:28: "and took him by the throat, saying . . ." For Lincoln's "thrust ("hurled") him into the street," see Jer 14:16, where the prophet says that the people heeding false prophets "shall be cast out in the streets of Jerusalem" (see also Luke 4:29). Lincoln's poignant remark, "The spirit of seventy-six and the spirit of Nebraska, are utter antagonisms," is introduced with the exhortation, "Let no one be deceived" (2:275). Lincoln may allude to Paul's words in Gal 6:7: "Be not deceived; God is not mocked: for whatsoever a man soweth, that shall he also reap." For this passage I am indebted to Fornieri (*Political Faith*, 129).

According to Lincoln, "The liberal party throughout the world, express the apprehension 'that the one retrograde institution in America, is undermining the principles of progress, and fatally violating the noblest political system the world ever saw.' This is not the taunt of enemies, but the warning of friends" (2:276). Both Jeremiah (24:9) and Ezekiel (5:15) tell their readers that the wicked people who remained in Judah, Jerusalem, and elsewhere after the conquest of Judah by Babylonia in 586 BC will be a reproach and a taunt wherever the Lord sends them. There, however, the taunt is that of enemies, not friends. Did Lincoln have that in mind when he uses "taunt of enemies"? Perhaps so, adapting it to his context.

Metaphorically, Lincoln says, "our republican robe is soiled, and trailed in the dust" (2:276). He exhorts his audience to "wash it white, in the spirit, if not the blood, of the Revolution" (2:276). The words about washing it white occur only here, but Lincoln had used "the blood of the Revolution" in his speech to the Young Men's Lyceum (1:112), and he uses it later in his speech at Lewistown, August 17, 1858 (2:547). The washing of the robe may be an allusion to Rev 7:9–17, where the persons "arrayed in white robes" are those who "have washed their robes, and made them white in the blood of the lamb" (Christ). The phrase "in the dust" is an idiom in the Old Testament for being relegated to a lower or inferior position or status. Despairing of hope for all, Job says. "They shall go down . . . to the pit, when our rest together is in the dust" (Job 17:16; see also Job 21:26). A psalmist says to the Lord that if he has done wrong let the enemy "tear down . . . mine honour in the dust" (Ps 7:5; see also Ps 45:23; Isa 47:1; Nah 3:18). After the metaphor of washing the Republican robe white, Lincoln exhorts his hearers about slavery:

> Let us turn slavery from its claims of 'moral right,' back upon its existing legal rights . . . to the position our fathers gave it . . . Let us re-adopt the Declaration of Independence, and with it, the practices, and policy, which harmonize with it. Let north and south— let all Americans—let all lovers of liberty everywhere—join in the great and good work. If we do this, we shall not only have saved the Union; but we shall have so saved it, as to make, and to keep

it, forever worthy of the saving. We shall have so saved it, that the succeeding millions of free happy people, the world over, shall rise up, and call us blessed, to the latest generations. (2:276)

Lincoln had used the phrase "to the latest generation" in his address before the Young Men's Lyceum of Springfield. Guelzo (*Redeemer President*, 193) says: "Lincoln could always fish up common [sometimes uncommon] biblical allusions on demand." This time, as frequently, Lincoln brings up a hybrid. He may allude to Luke 1:48, part of a poem composed by an unknown author and attributed to Mary, mother-to-be, of Jesus who says: "from henceforth all generations shall call me blessed." Or, Lincoln's allusion could just as well be a line from Mal 3:10–12, where the Lord tells his people that if they return to giving the proper tithes for the temple, "all nations shall call you blessed." However, the words "rise up," are not in either biblical passage mentioned but do appear in Prov 31:28 in praise of the virtuous woman: "Her children rise up and call her blessed" (see also Ps 72:17). Lincoln surely was not thinking of a particular context but of words he wanted to say, no matter from where they came.

Lincoln accused Judge Douglas of saying that he had assumed all the time that the Nebraska Bill would, in effect, extend slavery, which the Judge denied. Without wanting to reopen the argument, Lincoln said the world believed that from the start. "That was the intention. . . . This was the COUNTENANCE of the thing" (2:276). Lincoln says that the countenance of the situation cannot be changed by argument. "You can as easily argue the color out of the negroes' skin," as that the intention of the Nebraska Bill was not to extend slavery. "Like the 'bloody hand' you may wash it, and wash it, the red witness of guilt still sticks, and stares horribly at you" (2:276). This may allude to Pilate washing his hands after succumbing to the Jewish officials to have Jesus crucified, confessing his innocence of the blood of the just man Jesus (Matt 27:24). However, it is probably from Shakespeare's *Macbeth*, with which Lincoln was very familiar. Her Gentlewoman says of Macbeth: "It is an accustom'd action with her to seem thus washing her hands: I have known her continue in this a quarter of an hour." Macbeth responds: "Yet there's a spot . . . Out, damned spot! out, I say!" (Act 5, mid-scene 1). Lincoln's words about repeated hand washing confirm his use of *Macbeth*.

With respect to residents of a territory having the right to choose to have or not to have slavery, Lincoln says that Douglas had told him the choice between good and evil was as old as the creation of man. Douglas is really correct, because the point of the story is knowing the difference between good and evil. The tree and its fruit provide the concrete facility for the couple to make the choice. The penalty for disobeying the Lord was to be death. The best way out of the predicament for Lincoln was to make a facetious remark: "I should scarcely wish so strong a prohibition against slavery in Nebraska" (2:278).

Lincoln continues by saying that now the Judge has come to need some support from Whigs because his old friends are deserting him, leaving so few to go by. Therefore, he invokes the names of Clay and Webster, dead before the Nebraska case came up, so Lincoln asks "by what authority shall our Senator" say that they or other members of his party would be on his side now (2:282). The words by what authority are exactly those used by Jesus' critics about his teaching in the temple during his last days (Matt 21:23–27; Mark 11; 28–33; Luke 20:2–8). By applying the question to the Judge, the context is parallel to that of Jesus' critics in the gospels, but in doing so, Lincoln reverses the subject and the object of the question.

Lincoln summarizes that aspect of his criticism of Douglas with a biblical quotation: "He came to his own, and his own received him not, and Lo! he turns unto the Gentiles" (2:282). The first part of the sentence is an exact quotation of John 1:11, spoken about Jesus, although Lincoln has "to" instead of "unto" of the KJV. The second part is from Acts 13:46: "Lo, we turn to the Gentiles," put on the lips of Paul and Barnabas, who were beginning to preach to Gentiles after the Jews rejected them. Lincoln's "he" and "turns," instead of "we" and "turn," are adaptations to fit the occasion, and "unto" instead of "to" is imprecise memory, as is the change of prepositions in the first quotation. The exclamation point instead of the comma in Acts may be for emphasis indicated by the sound of his voice. The contrast in contexts is obvious. The biblical language was sufficient for Lincoln's argument.

6

A Self-Evident Lie

WHIGS MADE GREAT GAINS in the election of 1854. Lincoln was elected to the Illinois State Legislature on November 7, but he resigned about two weeks later to seek election to the U. S. Senate. Douglas was ever more antagonistic, but Lincoln's political star was shining brighter. He delivered a speech at Chicago, October 27, 1854 (2:283–84), and it was reported in the Chicago *Daily Journal*, October 30, 1854. Although the report dealt with "Lincoln's character and rise to prominence," an editor says that it "was as thorough an exposition of the Nebraska iniquity as has ever been made, and his eloquence greatly impressed all his hearers." He felt foolish, though, in arguing against non-existent arguments, and he "could not help feeling silly in beating the air before an intelligent audience" (2:283). Although the quoted words are those of the editor, they sound like those of Lincoln in reflecting biblical language. The Apostle Paul was fond of using athletic metaphors, and Lincoln's words "beating the air" might come from him: "so fight I, not as one that beateth the air" (1 Cor 9:26; see also 1 Cor 14:9). Lincoln repeated what he had said at Peoria about Senator Pettit of Indiana, saying that the Declaration of Independence was "a self-evident lie" and him being thrown into the street.

Because of Lincoln's increasing popularity and respect, he was approached about the merging of Whigs with rising Republicans into one party. He felt, however, that such a move was premature, and he began to think that the peaceful emancipation of the slaves was a lost hope. He became increasingly concerned about slavery dividing the Union vis-à-vis the principle of equality in the Declaration of Independence. He expressed his feelings in a letter to George Robertson, August 15, 1855 (2:317–19), lawyer, congressman, and law professor, who was counsel to Lincoln and heirs of Robert S. Todd, father of Mary Lincoln. Lincoln writes: "When we were the political slaves of King George, and wanted to be free, we called the maxim that 'all men are created equal' a self evident truth; but now when we have grown fat, and have lost all dread of being slaves ourselves, we have become so greedy to be *masters* that we call the same maxim 'a self-evident lie.' The fourth of July has not quite dwindled away; it is still a great day—*for burning fire crackers!!!*" (2:318). A phrase about growing fat occurs in Jer 50:11, where the author reports an oracle of the Lord who speaks about the coming overthrow of Babylon, the conqueror of Judah in 587–586 BC, and the Jews' return to Judah: "O ye destroyers of mine heritage, because ye are grown fat as the heifer at grass" (Jer 50:11).

In a letter to Speed, August 24, 1855 (2:320–23), Lincoln strongly disagrees with him on the matter of permitting slavery outside places where it already exists, especially over the admission of Kansas into the Union as a free state: "By every principle of law, ever held by any court, North or South, every negro taken to Kansas is free; yet in utter disregard of this—in the spirit of violence merely—that beautiful Legislature gravely passes a law to hang men who shall venture to inform a negro of his legal rights . . . If, like Haman, they should hang upon the gallows of their own building, I shall not be among the mourners for their fate" (2:321).

Lincoln acknowledges the decline of the Whig Party, which some even thought no longer existed. He is a Whig, and although in Congress he voted for the Wilmot Proviso, no one attempted to "unwhig" him for it. On February 22, 1856, Lincoln joined the budding Republican Party in Illinois. Engrossed in politics, he spoke at the Ohio State Republican Convention and was nominated as a presidential elector. At the national Republican Convention in Philadelphia on June 19, 1856, he was nominated for vice president but lost to John C. Fremont. According to a Fragment on Sectionalism, c. July 23, 1856 (2:349–53), Lincoln is concerned that in the Union some territories would be slave and some free and especially that slavery not be extended into the free territories. The question is dividing the North and the South, and Lincoln states his opinion succinctly: "Moral principle is all, or nearly all, that unites us in the North," whereas in the South, it is "pecuniary interest." The only solution is for one side to yield to the other. Lincoln asks if persons who believe slavery should not spread "really think that the *right* ought to yield to the *wrong?* Are they afraid to stand by the *right?*" (2:353).

Lincoln was becoming convinced that, if the principles of the Declaration of Independence and the Constitution were to be maintained, slavery must be eliminated.

Undaunted, his enthusiasm for the new party increased, and so did his personal political ambition. He hit the campaign trail by making a series of speeches, the first of which is a fragment of a speech at Peoria, Illinois, October 9, 1856 (2:379). According to an editor of the *Weekly Republican* of Peoria, Lincoln said that the forces of James Buchanan, a Democrat, and those of John C. Fremont, a Republican, whose supporters he joined, are now arrayed for battle, "one *for* and the other *against* slavery . . . our young, gallant and world-renowned commander was the man for the day—the man to right the ship of State, and, like the stripling of Israel, to slay the boasting Goliaths of slaveocracy that have beset the national capitol and defiled the sanctums of liberty, erected and consecrated by the old prophets and fathers of this republic." The literary style of these words assures their authenticity, and they allude to the remark of King Saul of Israel when he learned that the Philistine giant Goliath had been killed by David. Saul instructed his general Abner to "inquire . . . whose son the stripling is" (1 Sam 17:56).

In the elections of November 1856, the Republicans elected Colonel William H. Bissell, governor of Illinois, but the Democrats elected James Buchanan president (1857–1861). According to the Chicago *Democratic Press*, in a Speech at a Republican Banquet, Chicago, Illinois, December 10, 1856 (2:383–85), Lincoln encouraged the Republicans by saying that Buchanan was elected because their votes were split between Fremont and Millard Fillmore. Lincoln wants political differences among Republicans to be bygones. He exhorts his hearers to "reinaugurate the good old 'central ideas' of the Republic," especially the equality of men. "We *can* do it. The human heart *is* with us—God is with us" (2:385). The heart with is a Hebrew expression, for example, "uprightness of heart with thee" (1 Kgs 3:6) and "Went not mine heart with thee?" (2 Kgs 5:26; see also Prov 4:23; Ezek 25:6). A chief feature of the Hebrews' religion was their faith that God was with them and directing their lives and history. Many Lincoln scholars believe that Lincoln came to the same faith. For Lincoln's "God is with us," see Isa 8:10, where the Lord told Moses to say to the king of Egypt: "The Lord God of the Hebrews hath met with us" (Exod 3:18; 5:3). See especially "God with us" (Matt 1:23; see also 1 Kgs 8:57; Ps 46:11; 2 Chr 13:12). I wonder why italics are on *can* and the first *is* but not on the second *is*, used with God. Was Lincoln not sure enough to emphasize that God *is* with us? Of course, the emphases could be the work of editors, for whom the emphasis would be more likely. But remember that a very popular view is that Lincoln carefully supervised the printing of his speeches (White, *Greatest Speech*, 70); but if so, he did not change the implication of lack of emphasis.

On March 6, 1857, a decision by the United States Supreme Court eventually gave Lincoln and the Republicans a new challenge. Dred Scott, a Negro slave from Missouri, was taken by his master first to Illinois, a free state, and then to the Minnesota Territory, a free territory. After the death of his master, Dred Scott sued for his freedom because he had been taken into places free of slavery. In a 7–2 decision, the Supreme Court ruled that as a Negro Scott did not have the right to sue. Negroes were considered inferior to white men and, therefore, had no rights deserving of their respect. Because of his great respect for the whole judiciary, Lincoln did not immediately oppose the Court decision. But the fact that as a Negro Scot did not have the same rights guaranteed to all Americans by the Declaration and the Constitution angered Lincoln. His ambivalence toward the decision of the Supreme Court changed to opposition.

At first Douglas was dubious about the decision, but seeking a political advantage, he began to argue in favor of it. On June 7, 1857, he spoke in Springfield, Illinois, and strongly supported the Supreme Court decision. Lincoln's view of the equality of men as guaranteed in the Declaration of Independence was severely challenged. He met the challenge by replying to Douglas for the Republicans in a Speech at Springfield, Illinois, June 26, 1857 (2:398–410). Lincoln argued that the Nebraska Act was "a mere deceitful pretense for the benefit of slavery." Those persons who did not see that aspect in the Act "could not be made to see, though one should rise from the dead to testify" (2:399). Rising from the dead is language applied to Jesus and others (Mark 12:25; Luke 24:46; 1 Thess 4:16). See especially Luke 16:31: "neither will they be persuaded, though one rose from the dead" (see also Acts 26:23).

In the early days of slavery in the states, as Lincoln understands it, "masters could, at their own pleasure, emancipate their slaves," but recent legal restraints almost prohibited emancipation (2:404). The words "their own pleasure," which Lincoln uses also in 3:327, are biblical and occur exactly in Heb 12:10. In 4:43 and 6:474 Lincoln uses "your own pleasure," which occurs as "thine own pleasure" in Deut 23:24 and Isa 58:13. He echoes Matt 6:24 or Luke 16:13 when he says that "Mammon is after" the slave owner to hold the black man in bondage (2:404). He protests "the counterfeit logic" that concludes "because I do not want a black woman for a *slave* I must necessarily want her for a *wife*. I need not have her for either, I can just leave her alone. In some respects she certainly is not my equal; but in her natural right to eat the bread she earns with her own hands without asking leave of any one else, she is my equal, and the equal of all others" (2:405). This is another allusion to Adam earning his bread by the sweat of his face (Gen 3:19). The application to the text is obvious.

In discussing the part of the Declaration that declares all men are created equal, Lincoln says that it was of no practical use in gaining our freedom from Great Britain, but it was intended for future use. "Its authors meant it to be, thank God, it is now proving itself, a stumbling block to those who . . . might seek to turn a free people back into the hateful paths of despotism" (2:406). "The Declaration is of no practical use now—mere rubbish—old wadding left to rot on the battle-field after the victory is won" (2:407). Lincoln uses the biblical "thank God" (Rom 7:25; 1 Cor 1:14; 2 Thess 1:3; 2 Tim 1:3) for the first time here and only once or twice later. Indeed, it may have been a trite expression, as it is many times today.

"Stumbling block" represents the Greek noun *skandalon*, which in the Septuagint (the Greek translation of the Old Testament) translates Hebrew words meaning "a bait stick of a trap," hence "snare" or "stumbling block." It is used, for example, in Hebrew law: "Thou shalt not . . . put a stumbling block before the blind" (Lev 19:14). For different usages see 1 Sam 18:20–21; Isa 57:14; Ezek 3:20; 7:19; and 14:3–7. *Skandalon* occurs numerous times in the New Testament, but in the KJV it is translated as "stumbling block" only in Rom 11:9. Lincoln used the phrase to support his view that the Declaration was a stumbling block to those who wanted to turn a free people back to despotism.

Lincoln stresses his view that all African slaves should be transported to their native Africa where they would be a happy colony. That would be morally right and, at the same time, favorable to our interest. There would be a way to do it no matter how great the task might be. "The children of Israel, to such numbers as to include four hundred thousand fighting men, went out of Egyptian bondage in a body" (2:409). "Children of Israel" occurs hundreds of times in the Bible, sometimes with large numbers also mentioned. That makes it impossible to determine the source of Lincoln's numbers here, although he may have had in mind Judg 20:2, 17, where the number is "four hundred thousand footmen that drew sword," a context far different from that of Lincoln.

Lincoln uses stumbling block elsewhere only in a Speech in Carlinville, Illinois, August 31, 1858 (3:77–81), where he mentions it to support his view that Negroes should be returned to their native Africa, there to have "all the moral rights" of equality mentioned in the Declaration for "all mankind." The Declaration "has proved a stumbling block to tyrants, and ever will, unless brought into contempt by its pretended friends" (3:79).

For ten months after that Springfield speech on June 26, 1857, Lincoln devoted much of his time to the practice of law. However, he had not forgotten about politics and thought of running for the U.S. Senate to replace Douglas. Meanwhile, he decided to try a nonpolitical speech, so he came up with his First Lecture on Discoveries and Inventions, April 6, 1858 (2:437–42). Originally one treatise, it was divided into two parts, the first of which he delivered before The Young Men's Association in Bloomington, Illinois. Entirely devoid of politics, it is also devoid of anything else worthwhile. It is extremely simple, confused, and confusing, and it contradicts some things Lincoln says elsewhere. On several occasions when he delivered it, he was almost laughed out of town, and eventually only a few people came to hear him. In spite of all this, I consider the speech carefully because there are so many references to the Bible that enlighten our understanding of how he used it and the extent of his knowledge of it.

Lincoln probably used his Oxford Bible during the composition of the lecture. Although he mentions the Bible only three times, his speech is filled with quotations from and allusions to it that would be familiar to many of his hearers. Here Lincoln accepts the Bible, especially Genesis, as a record of history from the time of creation, and he also thinks it is the oldest account for the things he mentions. His dating of events indicates that he was familiar with and accepted the scheme of James Ussher. Sometimes Lincoln has Bible references, and sometimes he doesn't. References are mine unless "noted" is inserted after the biblical reference, and then I retain Lincoln's mixed style.

Lincoln begins with a metaphor: "All creation is a mine, and every man a miner. The whole earth, and all *within* it, *upon* it. . . ." Although the words "all creation" are not in the Bible, "the whole earth," which Lincoln uses as synonymous with them, occur often in the Old Testament and in Luke 21:35. Perhaps Lincoln was most influenced by "on the face of the whole earth" (Gen 8:9; 11:14; Isa 14:26; Dan 8:5) and "throughout the whole earth" (2 Chron 16:9; see also Exod 10:15; Zech 4:10). As a miner, man's existence, including his "physical, moral, and intellectual nature, and his susceptibilities, are the infinitely various 'leads' from which man, from the first, was to dig out his destiny" (2:437).

"In the beginning, the mine was opened, and the miner stood *naked* and *knowledgeless* upon it," an obvious allusion to the nakedness of Adam and Eve, and perhaps also to "the tree of the knowledge of good and evil" in the Garden of Eden story (Gen 2:9, 25; 3:7). Perhaps the words "in the beginning" are from Gen 1:1: "In the beginning God created . . ." Birds and animals, including beavers, and creeping things (see, e.g., Gen 7:23; 1 Kgs 4:33; Ezek 38:20; Acts 10:12) act just as they did five thousand years ago. "Ants, and honey-bees, provide food for winter," just as they did when Solomon "referred the sluggard to them as patterns of prudence" (2:437). Lincoln accepts the view of the KJV that Solomon was the author of Proverbs (Prov 1:1) and wrote: "Go to the ant, thou sluggard; consider her ways, and be wise" (Prov 6:6). Ants are mentioned elsewhere in the Bible only in Prov 30:25, but beavers are never mentioned, and bees are not mentioned in Proverbs. Lincoln was, apparently, writing about those creatures from personal observation, not from his depth of knowledge of the Bible. Five thousand years ago from Lincoln's time of 1858 coincides pretty well with Ussher's date of creation as 4004 BC.

Man's "first important discovery was the fact that he was naked; and his first invention was the fig-leaf-apron . . . made of leaves, seems to have been the origin of *clothing*" (Gen 2:25; 3:7). Lincoln relates the statement to his times when he says that almost half the labor of the human race has been expended on the making of clothing. The origin of spinning and weaving, so important in the making of clothing, are uncertain. "At the first interview of the Almighty with Adam and Eve, after the fall, He made 'coats of skins, and clothed them' Gen: 3–21" (noted), a literal quotation (2:437–38). Lincoln is not concerned with preciseness. He attributes the making of the apron to Adam, but the text of Gen 3:7 reads: "They sewed fig leaves together, and made themselves aprons." Lincoln uses his favorite designation for the deity—Almighty—instead of the Lord God (Gen 3:21).

"The fall" is an allusion to the universal belief that the disobedience of Adam and Eve by eating from the forbidden tree was "the fall of man," that is, the origin of sin. The belief was probably based on a dubious interpretation of Rom 5:12 and stated succinctly in a quip in *The New England Primer* of 1805: "In Adam's fall/ We sinned all." How Lincoln learned of the view, we cannot say, but the author of the Adam and Eve story does not mention "sin" before his story of Cain and Abel. There the Lord told Cain that in his thought of killing Abel "sin lieth at the door" (Gen 4:7). Lincoln is correct in saying that "the Bible makes no other allusion to clothing again, *before* the flood" (2:438). "Noah's two sons covered him with a *garment*; but of what *material* the garment was made is not mentioned. Gen. 9–23" (noted; 2:438). Lincoln does not mention the word Bible before this, although he has been using it from the start of the lecture. Garments of wool and linen are mentioned in the Bible, sometimes together, as in Lev 13:47: "whether it is a woolen garment, or a linen garment." The statement that Abraham's *"thread"* is "the oldest recorded allusion to spinning and weaving" and that they "were in use in his day—Gen—14.23" (noted) is half correct. "The oldest recorded" is incorrect, but the date of Abraham at "about two thousand years after the creation of man" is very nearly correct according to Ussher's date for the creation at 4004 BC. The age of the Patriarchs was about 2000–1700 BC. Exports from ancient Mesopotamia indicate that spinning and weaving were conducted there in the third millennium BC.

Lincoln states that "profane authors" think the arts mentioned originated in Egypt and that there is nothing in the Bible to contradict that fact (2:438). However, there is evidence in the Bible for it. Lincoln apparently was not aware that Ezekiel mentions "fine linen with embroidered work from Egypt" (Ezek 27:7; 44:18; see also Prov 7:16). It is interesting that he does not mention Pharaoh's arraying Joseph "in vestures of fine linen" (Gen 41:42; see also Lev 6:10).

Lincoln is correct that *"Linen breeches,"* are mentioned,—Exod. 28.42" (noted), that "all the women that were wise hearted did *spin* with their hands (35–25)" (noted), that "'all the women whose hearts stirred them up in wisdom, *spun* goat's hair (35–26)" (noted), and that "weaver is mentioned—(35–35)" (noted; see also Exod 28:37; 39:22, 27; 38:12; John 19:23). All the quotations are literal, except that Exodus has "goats' hair" instead of "goat's hair" and the insertion of a comma. "In the book of Job, a very old book, date not exactly known, the *'weavers shuttle'* is mentioned" (Job 7:6). Lincoln thought of Job as a historical person and that the book is a unity. Modern scholars think that Job is a compilation of sources, the dates of which are, indeed, "not exactly known," although some are "very old," as Lincoln says (2:438).

"The discovery of the properties of *iron*, and the making of *iron tools* must have been among the earliest of important discoveries and inventions." It is hard to conceive of anything made without iron. "An iron *hammer* must have been very much needed to make the *first* iron *hammer* with. A *stone* probably served as a substitute" (2:438). This is ridiculous, is it not? A hammer is mentioned in the familiar biblical story of Jael taking a hammer and driving a nail into Sisera's temple and killing him (Judg 4:21; 5:24–27). Was Lincoln not familiar with that story? The fact that he mentions copper (2:439) but does not mention "vessels of fine copper" (Ezra 8:27), nor does he mention the Sisera incident, indicates that he confined his research mostly to the Pentateuch.

"How could the *'gopher wood'* for the Ark, have been gotten out without an axe?" (Gen 6:14). Lincoln is correct that brass and iron are mentioned in the Bible, but Tubal-cain as its first user (Gen 4:22) is unlikely. The Iron Age began in Palestine about 1200 BC, so Lincoln's "about one thousand years before the flood" (2:438–39), according to Ussher, would be about 1348 BC, not too far off. Other iron things Lincoln mentions with correct references (noted) but given in the style used here are: "instruments of iron" (Num 30:16), "bed-stead [Bible, "bedstead"] of iron" (Deut 3:11), "iron furnace" (Deut 4:20), "iron tool" (Deut 27:5), "the ax [Bible, "axe"] to cut down the tree" (Deut 19:5), and iron and brass (Deut 8:9; 2:438).

As means of transportation, carriages, wagons, and boats "are the most important inventions" (2:439). Since the wheel and axle and chariot date about two millennia before the Bible was written, the words, "the oldest recorded allusion to the wheel and axle is the mention of a 'chariot' Gen: 41–43" (noted) is an anachronism (4:439). However, placing it in the Bible in the time of Joseph as the governor for the Pharaoh "about twentyfive [*sic*] hundred years after the creation of Adam" is approximately correct, according to Ussher's date of 4004 BC for the creation. That would be about 1504 BC, several decades after the rule of Egypt by the foreign Hyksos (c. 1650–1542 BC), who were probably the first people to introduce the horse and chariot into Egypt. The Israelite sojourn in Egypt, if historical, occurred about 1700–1300 BC. Lincoln also says that a wheeled-chariot drawn by horses is mentioned "at Exod. 14–25" and horses with chariots "in the same chapter, verses 9 & 23" (noted).

With respect to water transportation, Lincoln "concluded, without sufficient authority perhaps, to use the term 'boat' as a general name for all water-craft" (2:439–40). The use of the boat, "indispensable to navigation," depends upon "the *principle*, that any thing will float, which can not sink without displacing more than it's [*sic*] own *weight* of water." This is how the invention probably happened: "The sight of a crow standing on a piece of drift-wood floating down the swollen current of a creek or river, might well enough suggest the specific idea to a savage, that he could himself get upon a log, or on two logs tied together, and somehow work his way to the opposite shore of the same stream." That would be the beginning of navigation, and anything later would be only "improvements" or "auxiliaries" to it (2:440). The first biblical reference to a boat is 2 Sam 19:18 (see also John 6:22–23; Acts 27:16, 30, 32), again not in the Pentateuch, so perhaps that is why Lincoln does not mention it. "As man is a land animal, it might be expected he would learn to travel by land somewhat earlier than he would by water."

Up to this point it seems that Lincoln has taken Genesis literally with respect to the origins of things. Or was he being humorous and facetious? If serious, it is surprising that he calls man an animal. According to Gen 1:20–28, animals were created first, then man, and he was to have dominion over them and to name them (2:19–20). Lincoln's man as an animal does not coincide with his statement later: "The whole great family of man . . . stamped with the Divine image and likeness" (2:546). And his words about the Ark being a miraculous rather than a human invention cast doubt about the lore that Lincoln believed we should take all of the Bible we can on reason and the rest of it on faith. The first notice of "water-craft, is the mention of 'ships' by Jacob—Gen: 49–13" (noted). Lincoln is correct that not until Isaiah are "oars" and "sails" mentioned in the Bible (Isa 33:21–23). This reference to Isaiah is surprising in light of the omission of some more obvious things outside the Pentateuch. This suggests that here, as sometimes elsewhere, Lincoln used a concordance, perhaps the one by Alexander Cruden published in 1738.

Food was man's first necessity, so it was natural that his first care should be to assist in the vegetation that produced it. The first man was put "into the garden of Eden 'to dress it, and to keep it'" (Gen 2:15; comma inserted). "The first born man—the first heir of the curse—was 'a tiller of the ground,'" is an allusion to Gen 3:23: "to till the ground from whence he was taken." That harks back to Gen 2:7: "The Lord God formed man of the dust of the ground, and breathed into his nostrils the breath of life." The curse is an allusion to the Lord's words to Adam, "cursed is the ground for thy sake" (Gen 3:17). Man tilling the ground was the beginning of agriculture, and it is "the head of all branches of human industry." However, it has "derived less direct advantage from Discovery and Invention, than almost any other" (2:440).

It is interesting that, with the mention of food, tilling of the soil, invention of the plow (2:440), and grinding at the mill (2:442), Lincoln never mentions reaping and harvesting. "Seedtime and harvest" are mentioned already in Gen 8:22 and "wheat harvest" in Exod 34:21–22. Reaping is mentioned with reference to gleaning in Lev 19:9, "the days of wheat harvest" in Gen 30:14, and "when thou cuttest down thine harvest in thy field" in Deut 24:19. Reaping was done by holding a few stalks of grain and cutting them off with a small tool such as a sickle, made of flint and later of iron, inserted into a handle of wood or bone. See putting "the sickle to the corn" in Deut 16:9 (see also Deut 23:25; Jer 50:16). It is also interesting that Lincoln does not mention threshing, which occurs first in Lev 26:5.

With respect to beasts of burden, Lincoln says that "climbing unto the back of an animal, and making it carry us, might not, occur very readily," although of great importance (2:440–41). The earliest mention of such a matter is when "'Abraham rose up early in the morning, and saddled his ass,' Gen. 22–3" (noted)—a literal quotation. That animal was probably the domesticated wild ass, which may have originated in Africa centuries before the story of Abraham was written. According to Lincoln, the saddle indicates that people had been riding "bare-backed awhile, at least, before they invented saddles" (2:441). That is certainly not one of Lincoln's most profound insights. Species of animals other than the ass became riding ones, for example, camels and horses. Abraham's servant took "ten *camels*" with him in his search for a wife for Isaac, and

"'Rebekah arose, and her damsels, and they rode upon the camels, and followed the man' Gen 24–61" (noted). The quotations are literal.

The horse also became a riding animal. "Moses and the children of Israel sang to the Lord 'The *horse*, and his *rider* hath he thrown into the sea.' Exo. 15–1" (noted). In Exodus the introductory sentence reads: "Then sang Moses and the children of Israel this song unto the Lord." The differences in Lincoln's introductory sentence are obvious. He had the text before him, but he was not careful to get every word just right. The whole speech is an exercise in frivolity. His quotation about the horse and rider is exact, except for the comma. As with readers of the KJV and the people of his time, Lincoln thought Moses wrote the first five books of the Bible.

"Seeing that animals could bear *man* upon their backs, it would soon occur that they could also bear other burdens." Joseph's "brethren" in Egypt "'laded their asses with the corn, and departed thence' Gen. 42–26" (noted)—an exact quotation. Retaining the antiquated "laded" of the KJV indicates that Lincoln had it before him. It would also occur "that animals could be made to *draw* burdens *after* them . . . and hence plows and chariots came into use early enough to be often mentioned in the books of Moses—Deut. 22–10. Gen. 41–43. Gen. 46–29. Exo. 14–25" (2:441; all noted). Lincoln obviously used a concordance, and his use of it is as haphazard as most of his citations of biblical language.

The order of implements listed in the references is plow and chariot, the order in Lincoln's text instead of the alphabetical biblical order of chariot and plow in a concordance. Lincoln looked up plow first since he mentions it first, and Deut 22:10 is the first reference to it. However, there it is used as a verb, not as a noun: "Thou shalt not plow with an ox and an ass together." The references to Genesis are to chariot, but the reference in Exod 14:25 is to the wheels of the Egyptians' chariots, which the Lord took off in order to aid the Israelites in their pursuit of the Egyptians in crossing the Red Sea. And the first reference to chariot in Exodus is Exod 14:6, not 14:25. Did Lincoln's eye pass over Exod 14:6, or did he want Exod 14:25 because it has "chariot wheels"? If so, the context is also rather remote from the context of a chariot for carrying things.

As a source of power "the *wind* contains the largest amount of *motive power* . . . to move things. As yet it "is *an untamed*, and *unharnessed* force," and one of the greatest discoveries yet to be made will be the taming and harnessing of it (2:441–42). The difficulty in controlling wind power has "been perceived, and struggled with more than three thousand years," because the power was used for sailing vessels "at least as early as the time of the prophet Isaiah" (eighth century BC). See here Isa 33:23, part of a threat by the Lord to the security of the people: "The tacklings are loosed ... they could not spread the sail." Did Lincoln remember those words but did not give the source because he could not find it? In Isaiah ships are mentioned before that in Isa 18:2 and 33:21. The words of the first part of the paragraph have a contemporary sound.

Sailing ships are known from Egypt as early as 2650 BC and ships pictured with sails and oars from about 2500–2350 BC. During the time of the Judges in Palestine (c. 1200–1020 BC), ships sailed the Mediterranean Sea (Judg 5:17; see also Gen 49:13), and "king Solomon made a navy of ships in Ezion-geber . . . on the shore of the Red sea" (1 Kgs 9:26; see also 2 Chr 8:17–18; 9:20–21; 1 Kgs 10:21–22). King Jehoshaphat of Judah (873–849 BC) "made ships of Tharshish to go to Ophir" (1 Kgs 22:48; see also Jonah 1:5; Num 24:24; Ezek 27:3–10, 25–36). Again, Lincoln's knowledge of the Bible is neither deep nor profound, and his research was not very orderly or thorough.

"*Running streams*" provide motive power for mills and other machinery with the "'*water wheel*'—a thing now well known, and extensively used; but, of which, no mention is made in the bible, though it is thought to have been in use among the romans [*sic*]—(Am. Ency. Tit—Mill."[11] Lincoln is correct in saying that the water wheel is not mentioned in the Bible and that it was in use by the Romans (2:442). In the time of Jesus, Vitruvius Pollio, architect and engineer, wrote a work on architecture (*De Arichitectura*), about 40–10 BC, dedicated to Emperor Augustus (27 BC—AD 14) in which he mentions a water wheel and a mill.

Lincoln's words "'Two women shall be grinding at the mill'" is an exact quotation of Matt 24:41, and he refers to it as "the language of the Saviour." Lincoln adds the comment, "even in the populous city of Jerusalem, at that day, mills were operated by hand." Jesus' saying is part of an apocalyptic/eschatological context of the sudden coming of the Son of Man (Matt 24:37–41), a context that could not be less apt for that of Lincoln.

Did Lincoln overlook the death of "the firstborn of the maidservant that is behind the mill" (Exod 11:5)? Or did he ignore it for some reason? Was he unaware that Samson "did grind in the prison house" (Judg 16:21; see also Lam 5:13; Eccl 12:3–4; Isa 47:2)? Or is it more evidence that his knowledge of the Bible was neither profound nor inclusive? Or, since Lincoln delivered his lecture before the Young Men's Association in Bloomington, where he had spoken earlier and his audience was surely mostly Christians, did he find it expedient to use a saying of "the Saviour" near the end of his speech? Probably so.

In sum, Lincoln's lecture on discoveries and inventions provides ample evidence that his knowledge of the substance of the Bible, even when he had it before him, was neither deep nor profound. He was concerned only with its language, oblivious of contexts. His use of an ear catcher like "Saviour" was expedient to win any support he could to achieve his political ambitions.

7

A House Divided

LINCOLN'S UNPOPULAR LECTURE ON discoveries and inventions did not quench his political flare. As a candidate for the U.S. Senate in an effort to replace Douglas, Lincoln continues to attack him on the Kansas-Nebraska Act. He is now convinced that if the Union is to be saved slavery has to be abolished. He elaborates that point in a Fragment of a Speech, c. May 18, 1858 (2:448–54).

In contrast to Douglas, who has done nothing to make Kansas a free state or any other place free, Republicans think slavery is wrong. For them it is "not only morally wrong, but a 'deadly poison' in a government like ours, professedly based on the equality of men" (2:449). Lincoln's quotation marks may indicate that he had a specific phrase in mind, for which Jas 3:8 is the only possibility: "The tongue can no man tame; it is an unruly evil, full of deadly poison." The language is apt, but the context is far from relevant. According to Lincoln, the Kansas question is not confined to politics. Church denominational meetings and single churches "are wrangling, and cracking, and going to pieces on the same question. Why, Kansas is neither the whole nor a tithe of the real question" (2:452). Tithe is a biblical word that would be familiar to Bible-readers, and they would understand the implication of the magnitude of the slavery issue.

With the stage set for a major speech, Lincoln wrote letters to several persons on various matters. A letter to Ward H. Lamon, June 11, 1858 (2:458–59), his friend, law partner, political advocate, and future body guard, relates to our study. In objecting to the running of an independent candidate to oppose Owen Lovejoy, an avid abolitionist, for representative to Congress, Lincoln used metaphors of running a race. Such a move would not only be disastrous, but "while the race is in progress," such a candidate would be tempted "to trade with the democrats, and to favor the election of certain of their friends to the Legislature" (2:458–59). With respect to himself as a candidate and realizing that there is a chance some Republicans would favor Douglas, Lincoln uses an athletic metaphor: "That is one of the chances I have to run, and which I intend to run with patience" (2:458–59). Perhaps Lincoln was influenced by Heb 12:1, whose author gives a long list of faithful persons who remained faithful under difficult circumstances (Heb 11:1–40), to encourage his readers not to be overcome with sinning. They are to "run with patience the race that is set before us." The context in Hebrews could hardly be less appropriate for that of Lincoln, but the language is catching.

Five days after Lincoln wrote to Lamon about his chances in running against Douglas, he was nominated for the U.S. Senate by the Republican state convention at Springfield, Illinois, on June 16, 1858 (2:461–69). Immediately after his nomination, he delivered his house divided speech. The biblical allusion to a saying of Jesus about a house divided occurs in the introduction to the speech, where he applies it to the government that he believes "cannot endure, permanently half *slave* and half *free*. I do not expect the Union to be *dissolved*—I do not expect the house to *fall*—but I *do* expect it will cease to be divided. It will become *all* one thing, or *all* the other" (2:461).

Lincoln was greatly concerned about the possible division of the Union over the slavery issue. The house divided quotation first occurs in the campaign circular from a Whig committee, addressed to the people of Illinois, with three signatures, the first of which is "A. Lincoln" (1:318). It is possible that the words are not those of Lincoln, but the reference to Aesop later in the circular (1:315) suggests that the words are his. He uses the moral of the fable that "union is strength." And the words about the division of the Union occur exactly in a Fragment of a Speech, May 18, 1858 (2:448–54), a month before his acceptance speech in Springfield.

In his acceptance speech Lincoln had another motive for using the house divided metaphor. Douglas came to differences with President Buchanan over the issue of the spread of slavery, and Lincoln was concerned that some Republicans might become allied with Douglas and the Democrats.

Lincoln castigates Douglas for not caring if slavery spreads beyond the slave states. Douglas's supporters think that "*he* is a very *great man*, and that the largest of *us* are very small ones. Let this be granted. But 'a *living dog* is better than a *dead lion*,'" a literal quotation of Eccl 9:4. The author of Ecclesiastes is writing about the unknown fate of mankind, although all will die. Yet it is true that while one is among "all the living there is hope: for a living dog is better than a dead lion." If Judge Douglas is not a dead lion for what he is doing, he "is at least a *caged* and *toothless* one. How can he oppose the advances of slavery? He don't *care* anything about it. His avowed *mission is impressing* the 'public heart' to *care* nothing about it" (2:467).

The house divided citation is from Matt 12:25; Mark 3:24–25; or Luke 11:17, but Lincoln's words do not occur exactly in any gospel. Matthew reads: "Every kingdom divided against itself is brought to desolation; and every city or house divided against itself shall not stand." Mark reads: "If a kingdom be divided against itself, that kingdom cannot stand. And if a house be divided against itself, that house cannot stand." Luke reads: "Every kingdom divided against itself is brought to desolation; and a house divided against a house falleth."

In the context of the gospels, some Jews accuse Jesus of casting out demons by Beelzebub, the prince of devils, also called Satan. Jesus asks, "How can Satan cast out Satan?" The conditional sentences are not general conditions, but refer to the future. They are part of an early tradition about severe opposition Jesus faced that appears differently in Matthew and Luke. All gospel writers portray the opposition to Jesus' kingdom as the domain of Satan. The words of Lincoln, "A house divided against itself cannot stand," are an adaptation of Jesus' reply to the Jews' accusation.

In light of Lincoln's words "government," "Union," and "house," the gospel words about a kingdom would have been more apt for the context of his speech. This suggests that by Lincoln's time the gospel saying of the house divided had taken on an abbreviated form familiar to Lincoln. All of this again raises the question about the depth of his knowledge of the Bible and his concern for quoting every word exactly, especially for such a well-known saying of Jesus.

For the literary and political background of the house divided speech and its effects, see Donald (206–9, 232). He calls attention to the metaphorical and political nature of the first part of short sentences as indicated by the italicized words. "The idea behind the metaphor as he now used it, that slavery and freedom were incompatible, had been a standard part of the abolitionists' argument for decades" (Donald, 206). Fornieri (*Political Faith*, 43–46; see also 93–94) quotes the same part also

as illustrative of metaphor, and he also mentions some interesting inter-
pretations of Lincoln's use of the quotation.

Without quoting most of the first page of the speech, I should like
to add that the lines in the first part of the speech also contain features
of the literary form known as *parallelism*. The combination of the words
"*avowed* object" and "*confident* promise" and "*not ceased* and "*constantly
augmented*" are typical of synonymous parallelism, in which the idea expressed in the first pair of words is repeated in a second pair with different
words. See, for example, Ps 8:4: "What is man, that thou art mindful of
him? and the son of man, that thou visitest him?" The words "half *slave*
and half *free*, *all* one thing, or *all* the other," "*opponents* of slavery," and
"its advocates" and "*old*" and "*new*" and "*North*" and "*South*" are typical
of antithetic parallelism, in which the second word or phrase is in contrast to or opposite of the first. See Ps 1:6: "The Lord knoweth the way of
the righteous: but the way of the ungodly shall perish" and Prov 10:12:
"Hatred stirreth up strifes: but love covereth all sins."

Lincoln uses the house divided quotation for the last time in an entirely different context in a letter to Nathaniel P. Banks, November 5, 1863
(7:1–2). Ever since New Orleans fell to the Union forces in 1862, Lincoln
had hoped for the readmission of Louisiana to the Union as a free state.
However, he got little support from General Banks who was in charge of
government affairs there. He had asked Banks to register eligible voters
in the state for the purpose of holding a state constitutional convention.
He was afraid that a small group of men would succeed in setting up a
state government that would reinstate Louisiana as a slave state. That, says
Lincoln, "would be a house divided against itself" (7:2).

Slightly more than three weeks after Lincoln delivered his house divided
speech, Douglas spoke in Chicago on the evening of July 9, 1858, with
Lincoln present. Lincoln delivered a speech there, July 10, 1858 (2:484–
502), but Douglas was not present. In his house divided speech, Lincoln
had jested about Judge Douglas being a dead lion or, if not, at least a
caged and toothless one. In doing so he quoted Eccl 9:4 literally. Now
Lincoln jokes: "Why, my friend, the Judge, is not only, as it turns out, not a
dead lion, nor even a living one—he is the rugged Russian Bear!"(2:485).
The origin of this remark may be twofold. In the nineteenth century the
Russian nation was personified as a large and vicious bear, sometimes

with a lion pictured with it, and in the Old Testament the lion and the bear are mentioned together as ferocious creatures ready to attack their prey. David's ability to slay both the lion and the bear and take the prey from its mouth was a qualification for his challenge to fight the giant Goliath (1 Sam 17:34–37). See also Prov 28:15: "As a roaring lion, and a raging bear; so is a wicked ruler over the poor people" (see also Prov 19:12; 2 Sam 17:10; Prov 19:12; Lam 3:10; Amos 5:19; Nah 2:12). We have to wonder, though, how familiar Lincoln was with folk tales about bears that were the origin of personifying Russia as a rugged bear. Was he as familiar with them as he was with the accounts in the Bible about bears and lions? Do we have here statements compounded from both sources?

The Democrats "snub over" the fact that the Republicans were largely responsible for the defeat of the Lecompton Constitution, a document drawn up at Lecompton, Kansas, in September 1857, that supported the extension of slavery in a territory proposed for admission to the Union. It gave protection to the rights of slave holders and a referendum that gave voters a choice of allowing additional slaves in a territory. Ultimately, that constitution was rejected by Kansas, and it was admitted into the Union as a free state in 1861. Democrats, says Lincoln, do not seem to remember that Republicans "have an existence upon the face of the earth" (2:490). The phrase "upon the face of the earth" occurs often in the Old Testament, and "the face of the earth" occurs more often there and in Acts 17:26. Perhaps Lincoln was most influenced by Exod 33:16: "all the people that are upon the face of the earth" (see also Deut 7:6).

Lincoln repeats his house divided quotation (2:491) and discusses his views on self-government. He also repeats his view that individuals are entitled to do as they please with the fruit of their labor so long as what they do does not interfere with the rights of others (2:493). The majority of Americans think that slavery is "a vast moral evil." According to the Constitution, we have no right to interfere with slavery in states where it already exists. Lincoln says that we are "to stick by that Constitution in all its letter and spirit from beginning to end" (2:494). In the Bible "letter and spirit" do not occur exactly that way, but see, for example, Rom 2:25–29, where Paul is arguing that circumcision in the flesh does not make a real Jew because circumcision is a matter of the heart, "in the spirit, and not in the letter," and such a person is praised by God, not men (see also Rom 7:6; 2 Cor 3:6; 2 Thess 2:2). For Paul, the Hebrew scriptures were law, but the spirit is primary. For Lincoln, the Constitution was the law, and letter and spirit are equal, if the letter is not more important because he places it first. Besides this parallel, remote, real, or imagined, the contexts of the two could not be more adverse.

Lincoln exhorts the members of the Republican party to stand by their principles of opposing the spread of slavery and their hopes for its ultimate extinction. "As surely as God reigns over" them, inspires their minds, gives them a sense of propriety, and continues to give them hope, "so surely" they "will still cling to these ideas" (2:498). "God reigns" occurs in Ps 47:7–8: "God reigneth over the heathen," in which the psalm is celebrating a victory of God either over some event in Israel's history or in the glorious eschatological End (see also Isa 52:7).

Because the Judge had mentioned scripture, Lincoln turns to it: "My friend has said to me that I am a poor hand to quote Scripture. I will try it again, however." I am not sure what Lincoln's "poor hand" means. Does it mean not good at quoting the Bible or that Lincoln's behavior does not justify his using scripture or that he does not subscribe to Christian doctrine? Lincoln responds by saying: "It is said in one of the admonitions of the Lord, 'As your Father in Heaven is perfect, be ye also perfect.' The Savior, I suppose, did not expect that any human creature could be perfect as the Father in Heaven; but He said, 'As your Father in Heaven is perfect, be ye also perfect.' He set that up as a standard, and he who did most towards reaching that standard, attained the highest degree of moral perfection" (2:501).

Lincoln used the imprecise "one of the admonitions of the Lord," rather than mentioning precisely the Sermon on the Mount, with chapter and verse (Appendix 4). Chapters 5–7 of Matthew were known as the Sermon on the Mount at least as early as the Church Fathers Chrysostom (c. AD 354–407) and Augustine (AD 354–430), who both wrote about the Sermon. Surely many persons in Lincoln's audience were aware of the designation, so why did he not use it?

The quotation is an adaptation from Matt 5:48: "Be ye therefore perfect, even as your Father which is in heaven is perfect." Luke, the Gentile Christian, did not understand the saying as Matthew the Jewish Christian did because he puts Jesus' words another way: "Be ye therefore merciful, as your Father also is merciful" (Luke 6:36). The saying is in the context of love for one's enemies, in which the disciples are to surpass others. Lincoln reverses the clauses, and in doing so, by putting "be ye" last, the emphasis is on the hearers in order to win their support for his view on slavery. The omission of the words "therefore," "even," and "which" indicates that he was not concerned with repeating scripture precisely as it was written. Those words would have weakened the force of his statement.

This is one of the few times Lincoln interprets a passage from the Bible. However, his interpretation weakens the force of what the Jewish writer Matthew intended. In the Old Testament perfection of one kind or another, especially of character, was stressed. "Noah was a just man and perfect in his generations" (Gen 6:9). The Lord told Abraham: "Walk before me, and be thou perfect" (Gen 17:1). Lincoln was not a biblical scholar, so we could not expect him to know that. He directed the quotation to Douglas, and then he applied it to the principle that all men are created equal. If we cannot give freedom to every person, we must not do anything to impose slavery on any person, an allusion to the view that slavery should not spread to the free territories.

Lincoln's quotation is just one more incident that casts further doubt on the tradition that he could quote chapter and verse of much of the gospels. For his purposes, what biblical language he remembered, with adept manipulation, was profundity enough.

In Lincoln's campaign against Douglas for the U.S. Senate, the vote of German Americans was important for the Republicans, so he wrote about that to Gustave P. Koerner, a political supporter, July 15, 1858 (2:502–3). As a lawyer in Belleville, Illinois, Koerner was a main intermediary between Lincoln and German Americans and one of the delegates Lincoln chose to nominate him for president at the nominating convention in Chicago in 1860. He tells Koerner that in the Judge's "rampant indorsement of the Dred Scott decision he drove back a few republicans who were favorably inclined towards him. His tactics just now, in part is, to make it appear that he is having a triumphal entry into; and march through the country; but it is all as bombastic and hollow as Napoleon's bulletins sent back from his campaign in Russia" (2:502). The first biblical passage that comes to mind is Jesus' triumphal entry into Jerusalem from outside the city (Matt 21:1–9; Mark 11:1–10; Luke 19:28–38). However, Lincoln's words "march through the country" may suggest that he knew about the triumphal marches of famous Roman generals from city to city, sometimes with prisoners and booty. The march of Titus into the Roman Forum with captives and booty from the Temple in Jerusalem in AD 70 after his destruction of the city was especially well known. It is commemorated with The Arch of Titus, a beautiful sculpture, on the *Via Sacra* ("sacred way") at the east entrance into the Forum and depicts captives and booty taken by Titus.

Douglas spoke at Springfield on the afternoon of July 16, 1858, and Lincoln delivered his reply in a Speech at Springfield, Illinois, July 17, 1858 (2:504–21). Lincoln says that he was "made the standard-bearer in behalf of the Republicans" (2:506). Again, Lincoln ridicules Douglas about the Lecompton Constitution. Douglas had supported it, and Lincoln agreed with his position that the principle of the right of a people in a Territory in the process of becoming a State to form their own Constitution without outside influence. So then, is the Judge going to be transformed into a god and spend his life supporting a principle that "neither a man nor a mouse in all God's creation is opposing?" (2:509).

The idea of a man transformed into a god was known in Hebrew society and in the Greco-Roman world. According to Exod 7:1, the Lord said to Moses: "See, I have made thee a god to Pharaoh." According to Acts 12:22, Herod Agrippa I (AD 41–44), who treated the apostles cruelly, made a royal address, after which the people shouted, "It is the voice of a god, and not of a man" (see also Acts 28:5).

Lincoln remarks that Douglas said he has "a proneness for quoting scripture." If he were to do that now, it occurs that perhaps the Judge "places himself somewhat upon the ground of the parable of the lost sheep which went astray upon the mountains, and when the owner of the hundred sheep found the one that was lost, and threw it upon his shoulders, and came home rejoicing, it was said that there was more rejoicing over the one sheep that was lost and had been found, than over the ninety and nine in the fold" (2:510–11). The parable occurs in Matt 18:12–14 and Luke 15:3–7. "Parable" is mentioned only in Luke and Lincoln. In Matthew the context is Jesus' admonition that no one despise one of his disciples, whom he calls "these little ones." It is not the will of his Father in heaven that one of them should perish. According to Luke, the Pharisees and scribes complained that Jesus was welcoming publicans and other sinners and eating with them. Unlike Matthew, Luke does not mention God, so his readers are left to assume that Jesus was acting like the shepherd. Typically, Matthew omits the details about the shepherd laying the lost sheep on his shoulders and his invitation to friends and neighbors to rejoice with him at finding it. Rejoicing at the finding of the sheep is in Matthew, Luke, and Lincoln. Matthew says that the shepherd rejoices more over the lost sheep than over the ninety nine that did not go astray, but Luke emphasizes rejoicing by mentioning it three times in addition to joy in heaven.

According to Matthew, the sheep was lost in the mountains, which Lincoln mentions, but Luke does not. Luke says that the owner left the other sheep in the wilderness, which neither Matthew nor Lincoln has, and goes after the one lost. Lincoln concludes his description of the parable with "the ninety and nine in the fold," words not in either gospel. Lincoln's "in the fold" may reflect Matthew's "which went not astray." Matthew says nothing about the owner "laying" the sheep on his shoulders, only in Luke. According to Matthew, the owner rejoices more over that one sheep than over the ninety and nine (number in the three accounts) that did not go astray. According to Luke, the owner invites his friends and neighbors to rejoice with him because he found the lost sheep.

Both gospel writers begin with the man who owned the sheep and then tell about the one lost. Lincoln puts the one lost first and then brings in the owner and the other sheep. In this way he immediately draws the parallel between Douglas and the lost sheep. For Matthew the point of the parable is; "It is not the will of your Father . . . that one of these little ones [Jesus' disciples] should perish." For Luke the point is: "Likewise joy shall be in heaven over one sinner that repenteth, more than over ninety and nine just persons, which need no repentance." Lincoln ends the discussion of the parable by saying that the application made by the Saviour is: "Verily, I say unto you, there is more rejoicing in heaven over one sinner that repenteth, then over ninety and nine just persons that need no repentance," a free quotation of Luke's version. (2:511). Only Luke mentions sinning and repenting, which shows Lincoln's familiarity with his version, probably the more widely known and more applicable to current times. Lincoln's "Verily, I say unto you," is verbatim from Matt 18:13, which occurs in Luke 15:7, minus the "verily." Lincoln uses "that" throughout his story instead of "which," sometimes used in the KJV. These and other variations from the Bible show that Lincoln quotes from memory, perhaps mostly from Luke, to say that the Judge should repent and ask forgiveness. He should not think that he is the only just person and that the others are the ninety-nine sinners.

Lincoln's exact quotations are words easily remembered, and they are really all he needed to make his point. This is one of the few times that Lincoln shows familiarity with the biblical context from which his words are taken. So here we have a hybrid of biblical language taken from both Matthew and Luke, with more influence from Luke. As usual, the tradition about Lincoln quoting precisely whole sections from the Bible, sometimes mentioning chapter and verses is *demythed.*

Lincoln accuses the Judge of being in favor of Supreme Court decisions when he likes them and opposed when he does not. He has supported the Dred Scott case, "because it tends to nationalize slavery." Lincoln has never opposed any Supreme Court decision until the present time, while the Judge was never "in favor of any, nor opposed to any, till the present one, which helps to nationalize slavery" (2:518). Dramatically, Lincoln appeals to his audience: "Free men of Sangamon—free men of Illinois—free men everywhere—judge ye between him and me, upon this issue" (2:518). Judging between two parties was a part of Hebrew society and its laws, by which various persons did the judging. Moses says that when the people "have a matter, they come unto me; and I judge between one and another" (Exod 18:16). Sometimes the Lord is invoked as judge. Sarai (Sarah) says to Abram (Abraham) about his affair with Hagar, her maidservant: "The Lord judge between me and thee" (Gen 16:5; see also 1 Sam 24:12–15).

Lincoln continues to ridicule the Judge by saying that the previous evening he showed affection toward Americans and Whigs. "In a sort of weeping tone, he described to us a death bed scene. He had been called to the side of Mr. Clay, in his last moments, in order that the genius of 'popular sovereignty' might duly descend from the dying man and settle upon him, the living and most worthy successor" (2:519). Lincoln's words are reminiscent of death bed scenes in Hebrew society with dying men blessing their sons. See, for example, Jacob's (Israel's) blessing of Joseph's sons Ephraim and Manasseh and then of his own sons (Gen 48:8—49:27). For the biblical phrase "the living" see, for example, "He [Aaron] stood between the dead and the living" (Num 16:48; see also Ruth 2:0; Job 28:13; Ps 27:13; Eccl 4:2, 15).

The Judge "could do no less than promise that he would devote the remainder of his life to 'popular sovereignty;' and then the great states-man departs in peace." He promised himself that tears should run "down the cheeks of all old Whigs, as large as half grown apples" (2:519). For the weeping tone and tears running down the cheeks, see the previous discussion of Lincoln's speech to the Springfield Scott Club and the book of Lamentations, especially Lam 1:2, where the author says of the devastated city of Jerusalem: "She weepeth sore in the night, and her tears are on her cheeks" (see also Isa 16:9; Jer 31:15–16; Mal 2:13). For Lincoln's words, "if Mr. Clay cast his mantle upon Judge Douglas" (2:519), see "Elijah passed by him [Elisha], and cast his mantle upon him" (1 Kgs 19:19; see also 2 Kgs 2:8,13–14). Lincoln was certainly influenced by that language, and he used the metaphor several times elsewhere with respect to Clay and Douglas (2:545; 3:89, 244). The words "in all its glory" in the clause "when 'popular sovereignty' stood forth in all its glory" (2:519), echo biblical language. Perhaps Lincoln was most influenced by Matt 6:29: "Solomon in all his glory" (see also Isa 21:16; 1 Pet 1:24; Gen 31:1; John 2:11).

With respect to the argument of the superiority of the white man, Lincoln says that the Judge "is satisfied with any thing which does not endanger the nationalizing of negro slavery. It may draw white men down, but it must not lift negroes up." Lincoln asks: "Who shall say, 'I am the superior, and you are the inferior?'" (2:520). See the remarks of Job to Zophar: "I have understanding as well as you; I am not inferior to you" (Job 12:3; 13:2). In the context of eating the bread earned by his own hands, white and black men are equal, Lincoln says: "If more has been given you, you can not be justified in taking away the little which has been given him. All I ask for the negro is that if you do not like him, let him alone. If God gave him but little, that little let him enjoy" (2:520).

The idea of God giving something occurs many times in the Old Testament. For example, in his death bed blessing Isaac says to Jacob: "God Almighty ... give thee the blessing of Abraham" (Gen 28:4). Lincoln may have been influenced by a saying of Jesus in various forms in the first three gospels, especially Luke 8:18: "For whosoever hath, to him shall be given; and whosoever hath not, from him shall be taken even that which he seemeth to have" (see also Matt 13:12; 25:29; Mark 4:25; Luke 19:26). This is a difficult saying, and that is probably why it appears in different ways in the gospels. It is one of three sayings of Jesus stressing that his disciples should listen to what he says in his parables and do what he says. They will be given more to do. Those who do not do what he says will be deprived of the knowledge they think they have.

As the election for U.S. Senator drew nearer, Lincoln continued to accentuate the differences between him and the Judge on the slavery issue. His brief speech at Lewistown, Illinois, August 17, 1858 (2:544–47), is important for understanding his use of the Bible and its relationship to the documents of the founding fathers. Lincoln says that Douglas's position on slavery is as opposite to Clay's "as Beelzebub to an Angel of Light" (2:545). Beelzebub (Beelzebul) was an ancient mythological character known in Jewish and Christian literature as Satan (Matt 10:25; 12:24, 27; Mark 3:22–23; Luke 11:15–19). Paul says of his adversaries that as "false apostles" they transform themselves "into the apostles of Christ. And no marvel; for Satan himself is transformed into an angel of light" (2 Cor 11:13–14). In Jewish mythology that character was sometimes associated with the deception of Eve by the serpent in the Garden of Eden (Gen 3:4–6). In the gospel accounts, Beelzebub is generally portrayed as an adversary of Jesus, and there is nothing in any of them about Beelzebub being changed into an angel of light as in Paul. Is Lincoln's language a clever manipulation in order to emphasize the difference between Clay and Douglas on the issue of slavery? Who knows how much Lincoln was influenced here by ancient mythology and/or the Bible. But notice the difference in concept: Beelzebub being opposite to an angel of light is not the same thing as Satan being transformed into an angel of light.

I have suggested that for understanding Lincoln's position on slavery the Declaration of Independence and the Constitution are more important than the Bible. His superb rhetoric in the second half of the Lewistown speech is, perhaps, the best example of that. He quotes from the Declaration about all men being created equal and endowed by their Creator with unalienable rights of life, liberty, and the pursuit of happiness. For the founding fathers,

> This was their lofty, and wise, and noble understanding of the justice of the Creator to His creatures . . . *all* His creatures, to the whole great family of man. In their enlightened belief, nothing stamped with the Divine image and likeness was sent into the world to be trodden on, and degraded, and imbruted by its fellows. They grasped not only the whole race of man then living, but they reached forward and seized upon the farthest posterity. They erected a beacon to guide their children and their children's children, and the countless myriads who should inhabit the earth in

other ages. Wise statesmen as they were, they knew the tendency of prosperity to breed tyrants, and so they established these great self-evident truths, that when in the distant future some man, some faction, some interest, should set up the doctrine that none but rich men, or none but white men, were entitled to life, liberty and the pursuit of happiness, their posterity might look up again to the Declaration of Independence and take courage to renew the battle which their fathers began—so that truth, and justice, and mercy, and all the humane and Christian virtues might not be extinguished from the land; so that no man would hereafter dare to limit and circumscribe the great principles on which the temple of liberty was being built. (2:546–47)

Lincoln's exposition of the truths of the Declaration that are self-evident in the Lewistown speech is among his literary masterpieces, little mentioned before Wolf (96–97). Wolf says that Lincoln identifies the Declaration with the Genesis doctrine of the creation of man in the divine image and that Lincoln went on to establish the theological foundation of the Declaration. Then he quotes the paragraph from Lincoln given above. Lincoln is not primarily concerned with a theological doctrine of man, but with the equality of men, white and black, with each other as they have the unalienable rights of "life, liberty and the pursuit of happiness."

Lincoln's last, long sentence confirms the point that the three specific virtues mentioned, life, liberty, and the pursuit of happiness, are part of the divine image that Lincoln had in mind for *all men*. And morality from the Declaration overshadows theology, as we learn from what Lincoln continues to say in reflecting influence from the Bible besides the Genesis story, beginning with "the justice of the Creator to His creatures." Justice was an attribute of the Hebrew deity, "a just God" (Isa 45:21), and it was closely associated with judgment, as in Ps 89:14: "Justice and judgment are the habitation of thy throne; mercy and truth shall go before thy face" (see also Isa 59:4, 14). Notice the similar virtues of truth, justice, and mercy as in Lincoln's speech. His "humane and Christian virtues" are the same virtues, regardless of one's theology. Lincoln has not said anything with which morally sensitive persons would not agree. This is precisely the point Lincoln made in his speech at Chicago, when he said that being perfect is the standard for attaining "the highest degree of moral perfection . . . in relation to the principle that all men are created equal" (2:501).

Lincoln's "whole great family of man" and "whole race of man" reflect Luke 12:30: "the nations of the world" and Acts 17:26: "[God] hath made of one blood all nations of men for to dwell on all the face of the earth." In exhorting his hearers to return to the principles of equality and freedom of the Declaration, Lincoln uses a metaphor of a fountain and its waters: "Return to the fountain whose waters spring close by the blood of the Revolution" (2:547). It seems as though the words about a fountain and water might have been motivated by something in the Bible, but I am not sure. Perhaps the closest parallel to Lincoln's words is Jeremiah's lament that his people have forsaken the Lord, "the fountain of living waters" (Jer 2:13; 17:13). Is it not plausible to think that in the context Lincoln would emphasize the Declaration, not the Lord, as a fountain of life? Lincoln's words about people doing anything to him politically, even taking his life, and especially his dramatic conclusion tend to give credence to the idea.

In this speech at Lewistown, Lincoln's political ambition, as I continue to argue, played a major role in what he says with respect to his use of the Bible: "While pretending no indifference to earthly honors, I *do claim* to be actuated in this contest by something higher than an anxiety for office." He charges his audience "to drop every paltry and insignificant thought for man's success. It is nothing; I am nothing; Judge Douglas is nothing. *But do not destroy that immortal emblem of Humanity—the declaration of American Independence*" (2:547). That Declaration was the primary basis of Lincoln's faith, fortified by references from the Bible to win support for his political and moral position.

Naturally, it was thought that with each candidate, no matter what other factors motivated him, personal satisfaction played a role. According to a Fragment on Notes for Speeches, c. August 21, 1858 (2:547–53), Douglas has accused Lincoln of doing that. Lincoln responds by saying that by "mere burlesque on the art and name of argument" Douglas has fantastically arranged words "as prove 'horse-chestnuts to be chestnut horses'" (2:547). Lincoln protests that he has not entered the campaign for the Senate "solely, or even chiefly, for a mere personal object." But Lincoln clearly sees in Douglas "a powerful plot to make slavery universal and perpetual in this nation . . . I enter upon the contest to contribute my humble and temporary mite in opposition to that effort" (2:548). Mite is a biblical word, and Lincoln may have had in mind the poor widow who contributed her two mites, all she had, to the treasury (Mark 12:41–44; Luke 21:1–4; see also Luke 12:59). No matter what the likely source was for Lincoln, its meaning would be known to Bible-readers, and it would emphasize the magnitude of the slavery issue.

Lincoln accuses Chief Justice Roger B. Taney, who had ruled against Dred Scott, of falsifying reasons for his decision. Lincoln has the right to prove a conspiracy and the answer for it. "There is much more than the evidence of two witnesses to prove it" (2:549). Hebrew law required "the mouth of two witnesses, or three witnesses" (Deut 17:6; 19:15). With reference to Douglas, in dealing with the right of self-government as the essence of liberty, Lincoln thinks public opinion ought to be brought in. He asks rhetorical questions: "In the name of heaven, what barrier will be left against slavery being made lawful everywhere?" "Can you find *one* word of his, opposed to it? Can you *not* find many strongly favoring it? If for his life—for his eternal salvation—he was solely striving for that end, could he find any means so well adapted to reach that end?" (2:553). The phrase "eternal salvation" occurs in Heb 5:9, where the writer says that the perfect Jesus "became the author of eternal salvation" for all who obey him. Looking forward to a blissful ending for Israel, Isaiah says: "Israel shall be saved in the Lord with an everlasting salvation" (Isa 45:17). Again, Lincoln uses biblical language naturally, perhaps without being aware of it, and entirely out of context, to make his point for political advantage. Above all, it does not give any insight into Lincoln's personal belief in salvation.

From August 21 to October 15, 1858 (3:1–325), Lincoln and Douglas staged seven public debates, in which the Bible is rarely mentioned. When it is, we learn a lot about the extent and depth of Lincoln's knowledge of it.

8

The Almighty Gives No Audible Answer

There were supporters of the proslavery movement among the clergy, one of whom was the Rev. Frederick Augustus Ross (1796–1883) of First Presbyterian Church, Knoxville, Tennessee. He often preached on the subject of slavery, and he wrote a work on *Slavery Ordained of God* (1857). Lincoln replies to the proslavery view, perhaps to Ross in particular, in a Fragment on Pro-slavery Theology, October 1, 1858? (3:204–5). One of Lincoln's most interesting documents on slavery, it gives some interesting insights into his use of the Bible. He begins by saying: "Suppose it is true, that the negro is inferior to the white, in the gifts of nature; is it not the exact reverse justice that the white should, for that reason, take from the negro, any part of the little which has been given him? '*Give* to him that is needy' is the christian [*sic*] rule of charity; but 'Take from him that is needy' is the rule of slavery" (3:204).

The words about giving to the needy reflect a common biblical theme, not just a Christian one, but Lincoln's words as quoted do not occur in the Bible. However, see, for example, "Thou shalt open thine hand wide unto thy brother, to thy poor, and to thy needy" (Deut 15:11). Perhaps Lincoln was influenced by Eph 4:28, where the author exhorts the person who stole to steal no more but to work with his own hands "that he may have to give to him that needeth" (see also Matt 19:21; Mark 10:21; Luke 19:8). Again, Lincoln shows no concern about exact quotation, specific biblical book, or depth of biblical knowledge. On the basis of general knowledge of charity in the Bible, Lincoln invented the quotation on Christian charity, as he did for the rule on slavery which begins: "The sum of pro-slavery theology seems to be this: 'Slavery is not universally *right*, nor yet universally *wrong*; it is better for *some* people to be slaves; and, in such cases, it is the Will of God that they be such." Lincoln continues:

Certainly there is no contending against the Will of God; but still there is some difficulty in ascertaining, and applying it, to particular cases. For instance we will suppose the Rev. Dr. Ross has a slave named Sambo, and the question is 'Is it the Will of God that Sambo shall remain a slave, or be set free?' The Almighty gives no audable [sic] answer . . . and his revelation—the Bible—gives none—or, at most, none but such as admits of a squabble, as to it's meaning. No one thinks of asking Sambo's opinion on it. So, at last, it comes to this, that *Dr. Ross* is to decide the question. And while he consider[s] it, he sits in the shade, with gloves on his hands, and subsists on the bread that Sambo is earning in the burning sun. If he decides that God wills Sambo to continue a slave, he thereby retains his own comfortable position; but if he decides that God wills Sambo to be free, he thereby has to walk out of the shade, throw off his gloves, and delve for his own bread. Will Dr. Ross be actuated by that perfect impartiality, which has ever been considered most favorable to correct decisions? But, slavery is good for some people!!! As a *good* thing slavery is strikingly peculiar, in this, that it is the only good thing which no man ever seeks the good of, *for himself*. Nonsense! Wolves devouring lambs, not because it is good for their own greedy maws, but because it [is] good for the lambs!!! (3:204–5)

With respect to slavery and the Bible, Lincoln was treading on dubious ground. Both pro and antislavery parties accepted the Bible as authoritative and, therefore, both claimed that their will was the will of God. Differences hinged on interpretation. The precise phrase "the will of God" does not occur in the Old Testament, but it occurs twenty-two times in the New Testament, mostly in the absolute sense, that is, lacking an attribute or object. For exceptions see, for example, 1 Thess 4:3: "This is the will of God . . . that ye should abstain from fornication" (see also 1 Thess 5:17–18; 1 Pet 3:17; 4:19). The author of Ephesians writes: "Walk circumspectly, not as fools, but as wise . . . .Be ye not unwise, but understanding what the will of the Lord is" (Eph 5:15–17). Was Lincoln, perhaps subconsciously, influenced by this passage when he wrote that in the Bible "the Almighty gives no audible answer" to what the will of God is, "none but such as admits of a squabble, as to its meaning," with respect to a slave being set free?

Impartiality in making decisions was a part of the religion of Judaism and Christianity. The prophet Malachi says that his people "have been partial in the law" in not obeying the laws of the Lord (Mal 2:9). In the KJV the same idea is expressed most often in the form of respecting or not respecting persons, for example, "Ye shall not respect persons in judgment" (Deut 1:17; see also Deut 16:19). In later translations the idea is conveyed as being partial or impartial, for example, the phrase "without respect of persons judgeth" in the KJV is "judges all people impartially" in the NRSV (1 Pet 1:17; see also Gal 2:6; Rom 2:11; Acts 10:34). In 1 Tim 5:21 both forms of the idea occur, where the author charges his readers to act "without preferring one before another, doing nothing by partiality." Lincoln's "perfect impartiality" may be most influenced by Jas 3:17, where the author writes: "The wisdom that is from above is . . . without partiality, and without hypocrisy."

Lincoln's statement that the Bible gives no evidence for the retaining or freeing slaves is incorrect, even though he says "a squabble" arises over it. Slavery was an integral part of the economic, social, and religious life of the Jews and the early Christians, as is clear from the frequent use of the word "servant," both male and female, in the Bible. Although considered a part of Hebrew and early Christian households, slaves were bought and sold, imported and exported, and manumitted. Sometimes a free person and a slave were married (1 Chr 2:34–35; Exod 21:1–11, 16; 23:15–16; 24:7). As members of households, slaves, like their masters, were to observe the commandments (Exod 20:10; Deut 5:14). There were laws for punishing servants and for masters who abused them. And, at the end of six years of service, slaves were to be set free without any circumstances detrimental to them (Exod 21:2–6; Deut 15:12–18). For Hebrew laws on slaves see Exodus 21, Leviticus 24, and Deuteronomy 15.

If slavery were objectionable, the figure of servant would not have gotten into the theology of both the Old Testament and New Testament. In the Old Testament the one chosen by God to redeem Israel was called servant. "Behold my servant, whom I uphold; mine elect . . . I have put my spirit upon him: he shall bring forth judgment to the Gentiles" (Isa 42:1; see also Isa 41:8–9; 49:5–6). The passage from Isa 42:1 is quoted by Jesus of himself in Matt 12:15–18, and he says to his disciples: "He that is greatest among you shall be his servant" (Matt 23:11; see also Matt 10:24; 24:45–50). Paul says that Christ "took upon him[self] the form of a servant, and was made in the likeness of men" (Phil 2:7). Paul and other believers in Jesus thought of themselves as servants of Christ (Rom 1:1; Phil 1:1; Jas 1:1; 2 Pet 1:1). Paul asks Philemon, whose slave Onesimus had run away, to take him back forever, "not now as a servant, but . . .

a brother beloved" (Phlm 1:16). Servants are to obey their masters, who are to treat them well, knowing that their Master is in heaven (Eph 6:5–9; see also Col 3:22; 4:4:1; Titus 2:9; 1 Pet 2:18).

Although Paul never says that slavery is wrong, he goes beyond the social to the moral issue when he teaches: "For as many of you as have been baptized into Christ . . . there is neither Jew nor Greek, there is neither bond nor free, there is neither male nor female: for ye are all one in Christ Jesus" (Gal 3:27–28). It is doubtful that this passage influenced Lincoln, because his concept of the equality of men was derived directly from the Declaration of Independence, not the Bible (*pace* Fornerie, *Political Faith*, 84, 136; but see his excellent discussion, 70–91).

It would be interesting to have a reply from Ross. Lincoln's thought and feeling, rather than theology, played an inestimable role in the resolution of the slavery question, for which the story about Sambo is a superb example. Speaking of theology, characteristically, Lincoln uses different titles for the deity—God and Almighty, which reflects his inner struggle to understand the Divine (Appendix 3). The will of God is left undetermined, and the Almighty is not almighty, because he gives no certain answer to Lincoln's great concerns about slavery. On the other hand, the Rev. Dr. Ross, a true believer, thought that his opinion was the will of God. Lincoln was writing to a theologian, and he was turning Ross's own theology against him, not proclaiming his own personal theology, but his own morality.

In the Seventh and Last Debate with Stephen A. Douglas at Alton, Illinois, October 15, 1858 (3:283–325), Lincoln mentions the Bible three times in his reply to Douglas. The slavery question has heated up, and the Union is threatened. Douglas had referred to Lincoln's quotation of a house divided against itself in his speech at Springfield, to which Lincoln responds by quoting the relative part of that speech and then says that sentiments expressed in it "have been extremely offensive to Judge Douglas. He has warred upon them as Satan does upon the Bible. His perversions upon it are endless" (3:305). Although such humorous sarcasm invoked laughter in the audience, the words "as Satan does" may reflect a likely view of many of Lincoln's hearers that Satan is always opposing precepts of the Bible, the word of God. Lincoln's "warring upon" does not occur in the Bible, but "warring against" occurs in 2 Kgs 19:8 and Isa 37:8, both of military action. In Rom 7:22–23 Paul soliloquizes that "another law" (not "the law of God"), in his body is "warring against the law" of his mind. It is more likely that Lincoln had in mind the story of Jesus' temptations, in which Satan quotes scripture to tempt Jesus, who replies by quoting scripture (Matt 4:1–11; Luke 4:1–13). Lincoln has coined an expression that was bound to appeal to his hearers to support his political opposition to Douglas.

According to Lincoln, Douglas "tries to show that variety in the domestic institutions of the different States is necessary and indispensable" (3:309). Lincoln has no quarrel with that idea and proceeds to speak with a typical mixture of humor and sarcasm. He argues that "it would be foolish for us to insist upon having a cranberry law here, in Illinois, where we have no cranberries, because they have a cranberry law in Indiana, where they have cranberries." Wherever slavery has tried to spread itself, there has been "difficulty and turmoil" (3:309–10). Lincoln does not want his hearers to think, as Douglas had implied, that the difficulty regarding slavery "is the mere agitation of office seekers and ambitious Northern politicians" and that Lincoln wanted to get Douglas's political office. Lincoln continues: "The Bible says somewhere that we are desperately selfish. I think we would have discovered that fact without the Bible." Lincoln does not claim to be less selfish than the average person, but he does claim that he is "not more selfish than Judge Douglas" (3:310).

There are no words in the Bible about persons being "desperately selfish," and neither the word selfish nor selfishness occurs in the KJV. What an excellent example of Lincoln's lack of inclusive knowledge of the Bible and of his habit of quoting chapter and verse from it exactly. What he says is dead wrong. Recall our earlier discussion of this observation in connection with the assumed depth of Lincoln's knowledge of the Bible.

The last debate with Douglas took place just two and a half weeks before Lincoln lost the election to the U.S. Senate to him. However, the Republican plurality in Illinois and other hopeful signs set the stage for the presidential election of 1860. Meanwhile, Lincoln continued to make public speeches and write to friends and political supporters. In those communications there are few, if any, instances of biblical influence. Among those speeches is Lincoln's Second Lecture on Discoveries and Inventions, February 11, 1859 (3:356–63), delivered before the Phi Alpha

Society of Illinois College, Jacksonville. A literary society for men, it was organized by seven college students on September 25, 1845, and its purpose was to attain truth, improve literary skills, and further their democratic heritage. Lincoln was inducted as the first honorary member on February 4, 1859. His second lecture was probably an induction speech he had been invited to give, and it is most likely a continuation of the first lecture delivered before the Young Men's Association of Bloomington, Illinois.

In the first lecture, the Bible was Lincoln's chief source, but in his second, he mentions the Bible only once, although he alludes to it several times in interesting ways. Lincoln begins his speech metaphorically concerning the youth of America, about whom all have heard. They are the "he" in what follows: "He is the most *current* youth of the age. Some think him conceited, and arrogant; but has he not reason to entertain a rather extensive opinion of himself?" Lincoln also asks: "Is he not the inventor and owner of the *present*, and sole hope of the *future?*" (3:356). After repeating some of the material from his first lecture, Lincoln uses Old Fogy as a metaphor for people, beginning with Adam. He [the youth] has "considerable advantage of Old Fogy. Take, for instance, the first of all fogies, father Adam," whom Lincoln considered the father of the human race (3:357).

Lincoln continues to arouse the interest of the young men in his audience. According to poets and painters, Adam "stood, a very perfect physical man . . . but he must have been very ignorant, and simple in his habits." He did not learn much by observation, since "he had no near neighbors to teach him anything. No part of his breakfast had been brought from the other side of the world; and it is quite probable, he had no conception of the world having any other side" (3:357).

Lincoln is more entertaining than displaying insightful understanding of Adam and the Bible. He says that Adam had the advantage of having land and livestock and that he had dominion over the earth and all things on it, which reflects Gen 1:26–28. In his first lecture Lincoln sometimes gives references to the Bible for what he says, but in the second there are none. "The great difference between Young America and Old Fogy, is the result of *Discoveries, Inventions,* and *Improvements.* These, in turn, are the result of *observation, reflection* and *experiment*" (3:358). Adam at first was not a very observant man, because he went around naked for a long time before he discovered the fact, but his lack of observation led to *the fig-leaf apron* as the first invention (3:359). Up to this time Lincoln has said nothing about the woman (Gen 2:25), but later he says he did not notice that making the apron must have been "a joint operation," and since sewing came down from then to the present as a woman's work, Eve must have played the main role, perhaps while Adam stood ready "to thread the needle" (3:359–60). Lincoln says nothing about the couple's disobeying of God's command not to eat the forbidden fruit and that after God appeared to them they knew they were naked and made the aprons. Lincoln's way of putting it was much more entertaining than if he had conveyed the text precisely. Does this imply that he did not regard the Bible as holy scripture and therefore sacred and authoritative?

"The inclination to exchange thoughts with one another is probably an original impulse of our nature." People want to communicate about their pain and to seek sympathy and to help and share joyful emotions. For such communication "some *instrumentality* is indispensable . . . Accordingly Speech—articulate sounds rattled off from the tongue—was used by our first parents." Adam used speech before Eve was created in naming the animals (see Gen 2:19–20). While she "was still a bone in his side," Adam "broke out quite volubly when she first stood before him" (3:359). According to Gen 2:21–22, God took "a rib" from Adam and made a woman from it. After the Lord took the woman to Adam, Adam said: "This is now bone of my bones, and flesh of my flesh" (Gen 2:23).

According to Lincoln, "Speech was not an invention of man, but rather the direct gift of his Creator. But whether Divine gift, or invention," but if left to invention, "*speech* . . . was the superior adaptation . . . of the organs of speech, over every other means within the whole range of nature" (3:359). Lincoln does not take everything in the Bible that cannot be explained by reason on the basis of faith.

The breaking out "quite volubly" may be an allusion to Gen 3:8–12 when the Lord God asked Adam where he was. Adam said that he heard God's voice in the garden and was afraid because he was naked. God said: "Who told thee that thou wast naked? Hast thou eaten of the tree, whereof I commanded thee that thou shouldest not eat? And the man said, The woman whom thou gavest to be with me, she gave me of the tree, and I did eat."

The precise time of the invention of writing is not known, but certainly "as early as the time of Moses; from which we may safely infer that its inventors were very old fogies." The origin of writing, however, goes back to ancient Mesopotamia, several millennia before Lincoln's old fogies and Moses.

Many generations have passed from the time of Adam to Lincoln's time without the invention of *phonetic* writing, "which distinguishes us from savages. Take it from us, and the Bible, all history, all science, all government, all commerce, and nearly all social intercourse go with it" (3:361). How significant is it that Lincoln puts the Bible first and does not include religion? Did he think it was included with the Bible, and does it represent literature, also omitted? In his first communication to the public, Lincoln wrote that education was most important because it enables all "to read the scriptures and other works, both of a religious and moral nature" (1:8). There, as we have learned, Lincoln regarded the Bible as literature, not as sacred or authoritative scripture. Or, did he put the Bible first because he had used it in preparation for his lecture?

Lincoln was advised that in his campaign for president he should lambaste Douglas even stronger on the status of Negroes. An example of that is his sarcastic but effective style in Notes for Speeches at Columbus and Cincinnati, Ohio, September 16, 1859 (3:425–36). Lincoln says that at Memphis Douglas told his audience that he was "for the negro against the crocodile, but for the white man against the negro" (3:431). According to Lincoln, that was not a spontaneous remark but one mentioned before, as a sort of proposition. "As the negro is to the crocodile, so the white man is to the negro. As the negro ought to treat the crocodile as a beast, so the white man ought to treat the negro as a beast'" (3:432). Then comes the sarcasm: "Gentlemen of the South, is not that satisfactory? Will you give Douglas no credit for impressing that sentiment on the Northern mind for your benefit? Why, you should magnify him to the utmost, in order that he may impress it the more deeply, broadly, and surely" (3:431–32). It seems a bit strange that here Lincoln, thought to have such profound knowledge of the Bible, would let Douglas get away with such a degradation of human beings without quoting something from the Bible to mitigate it. See, for example, the equality of all men as part of the image of God, mentioned earlier, and the command to love one's neighbor as oneself.

After Lincoln wrote his notes for speeches, he delivered a very long Speech at Cincinnati, September 17, 1859 (3:438–62), eight months before he was nominated for president at the Republican Convention in Chicago, May 18, 1860. Lincoln reiterates his views that a house divided against itself cannot stand, that he does not expect it to fall and the Union to be dissolved, and that it would eventually become either all slave or all free. He repeats his belief that "Slavery is wrong, morally, and politically," and he is concerned that it not spread beyond the slave states (3:438–41). Note the absence of religiously in the list.

Delivered on the border of a free state and a slave state, that speech was a way of introducing himself to some of the Bible-reading people of Kentucky, a slave state. It was an ideal occasion for mentioning the Bible, which indeed he does—five times. The people of Kentucky, and perhaps also in many slave states, "are trying to establish the rightfulness of Slavery by reference to the Bible . . . that slavery existed in the Bible times by Divine ordinance. . . . Douglas knows that whenever you establish that Slavery was right by the Bible, it will occur that that Slavery was the Slavery of the *white* man—of men without reference to color." Douglas uses the Bible to his advantage, in order to argue "that the slavery of the *black* man, the slavery of the man who has a skin of a different color from your own, is right." However, Northerners will not support that argument. Douglas believes that slavery of the *black* man is right, so he brings to your support "Northern voters who could not . . . be brought by your own argument of the Bible-right of slavery."

Lincoln's remark about slavery in the Bible as that of the white man is essentially correct, especially in saying "men without reference to color" (3:445). Ethiopians, who were black, are mentioned in the Old Testament, but they are not referred to as black men. According to Num 12:1, 10–15, Miriam criticized Moses because he had married an Ethiopian woman. The objection was made because she was a foreigner, not because of her skin color. And the Lord punished Miriam by afflicting her with leprosy, not because of her marriage, but because she was challenging Moses' authority as the supreme messenger of the Lord's will for his people. According to Jer 13:23, the people of Judah had become so wicked that it had become a natural condition, completely setting them off from the Lord, with no hope: "Can the Ethiopian change his skin, or the leopard his spots?" The language is metaphorical, not racial. Jeremiah says that King Hezekiah of Judah had a servant named Ebed-melech, "the Ethiopian," but he is referred to as a member "in the king's house," not as a slave, although he served as one (Jer 38:7–16).

With a view to the presidential election in 1860, Lincoln uses the personal pronouns we, our, and us with rhetorical effect to convince his audience about what should be done, within the bounds of the constitution, to prevent the spread of slavery where it does not exist. Lincoln proclaims a political faith and even says, "We believe": "We believe that the spreading out and the perpetuity of the institution of slavery impairs the general welfare. We believe that . . . is the only thing that has ever threatened the perpetuity of the Union. . . . The people of these United States are the rightful masters of both Congresses and courts not to overthrow the constitution, but to overthrow the men who pervert that constitution" (3:460).

Among the many things "we" must do are "keep in view our real purpose" and not act adverse to it. If we adopt a platform that does not express our purpose, "or elect a man that declares himself inimical to our purpose, we not only take nothing by our success, but we tacitly admit that we act upon no [other] principle than a desire to have 'the loaves and the fishes,' by which, in the end our apparent success is really an injury to us" (3:461). In using the personal pronouns, Lincoln includes himself in stating his political faith derived from the constitution. This differs greatly from the times when he speaks of the Bible and aspects of Christian faith and conspicuously excludes himself.

Although the words Lincoln quotes do not occur exactly in the Bible, the allusion to Jesus feeding the multitude is obvious, where loaves and fishes are mentioned together (Matt 14:16–21; 15:34–26; Mark 6:37–44; Luke 9:12–17; John 6:1). He introduces the words abruptly, so it is hard to see how they fit into the context of his speech. He seems to want fellow politicians not to be satisfied with the personal gains which come from being elected as the multitude was satisfied after being fed. Would persons not familiar with the Bible understand Lincoln's words that are unrelated to the context of his speech?

Lincoln concludes his speech at Cincinnati with a political pitch for any persons who can vote for him, provided they will sympathize with his purpose. Unless voters on either side of the political campaign do so, matters will get worse, and there can be no success on either side. Then he adds: "The good old maxims of the Bible are applicable, and truly applicable to human affairs, and in this as in other things, we may say here that he who is not for us is against us; he who gathereth not with us scattereth" (3:462). Lincoln had used the same quotation in conclusion to his Notes for Speeches at Columbus and Cincinnati.

The words of Lincoln are a loose conflation of several New Testament passages, the first of which is probably Luke 9:50: "He that is not against us is for us." The saying occurs also in Mark 9:40: "He that is not against us is on our part." The second part of the quotation about gathering is from Matt 12:30: "He that is not with me is against me; and he that gathereth not with me scattereth abroad" (= Luke 11:23, except for the omission of abroad, which is included in the Greek verb). The saying in Luke 9:50 and in Mark 9:40 is Jesus' response to the disciple John who called Jesus' attention to a man casting out demons in Jesus' name. The disciples "forbad him, because he followeth not with us." The context of Matt 12:30 is the Pharisees' charge that Jesus casts out demons by the prince of demons and Jesus' response that a house divided against itself cannot stand. Satan is portrayed as a strong man that Jesus has bested, so his kingdom is not divided. Lincoln may have in mind the multitudes who "were scattered abroad, as sheep having no shepherd" in Matt 9:36.

Observe how Lincoln uses the biblical texts. He reverses the words of Luke's order of against us and for us to for us and against us, and in doing so, he made the words more "applicable" to the situation (3:452). The words "on our part" of the KJV (Mark 9:40) are an inept rendering of the Greek "for us." Lincoln changes the "me" of Matt 12:30 to "us" to fit the context. He adapted the loose combination of quotations, oblivious of their contexts, in trying to win some Southern Republicans and Democrats to his political campaign.

Lincoln had his mind set on the presidency, so when Henry Ward Beecher invited him to speak in his Brooklyn church at the end of February 1860, he readily accepted. He realized that it would be an excellent occasion to make his views on slavery known to people in the eastern states who had never heard him. As fate would have it, when he arrived at his destination, he was informed that his speech was being sponsored by the Young Men's Central Republican Union and that it would be presented in the Union building on Broadway, New York, not in Beecher's church, as planned. Among members of the Union were William Cullen Bryant and Horace Greeley, so Lincoln's audience was the most sophisticated he had ever faced. Moreover, the political goal of the Cooper Union was to prevent William H. Seward from being nominated for president at the national Republican Convention. Lincoln knew, then, that he was among some of his own supporters and that the speech would make him a viable candidate in New England. As a result, he delivered one of his best political speeches, the Address at Cooper Institute, New York City, February 27, 1860 (3:522–50).

Lincoln set the political tone of his speech by beginning with a quotation from Douglas reported in the *New York Times* about the framers of the Constitution and the slavery issue. Based on the facts of history behind it, Lincoln argued that there is nothing in the Constitution that prohibits the Government from preventing the spread of slavery into the Territories. In such a favorable political setting, Lincoln's use of the Bible would have been superfluous. On the other hand, before an audience not committed to a candidate, Lincoln's use of the Bible would be more beneficial, if not necessary, in order to further his own political ambition. Only toward the end of his speech does he allude to a passage in the Bible that would be familiar to many of his hearers. Lincoln stresses again that slavery is wrong, although we can let it alone where it exists, but it must not spread to the Territories. He exhorts his hearers:

> Let us be diverted by none of those philosophical contrivances wherewith we are so industriously plied and belabored—contrivances such as groping for some middle ground between the right and the wrong . . . a policy of 'don't care' on a question about which all true men do care—such as Union appeals beseeching true Union men to yield to Disunionists, reversing the divine rule, and calling, not the sinners, but the righteous to repentance (3:550). Supporters of the Union are morally right, and as righteous men they must not change. The framers of the Constitution were right, and the Disunionists men must not undo the work of Washington.

The "divine rule"—another ambiguous designation of Lincoln's for something Jesus said (Appendix 4)—being reversed is an allusion to Matt 9:13: "I am not come to call the righteous, but sinners to repentance" (see also Mark 2:17; Luke 5:32). The gospel context is Jesus calling a tax collector named Matthew in Matthew's gospel, but named Levi in Mark and Luke. Pharisees regarded such persons as sinners and, therefore, criticized

Jesus for associating with them. Oblivious of the biblical context, Lincoln adapts a more familiar passage from the Bible to reinforce something he says. Persons familiar with the gospels would recognize it and sense the application as Lincoln intended, irrespective of the biblical context. And what better way to win support for his political ambition from any doubters than to link words from the Bible with the name of Washington?

Lincoln's concluding exhortation is emphatic: "Let us have faith that right makes might; and in that faith, let us, to the end, dare to do our duty as we understand it." Here Lincoln's faith is used abstractly, but it refers to the political faith of the righteousness of the Unionists as against the unrighteousness of the Disunionists. Lincoln shares the faith and action of the Unionists, so he includes himself in it—"we" and "us."

There was an old saying, "might makes right," that originated when persons in power were mighty enough to persuade or force others to obey their commands. Lincoln reverses the words, as he did the biblical text, to stress the moral right of Unionists. Conspicuously absent is any reference to God, as it is also in the Gettysburg Address, except as an after thought. This is in sharp contrast to the Second Inaugural Address, reasons for which we shall learn. One might wonder if there was anything implying religious faith in his speech originally prepared for delivery in Beecher's church. For comments on the Cooper Union speech and the favorable responses to it see Donald (239–40).

In an especially well received Speech at New Haven, Connecticut, March 6, 1860 (4:13–30), Lincoln again stresses that slavery is "a great moral wrong." Slave owners think of slavery only as it will favorably affect their value as property and the money slaves bring them. That helped to persuade the owners that there was nothing wrong with slavery and therefore right. Lincoln concocted a story about how a "dissenting minister, who argued some theological point with one of the established church, was always met by the reply, 'I can't see it so.' The dissenting minister opened the Bible, and pointed him to a passage, but the orthodox minister replied, 'I can't see it so.' Then he showed him a single word—'Can you see that?' 'yes, I see it,' was the reply. The dissenter laid a guinea over the word and asked, 'Do you see it now?'" No response. Lincoln doesn't want to say if slave owners really see their property as it is. "If they do, they see it as it is through 2,000,000,000 of dollars, and that is a pretty thick coating" (4:16).

As Lincoln faced the ultimate challenge of his political career, he increasingly stressed that slavery is morally wrong. The morality of the Unionists is set against the unrighteousness of the Disunionists. And the primary bases for that morality are the Declaration of Independence and the Constitution, not the Bible. However, he makes good use of the Bible again in his last public speeches, especially in his Second Inaugural Address.

Lincoln was elected President on November 6, 1860, and within eleven days after he was inaugurated on March 4, 1861, South Carolina declared its independence of the Union, Confederate forces shelled Fort Sumter, Lincoln issued a call for 75,000 volunteers, ordered a blockade of the rebelling states, and the Civil War began.

Although Lincoln made a first draft of an emancipation proclamation July 22, 1862 (5:336–38), he continued to have doubts about the wisdom of such action. On September 13, 1862, the Reverends Wilson W. Patton, a Congregationalist, and John Dempster, a Methodist, both strong abolitionists, presented Lincoln a memorial on emancipation adopted at a public meeting of denominational Christians in Chicago on September 7, 1862. In his reply, September 13, 1862 (5:419–25), only a few paragraphs are quoted as Lincoln's words, presumably by the editors of the Chicago *Tribune* and the *National Intelligencer*. Lincoln is to have said that suppose by such a proclamation and, induced by it, the slaves "throw themselves upon us, *what should we do with them?* How can we feed and care for such a multitude?" (5:420). The words quoted are probably an allusion to the feeding of the five thousand persons reported in the four gospels (Matt 14:14–21; Mark 6:30–44; Luke 9:10–17; John 6:5–14). There the crowds are a consideration, and in the first three gospels, the disciples suggest that Jesus send them away because it was time for the evening meal (Mark 6:35–36; Matt 14:15; Luke 9:12). The people were rushing to get to Jesus (Matt 14:13; Mark 6: 33–34), but there is no indication that they threw themselves upon Jesus and his disciples, obviously an overstatement by Lincoln or an editor. The italicized words may reflect the disciples' words about sending them away to get food for themselves. Lincoln's word "multitude" occurs in Matt 14:15, 19 and Luke 9:12, 16 but is "much people" in Mark 6:34.

One of the most difficult things for me to decide is how sincere Lincoln was in his use of Providence and the Divine will. Lincoln's reply to the emancipation memorial is a typical example of why I have doubt.

> I hope it will not be irreverent for me to say that if it is probable that God would reveal his will to others, on a point so connected with my duty, it might be supposed that he would reveal it directly to me; for, unless I am more deceived in myself than I often am, it is my earnest desire to know the will of Providence in this matter. *And if I can learn what it is I will do it!* These are not, however, the days of miracles, and I suppose it will be granted that I am not to expect a direct revelation. I must study the plain physical facts of the case, ascertain what is possible and learn what appears to be wise and right. The subject is difficult, and good men do not agree. (5:420)

Considering the slavery situation, his position as commander-in-chief of the military, and the war, Lincoln asked those presenting the memorial, "What possible result of good would follow the issuing of such a proclamation as you desire?" Lincoln has the right to take any measure to help subdue the enemy, and he has no moral objections to doing so in light of possible insurrection and massacre in the south. He considers it "a practical war measure, to be decided upon according to the advantages or disadvantages it may offer to the suppression of the rebellion" (5:421).

Notice here the pervading uncertainty of Lincoln's knowledge of the will of God as late as September 1862: "If it is probable," "it might be supposed that he would reveal it directly to me," "my earnest desire to know the will of Providence," "*if I can learn what it is*," "not the days of miracles," and "granted that I am not to expect a direct revelation." Lincoln himself will study the plain physical facts of the case and determine what is wise and right based on them. These observations temper phrases that Lincoln used earlier: "God is with us" (2:97); "the Providence of God was given us" (2:132); "May the God of the right, give you the victory" (2:395); "as surely as God reigns over you" (2:498). The phrases in the emancipation memorial also temper some of Lincoln's words about God mentioned later in this chapter.

In commenting on Lincoln's remarks, the editors report that the memorial from the Chicago Christians "contained facts, principles, and arguments which appealed to the intelligence of the President and to his faith in Divine Providence; that he could not deny that the Bible denounced oppression as one of the highest of crimes, and threatened Divine judgments against nations that practice it . . . so that there is the amplest reason for expecting to avert Divine judgments by putting away the sin [of slavery and its spread], and for hoping to remedy the national troubles by striking at their cause" (5:421–22).

Oppression was a universal experience of the Israelites, and God knew their oppression, especially of the poor by the rich (Exod 3:8; Deut 26:7; 2 Kgs 13:4). Such oppression was condemned by the prophets (Isa 5:7; 30:12; Ezek 2:7, 29), and psalmists decried it (e.g., Pss 12:5; 42:9; 107:39; 119:34). The fact that several times Lincoln draws a parallel between the slavery of the Israelites in bondage in Egypt and American slavery gives credence to what he says about the Bible denouncing oppression. But the part about diverting Divine Judgment "by putting away the sin" of slavery is the thought of the editors, not the language of Lincoln. This assumption is confirmed by the editors' later statement: "We felt the deepest personal interest in the matter as of national concern, and would fain aid the thoughts of our President by communicating the convictions of the Christian community from which we came, with the ground upon which they were based" (5:422). Moreover, Lincoln never would have used the word "sin" for the offense of slavery on the part of either the South or the North (see discussion of his Second Inaugural Address in the next chapter).

Lincoln elaborates his concern that white men were earning their bread from the labor of Negroes in his response to the delegation of Baptists George B. Ide, James R. Doolittle, and A. Hubbell, May 30, 1864 (7:368). Lincoln begins by thanking the Christian communities for their support and liberty, which he believes is a moral issue: "It is difficult to conceive how it could be otherwise with any one professing Christianity, or even having ordinary perceptions of right and wrong." As usual, his language separates him from the Christian religion, and then he attacks the holy men in the South: "To read in the Bible, as the word of God himself, that 'In the sweat of *thy* face shalt thou eat bread,' and to preach there-from that, 'In the sweat of *other mans* [*sic*] faces shalt thou eat bread,' to my mind can scarcely be reconciled with honest sincerity" (7:368). Lincoln is being sarcastic because it was the view of Baptists, including George B. Ide, a well-known minister and author in Springfield, Massachusetts. Lincoln hopes: "When brought to my final reckoning, may I have to an-swer for robbing no man of his goods; yet more tolerable even this, than for robbing one of himself, and all that was his."

Lincoln questions the sincerity of those professedly holy men of the South, met in the semblance of prayer and devotion, and, in the name of Him who said, 'As ye would all men should do unto you, do ye even so unto them' appealed to the christian [*sic*] world to aid them in doing to a whole race of men, as they would have no man do unto themselves, to my thinking, they contemned and insulted God and His church, far more than did Satan when he tempted the Saviour with the Kingdoms of the earth. The devil's attempt was no more false, and far less hypocritical. But let me forbear, remembering it is also written 'Judge not, lest ye be judged.'

The quotation of doing unto others is a loose combination of Matt 7:12 and Luke 6:31, lacking in Mark. Matthew reads: "All things whatso-ever ye would that men should do to you, do ye even so to them"; Luke has: "As ye would that men should do to you, do ye also to them likewise." If Lincoln quoted from memory, and if he was accustomed to memoriz-ing so much from the Bible by chapter and verse, as tradition says, it is strange that he did not quote precisely from that part of Jesus' Sermon on the Mount, which among Christians, became known as the Golden Rule long before the time of Lincoln. The most significant difference from both biblical texts is Lincoln's insertion of "all" before men, a subtle inference that whites should include blacks in their actions. Matthew's "All things whatsoever" puts the emphasis on deeds, whereas Lincoln writes to em-phasize both the persons and their deeds, which may be closer to Luke's version. The mention of Satan is an allusion to the story of the tempta-tions of Jesus in Matt 4:8; Mark 1:12–13; and Luke 4:6. Matthew mentions both the devil and Satan; Mark has only Satan; Luke has only devil. Both Matthew and Luke have "all the kingdoms of the world" (from Isa 23:17 or Jer 25:26). Lincoln has "the Kingdoms of the earth," used only here by him. Lincoln lacks "all," which is included with the phrase eleven times in the Old Testament, and he has a capital "K." Mark lacks the words about the kingdoms. These observations are further evidence against the tradition of Lincoln's practice of precise quotation from the Bible.

Lincoln's allusion to judging in Matt 7:1 or Luke 6:37, also from Jesus' Sermon, is interesting for several reasons. Matthew reads: "Judge not, that ye be not judged" and Luke: "Judge not, and ye shall not be judged." Lincoln changes the meaning by saying, "Judge not, lest ye be judged," a subtle rebuke of Ide and other Baptists about their defense of slavery. Douglas had used the quotation about judging in the sixth debate, where he rebukes Lincoln for telling the people of Kentucky that their views are in violation of the law of God. It were better for him to adopt the doctrine of "judge not lest ye be judged" (3:275), the same alteration to fit his criticism of Lincoln. Both men changed the biblical statement in the same way to adapt it to their respective situations. Lincoln uses the quotation about judging again but in another way in his Second Inaugural Address.

Lincoln's address at the dedication of the cemetery at Gettysburg, November 19, 1863 (7:17–21), of less than a page, is probably the best known and most quoted of his speeches. In his definitive work on that speech, Boritt (*Gospel*, 108, 120, 122, 186) mentions influence from the Bible on Lincoln's thought and language. I suggest some other influence from the same source.

From the time of the patriarchs (called "our fathers" innumerable times in the Old Testament and in 1 Cor 10:1), the Hebrews/Israelites believed that they were a unique people. The author of Deuteronomy stated their religious/political faith succinctly: "an holy people unto the Lord thy God, and the Lord hath chosen thee to be a peculiar people unto himself, above all the nations that are upon the earth" (Deut 14:2; see also Deut 4:7–8; 26:18–19). Israel was the peculiar people of God, and Yahweh was the peculiar "God of Israel," a phrase that occurs 201 times in the Old Testament and in Matt 15:31 and Luke 1:68. Although Lincoln's "our fathers brought forth . . . a new nation" and "one nation, under God" allude to the nation's founding, perhaps the biblical idea of a peculiar nation was in his mind when he penned those words. Lincoln had used the phrase "under God" in his Reply to Governor Curtin at Harrisburg, Pennsylvania, February 22, 1861 (4:243), so he did not use it for the first time at Gettysburg. He also used it later in a speech at the Great Central Sanitary Fair, Philadelphia, June 16, 1864 (7:395).

When Lincoln speaks about "brave men, living and dead," the phrase living and dead is biblical and occurs twenty-one times in the Old Testament and sixteen in the New Testament. Sometimes one subject comes first and then the other, as, for example, in Num 16:48; Ruth 2:20; Matt 22:32; and Luke 24:5. And Lincoln's words "the living," which he uses many times elsewhere, are also biblical, especially in Ecclesiastes, for example, 4:15; 6:8; 7:2; 9:4–5 (see also Job 33:30; Pss 27:13; 56:13; Dan 4:17; Matt 22:32). A most apt passage is Eccl 4:2: "Wherefore, I praised the dead which are already dead more than the living which are yet alive." Both the writer of Ecclesiastes and Lincoln praised the dead and challenged the living. Finally, Lincoln's concluding words, "shall not perish from the earth," are stated positively about the fate of the wicked in Job 18:17: "His remembrance shall perish from the earth." In Jer 10:11 the same thing is said about idols. The words "let" and "perish" occur together often in the Old Testament, for example, those in the boat with Jonah prayed to the Lord: "Let us not perish for this man's life" (Jonah 1:14).

In discussing Lincoln's reply to the "Loyal colored people of Baltimore," who presented Lincoln a Bible, September 7, 1864 (7:542–43), Wolf (135–6) relies too much on the work by Lucius E. Chittenden (448–50). According to Chittenden, Register of the Treasury during Lincoln's administration, Lincoln is to have said: "The character of the Bible is easily established, at least to my satisfaction. We have to believe many things that we do not comprehend. The Bible is the only one that claims to be God's book . . . It contains an immense amount of evidence of its own authenticity. It describes a Governor omnipotent enough to operate this great machine, and declares that He made it." Lincoln says that we should treat the Bible with fairness equal to the true testimony of a witness in court. "I decided a long time ago that it was less difficult to believe that the Bible was what it claimed to be than to disbelieve it. It is a good book for us to obey—it contains the Ten Commandments, the Golden Rule, and many other rules which ought to be followed." This language is quite uncharacteristic of Lincoln. "Comprehend" is not a favorite word of his, and although he uses it several times (3:122, 331, 384, 418; 6:518; 7:10; 8:369), he never does so with reference to the Bible. He never mentions believing in the Bible or faith with reference to it.

Lincoln never uses "Omnipotent" as a title for God, but in his Eulogy on Benjamin Ferguson, February 8, 1842 (1:268–69), he commends Ferguson to Almighty God and implores "the aid and protection, of his omnipotent right arm, for his bereaved and disconsolate family" (1:269). This is the only time Lincoln uses "omnipotent," and it is what we might expect from him in a eulogy and the fact that it was delivered before the Springfield Washington Temperance Society just two weeks before he addressed that Society. Then Lincoln used "omnipotence" of the deity when he said that some who do not want to join the society say: "'We are no drunkards; and we shall not acknowledge ourselves such by joining a reformed drunkard's society, whatever our influence might be.'" Then Lincoln's pertinent comment follows: "Surely no Christian will adhere to this objection. If *they* believe, as *they* profess, that Omnipotence condescended to take on himself the form of sinful man, and, as such, to die an ignominious death for *their sakes*, surely *they* will not refuse submission to the infinitely lesser condescension, for the temporal, and perhaps eternal salvation, of a large, erring, and unfortunate class of *their own* fellow creatures" (my italics; 1:277–78). Lincoln conspicuously does not include himself among the Christians who believe in Omnipotence. According to Chittenden, Lincoln used "a Governor omnipotent" of the deity, but Lincoln used Omnipotence with reference to Jesus.

With respect to the good book for us to obey containing the Ten Commandments, the Golden Rule, and other rules mentioned by Chittenden, Lincoln never mentions the Decalogue, and he does not mention the Golden Rule, even when he quotes from it. With Chittenden's "this great machine" for the universe, compare Lincoln's "all creation is a mine" (2:437), "in all God's creation" (2:509), "the creation of the world" (7:254), "the economy of the Universe" (2:546), and "this Universe" (3:399). Such observations raise doubt about the validity of Chittenden's remarks about Lincoln's "great machine" for the earth.

After Lincoln apologizes to the "loyal colored people of Baltimore" for such a brief response to an occasion worthy of a longer one, he expresses his sentiment "that all mankind should be free," that he has done what he thought "to be right and just . . . for the good of mankind generally." He continues: "In regard to this Great Book, I have but to say, it is the best gift God has given to man. All the good the Saviour gave to the world was communicated through this book. But for it we could not know right from wrong. All things most desirable for man's welfare, here and hereafter, are to be found portrayed in it . . . the great Book of God which you present" (7:542).

Persons interested in Lincoln often take the words of this speech, his most numerous and pious about the Bible, as of major importance for his views about it and for his religion as well. That we should be cautious in making such a generalizing judgment is clear from what we have already learned. Moreover, his words before the "loyal colored people of Baltimore" are not harmonious with those in his last debate with Douglas when he said that we could have discovered the fact of our selfishness "without the Bible." Nor are his words consistent with those to Mary Speed about his Oxford Bible that it would be "the best cure for the 'Blues' could one take it according to the truth." And Lincoln's words without the Bible, as late as October 15, 1858, raise further doubt about both the validity of Chittenden's words earlier and the sincerity of Lincoln's words in his speech to the "loyal colored people of Baltimore."

If we consider affairs before this speech, we can better understand its contents. Politically, there was discontent among some Republicans and a crisis in the cabinet over the antislavery issue and the management of the war. It was just two months before Lincoln was to defeat his Democratic opponent, George B. McClellan. Personally, Lincoln was under severe emotional strain because of the slavery issue and the state of the Union, intensified by the death of his son Willie about two years earlier and the problems with Mary's health. Before his speech to the "loyal colored people of Baltimore," Lincoln had been a very busy man. Representatives from them had written three times unsuccessfully to arrange a date with him for the presentation.[12]

Speaking impromptu, Lincoln begins by saying that a lengthy response would be appropriate, but he is not prepared to make one, and if he were to promise to respond in writing, experience has taught him that "business will not allow me to do so." If we study the Annotation to the speech (7:542–3), we learn that Lincoln was a good listener. Indeed, it seems to have provided a rough outline for his impromptu reply. Here are comparisons of the presentation speech (P) with the acceptance by Lincoln (L).

P: Your humane conduct towards the people of our race.

L: Always acted as I believed to be right and just.

P: The Friend of Universal Freedom (inscription) and "furtherance of the cause of the emancipation of our race.

L: It has always been a sentiment with me that all mankind should be free.

P: Our incorporation into the American family.

L: I have done all I could for the good of mankind generally.

P: This copy of the Holy Scriptures.

L: This Great Book . . . the best gift God has given to man . . . the great Book of God.

P: Our children . . . will be told of your worthy deeds.

L: But for it [Bible] we could not know right from wrong. All things most desirable for man's welfare, here and hereafter, are to be found . . . in it.

P: May you be borne to the bosom of your Saviour and your God.

L: All the good the Saviour gave to the world and the mention of God twice.

P : When you pass from this world to that of eternity.

L: All things most desirable for man's welfare, here and hereafter.

Moved by what he heard in the presenter's speech, Lincoln rose admirably to the occasion by using such pious language, saying what his audience hoped to hear about the Bible. That Lincoln does not call it the Holy Scriptures (used by the presenter) or use the words "holy" or "sacred" with it is significant.

9

No Difference in Soil or Climate

INTRODUCTION

Lincoln's last words in his Cooper Union Address anticipated similar feelings expressed in his Second Inaugural Address, March 4, 1865 (8:332–33), where he mentions the Bible for the last time. Lincoln rose admirably to the occasion, but many in the divided nation were unwilling to listen. For the setting and comments on the speech see Donald, 565–68, and for an account of the day of the inauguration see White, *Greatest Speech*, 21–48.

Military victories at Gettysburg on July 3, 1863, and at Chattanooga on November 23–25, 1863, were turning points in the war. Lincoln issued his Proclamation of Amnesty and Reconstruction on December 8, 1863 (7:53–56). Subsequent victories by General Grant at Vicksburg and elsewhere, and General Sherman's eventual conquest of Atlanta hastened the end of the war, and the Union was preserved. On November 8, 1864, Lincoln was reelected president. On January 31, 1865, Congress passed the Thirteenth Amendment to the Constitution: "Neither slavery nor involuntary servitude, except as a punishment for crime whereof the party shall have been duly convicted, shall exist within the United States, or any place subject to their jurisdiction."

Despite the fact that Lincoln was elected to a second term, perhaps mostly on the basis of recent military victories, he lacked credibility among many (*pace* White, 84). The war was ending, but the Cabinet was troublesome, and the feelings concerning slavery were far from soothed between the North and the South. The proof of these things is the turmoil that preceded and followed Lincoln's death. The times demanded healing, reconciliation, recovery, and the reunion of the Nation, and Lincoln confronted those issues in addressing people of both South and North.

Antecedent Documents

Lincoln anticipated the thought and language concerning the slavery issue and the war in several documents that provide some background for understanding the Second Inaugural Address (hereafter Address). The first one is a speech at Bloomington, Illinois, September 12, 1854 (2:230–33). According to an editor, Lincoln declared "that the Southern slaveholders were neither better, nor worse than we of the North, and that we of the North were no better than they. If we were situated as they are, we should act and feel as they do; and if they were situated as we are, they should act and feel as we do; and we never ought to lose sight of this fact in discussing the subject" (2:230).

Lincoln never lost that sense of not blaming either party. In a speech at Indianapolis, Indiana, September 19, 1859 (3:463–70), he said: "Now, it so happens that the country south of the Ohio is slave, and the country north, free. What caused this? . . . There is no difference in soil nor in climate. . . . He [Douglas] never heard that the left bank of the Ohio was more favorable to slavery than the right. It could not be because the people had worse hearts. They were as good as we of the North—the same people" (3:467).

In the two speeches Lincoln was careful not to accuse either the North or the South of being responsible for the war. This is true also in the documents that follow, in which I compare some of the language and thought among them with that in the Address. I do not aim for completeness or perfection.

In his Meditation On the Divine Will, September 2, 1862 (5:403–4), Lincoln writes:

> The will of God prevails. In great contests each party claims to act in accordance with the will of God. Both *may* be, and one *must* be wrong. God can not be *for*, and *against* the same thing at the same time. In the present civil war it is quite possible that God's purpose is something different from the purpose of either party— and yet the human instrumentalities, working just as they do, are of the best adaptation to effect His purpose. I am almost ready to say this is probably true—that God wills this contest, and wills that it shall not end yet. By his mere quiet power, on the minds of the now contestants, He could have either *saved* or *destroyed* the Union without a human contest. Yet the contest began. And having begun He could give the final victory to either side any day. Yet the contest proceeds.

Compare these phrases between the Meditation and the Second Inaugural Address, and note that both lists leave the role of God in the war uncertain.

M: The will of God prevails

A: The Almighty has His own purposes

M: If God wills that it shall not end yet

A: If God wills that it continue

M: To effect His purpose

A: The Almighty has His own purposes

M: Yet the contest began

A: And the war came

M: Yet the contest proceeds

A: Yet, if God wills that it continue

Lincoln wrote the Meditation when he was struggling whether he should issue a proclamation of emancipation. Many scholars, it seems to me, have gone too far in assuming that the Meditation provides an accurate insight into Lincoln's personal faith in Divine Purpose or in Predestination. According to Wolf (147–48), "The meditation reveals theological profundity and legal precision of definition" (147). He also says that the decision to proclaim the proclamation was "preceded by the blood, sweat, and tears of a struggle to know the will of God on the Union and on slavery" and related matters and then quotes James G. Randall: "In reaching his important decision there is ample reason to believe that Lincoln had not only endured anxious hours, but had undergone a significant inner experience from which he emerged with quiet serenity" (Wolf, 148 and 207 n. 8). That would have made Lincoln a good Quaker.

According to Fornieri (*Political Faith*, 40–41), Lincoln's statement about God not being for and against something at the same time "presumes the ability of reason to grasp something about the nature of the divine . . . Nevertheless, God's overall design was ultimately mysterious and unfathomable to both sides of the conflict. Neither side could claim perfect certitude; neither could claim perfect rectitude. Both were culpable before God." Lincoln uses the phrase "the will of God" with respect to the people of both North and South. In reality, both sides of the slavery issue thought they were right and that God was on their side. The fact that representatives from both sides of the slavery issue came to present their case to Lincoln confirms the view presented here. At first glance, it seems that in the Address both were culpable. God "gives to both North and South, this terrible war." But in both the Meditation and the Address the outcome is ultimately up to God.

Fornieri (*Political Faith*, 41 and 182 n. 13) quotes Guelzo (*Redeemer President*), who "sees the Meditation as a sincere and mature expression of Lincoln's biblical faith, which was implicit from his youth but which deepened and developed throughout the experience of personal suffering during the war." Fornieri himself argues that the Meditation "is particularly relevant to an analysis of Lincoln's biblical faith . . . Lincoln used biblical language in a civil theological sense as a normative standard to judge public life." Fornieri (40–41) also says that Lincoln's Meditation is "an authentic private reflection . . . particularly relevant to an analysis of Lincoln's biblical faith." However, in biblical faith God is its object, but in the Address Lincoln separates himself from that faith when he says, "the believers in a Living God" (8:333). Lincoln is concerned with the nation and its welfare, as the concluding paragraph of the Address shows. In contrast to that Address, anything suggested as biblical is read into the Meditation.

In the Meditation there is nothing conclusive about Lincoln's position on the war and God's part in it. At the end of his pensive debate with himself, he says that God "*could have* either *saved* or *destroyed* the Union, and he "*could give* the final victory to any side either day. Yet the contest proceeds."

The last four words are most important. The war is running its course, and Lincoln is still uncertain about God's will concerning it and the emancipation of the slaves. His words in the reply to the emancipation memorial presented by Chicago Christians (September 13, 1862) less than two weeks after his Meditation confirm that fact. "*If* [my Italics] it is probable that God would reveal his will to others, on a point so connected with my duty, it might be supposed he would reveal it directly to me." Lincoln earnestly wants "to know the will of Providence" about emancipating the slaves. "*And if I can learn what it is I will do it!*" (Lincoln's emphasis). What he proceeds to say leaves doubt about him being so closely atoned to the will of God as some traditions maintain. "These are not, however, the days of miracles, and I suppose it will be granted that I am not to expect a direct revelation [contrast Randall's "significant inner experience"]. I must study the plain physical facts of the case, ascertain what is possible and learn what appears to be wise and right" (5:420). These words are not those of one suffering blood, sweat, and tears, but the calm, cool, calculating mind so characteristic of the man.

In a letter to Albert G. Hodges, April 4, 1864 (7:281–83), editor of the *Commonwealth* of Frankfort, Kentucky, Lincoln writes: "I am naturally anti-slavery. If slavery is not wrong, nothing is wrong," and he has always felt that way. As president, he took the oath to abide by the Constitution of the United States, and he understood that "in ordinary civil administration this oath" forbade him the right to indulge his "primary abstract judgment on the moral question of slavery." Having publicly declared that view many times, he still avers it. At the same time, he understood that the oath imposed upon him "the duty of preserving . . . that government— that nation—of which that constitution was the organic law" (7:281).

After elaborating those points, probably with a view to the coming military campaigns of the Union troops, Lincoln concludes the letter to Hodges: "I claim not to have controlled events, but confess plainly that events have controlled me. Now, at the end of three years struggle the nations' condition is not what either party, or any man devised, or expected. God alone can claim it. Whither it is tending seems plain. *If* [my Italics] God now wills the removal of a great wrong, and wills also that we of the North as well as you of the South, shall pay fairly for our complicity in that wrong, impartial history will find therein new cause to attest and revere the justice and goodness of God" (7:282).

I compare Lincoln's words to Hodges with those in the Address.

H: not what either party, or any man devised, or expected

A: Neither party expected. . . . Neither anticipated

H: If God now wills the removal of a great wrong

A: American slavery. . . . He now wills to remove

H: If God now wills . . . that we of the North as well as you of the South, shall pay fairly for our complicity in that wrong

A: He [God] gives to both North and South, this terrible war

H: the justice and goodness of God

A: the judgments of the Lord, are true and righteous

At the Sanitary Fair in Baltimore, Maryland, April 18, 1864 (7:301–3), Lincoln calls attention to the change in Baltimore with respect to the Union, and that it is only part of greater change. "When the war began, three years ago, neither party, nor any man, expected it would last till now. Each looked for the end, in some way, long ere to-day. Neither did any anticipate that domestic slavery would be much affected by the war. But here we are; the war has not ended, and slavery has been much affected—how much needs not now to be recounted. So true it is that man proposes, and God disposes" (7:301). Here are comparisons with Hodges, Fair, and the Address:

> H: Now, at the end of three years struggle

> F: When the war began, three years ago, neither party, nor any man, expected it would last till now

> F: Now, three years having past

> A: Now, at the expiration of four years

> F: Each looked for the end, in some way, long ere to-day

> A: Neither party expected for the war, the magnitude, or the duration, which it has already attained

Recall a similar comparison of the last lines with words of Lincoln to Hodges.

The words at the Fair, "So true it is that," are a clue that what follows is a quotation from some ancient literary work that had become famous. Recall the one from Browning in Lincoln's letter to Mary Speed (1:260). The present one is a line translated from the Latin work by Thomas à Kempis (c. 1380–1471) as "Man proposes but God disposes" (Book 1, Chapter 19).

Sometimes Lincoln did not wait for God to dispose. He frequently disposed of matters with his military generals. A good example of this is his reaction to the massacre of black Union soldiers by the Confederates when they captured Fort Pillow in Western Tennessee on April 12, 1864. Lincoln made plans to dispose the situation himself. At the Fair Lincoln says that the situation is grave, but in this case retribution must come (7:303). Congressman John F. Farnsworth had urged Lincoln to follow General Hurlbut's demand for a court inquiry into the event. Lincoln wrote to Stephen A. Hurlbut, May 2, 1864 (7:327), advising him not to "allow Gen's Grant and Sherman to be diverted by it just now." That Lincoln further disposes of the matter is affirmed in a later communication to Cabinet Members, May 3, 1864 (7:345–46). They are to give him an opinion "in writing . . . as to what course, the government should take in the case" (7:328). The outcome of the incident is not known because attention centered on Grant's continuing campaign, but Lincoln had begun a process for disposal.

On September 4, 1864 (7:535), Lincoln wrote a letter to Eliza P. Gurney in reply to one she had written to him on August 8, 1863 (7:536). He repeats thoughts about God in the documents we have been considering, and, like them, it foreshadows some of the thought and language in the Address. All are important for insight into what Lincoln says about the North and South in the body of that Address.

Lincoln acknowledges that Mrs. Gurney's purpose is to strengthen his "reliance on God." However, he avoids saying that it has done so (*pace* Fornieri, *Political Faith*, 64). Why would she try to strengthen Lincoln's reliance on God if his biblical faith was so clear? Instead of thanking her for her purpose, Lincoln expresses his indebtedness "to the good christian people of the country for their constant prayers and consolations," and to none more than to her. Lincoln continues: "The purposes of the Almighty are perfect, and must prevail, though we erring mortals may fail to accurately perceive them in advance. We hoped for a happy termination of this terrible war long before this; but God knows best, and has ruled otherwise. We shall yet acknowledge His wisdom and our own error therein. Meanwhile we must work earnestly in the best light He gives us, trusting that so working still conduces to the great ends He ordains. Surely He intends some great good to follow this mighty convulsion, which no mortal could make, and no mortal could stay" (7:535).

G: The purposes of the Almighty are perfect, and must prevail

A: The Almighty has His own purposes

G: We hoped for a happy termination of this terrible war long before this

A: Fondly do we hope . . . that this mighty scourge of war may speedily pass

G: but God knows best, and has ruled otherwise

A: Yet, if God wills that it continue

Although these words seem too pious for Lincoln, like those to the "Loyal Colored People of Baltimore," they would be soothing to Mrs. Gurney, and they really imply that Lincoln is saying God is responsible for the war, which he has not yet disposed. This is affirmed in what follows. Lincoln acknowledges the dilemma confronting the Quaker Friends regarding the war, and he promises that for those who oppose it, "I have done, and shall do, the best I could and can, in my own conscience, under my oath to the law." He does not doubt that she believes what he says, and he shall still receive her "earnest prayers to our father in Heaven." What more assuring words could he say to a woman of great faith and prayer?

Again, there is nothing reassuring about Lincoln's personal faith, and there is no suggestion of biblical influence on what he says. It may be almost blasphemous to say that he writes what Mrs. Gurney and "the [not our] good christian people of the country" would be consoled to hear. Lincoln's words have to be considered in light of the two letters Mrs. Gurney wrote to him, the first on August 8, 1863 (7:535–36 n. 1), and the second, on September 8, 1864, in response to Lincoln's letter to her just mentioned, in which he says that it has been her purpose to strengthen his reliance on God. In neither letter to Lincoln (7:536) does Mrs. Gurney acknowledge any hint of religious faith on the part of Lincoln. Rather, in the first letter she gives her own and that of many thousands of "continued hearty sympathy in all thy burdens and responsibilities" in his effort to "'burst the bands of wickedness, and let the oppressed go free.'" Perhaps she realized that for him the significant thing was his own conscience under his oath to the law. Lincoln's commitment to his oath as president, so strongly affirmed to Hodges and reiterated to Mrs. Gurney, was a matter of political, not religious, faith. That oath and the law were determining factors for Lincoln's faith.

In response to a serenade, November 10, 1864 (8:100–101), after his election to a second term, Lincoln delivered a short speech that, insofar as I know, has been neglected in the study of Lincoln's concern for the Union after the War. It also anticipates some thoughts of his Second Inaugural Address. In his response to the serenade, he says: "The rebellion brought our republic to a severe test; and a presidential election occurring in regular course during the rebellion added not a little to the strain. If the loyal people, *united*, were put to the utmost of their strength by the rebellion, must they not fail when *divided*, and partially paralized, by a political war among themselves?" Compare those statements with the ones of Lincoln in the Second Inaugural about parties trying to save or destroy the Union: "Both parties deprecated war; but one of them would *make* war rather than let the nation survive; and the other would *accept* war rather than let it perish."

Lincoln proceeds to say to the serenaders that, as in the present situation, there will always be a diversity of human natures in any future national emergency. He exhorts his audience: "Let us, therefore, study the incidents of this, as philosophy to learn wisdom from, and none of them as wrongs to be revenged."

Those thoughts and the ones in the quotation below provide the philosophical background, central theme, and the first part of the conclusion to the Address. Lincoln continues speaking to the serenaders: "The rebellion continues; and now that the election is over, may not all, having a common interest, re-unite in a common effort, to save our common country? . . . May I ask those who have not differed with me, to join with me, in the same spirit towards those who have?" In the Address the words "the rebellion continues" become "Yet, if God wills that it continue." With the last sentence quoted, recall Lincoln's "With malice toward none, with charity for all."

God Responsible for the War

The common theme in the antecedent documents is the implication that the responsibility for the war does not rest with either the North or the South, but with God. With the introduction of God in the Address, Lincoln brings that theme to a climax (all quotations): The Almighty has His own purposes; his appointed time; He now wills to remove; He gives to both North and South, this terrible war, as the woe due to those by whom the offence came; Yet if God wills that it continue; and 'the judgments of the Lord are true and righteous altogether.'

By the time of the Address, March 4, 1865, Lincoln's ambitions were to reconcile all the people and unite them in the problems of restoring the Union. The fact that there is not a hint of biblical influence on Lincoln's language in the antecedent documents confirms the main thesis of this work: Lincoln uses the Bible to win support for his ambitions, and it is consummated in the Address. After his reelection as president, as with his earlier political ambitions, he used the Bible, with several references to the deity, in order to win the support of the people to accomplish his goals.

The Address and the Bible

In the first half of the Address, Lincoln compares and contrasts the situations at the time of the first and second inaugurals. Stylistically, notice the antithetic parallelism: saving and destroy; make war and accept war; one of them and the other; and survive and perish. Up to this point Lincoln carefully avoids mentioning the North and the South and, instead, uses "both parties," the first step toward the healing and the reunion of the nation for which he hoped. That sets the scene for his introduction of the Bible, whereby he turns from the past to the future. Lincoln introduces the Bible and God, common grounds for both parties, into the agony of deciding the responsibility for the war. In doing so, he uses two of his favorite biblical texts, those about earning bread by the sweat of other men's faces and not judging. God becomes the center of the stage, and ultimately the case rests with him, whose judgments are infallible. There is to be no revenge taken toward anyone in a reunited Union. "Both read the same Bible, and pray to the same God; and each invokes His aid against the other. It may seem strange that any men should dare to ask a just God's assistance in wringing their bread from the sweat of other men's faces; but let us judge not that we be not judged" (8:333).

As with Lincoln's other major speeches, the Address shows how and why he used the Bible to win supporters of his political ambition that now differs from his former ambitions. The war is coming to an end, and as president his ambition is the reconciliation of people in both North and South and the restoration of the Union.

White (*Greatest Speech*, 102–8) writes about a proliferation of the publication and distribution of Bibles during the war. He says, "The centrality of the Bible in nineteenth-century America cannot be overemphasized" (103). Of course, that would be ample reason for Lincoln using the Bible in his speeches, culminating with his Second Inaugural where he was addressing *all* persons of North and South.

According to White (115), Lincoln "asked how it was possible for soldiers to read their Bibles and come up with such a '*strange*' practice as slavery, which went against all the precepts taught in the Bible" (see also 101–2). There really is nothing in the Bible that goes against "such a '*strange*' practice as slavery," which was universally accepted as a common phenomenon in the world of the Bible. It is highly unlikely that Lincoln had in mind soldiers at all. Their role was almost over, as the war was ending. He had in mind the people of both North and South who both read the same Bible. The Address looks toward the future in light of the past. Lincoln is addressing slave owners and supporters of slavery in both the South and the North. Key words are "both parties," "neither party," "neither," "both," and "North and South." He had become convinced that slavery was incompatible with a free government. Lincoln's "the same God," occurs exactly in 1 Cor 12:6, and "a just God," exactly in Isa 45:21, all in contexts unrelated to those of Lincoln.

In the Address Lincoln reinforces the conviction that slavery is incompatible with a free government. We hear again his moral argument against slavery that slave holders were earning their bread by the sweat of other men's faces. They are the "any men" and "both," whether of the North or the South, who had asked a just God's help in doing it. That sets the stage for the judgment quotation that follows. Slavery belongs to the past, so Lincoln exhorts his hearers: "But let us judge not that we be not judged."

We dealt with the biblical quotation of Matt 7:1 (Luke 6:37) in the discussion of Lincoln's letter to the Baptist ministers George B. Ide and others (7:368). There Lincoln was incisive in his criticism of individuals who eat their bread at the sweat of others: "professedly holy men of the South, met in the semblance of prayer and devotion, and, in the name of Him who said 'As ye would all men should do unto you, do ye even so unto them' appealed to the christian [sic] world to aid them in doing to a whole race of men, as they would have no man do unto themselves." Those words anticipate the ones in the Address about asking "God's assistance in wringing their bread from the sweat of other men's faces." In the letter to the Baptists, after his incisive remarks, Lincoln says of himself, "But let me forbear, remembering it is also written 'Judge not, lest ye be judged.'" The quotation he adapts at the end is his criticism of the Baptists. By the time of the Second Inaugural, such criticism is to be ended, so Lincoln intends the quotation to apply to everyone, including himself. Therefore, the exhortation is: "But let *us* not judge that *we* be not judged" (italics mine), well adapted to the situation at hand.

In both the Bible and Lincoln, the implication of the quotation is that God will do the judging. In the Address the quotation serves as an introduction to the discussion of God's responsibility for the war. "The prayers of both could not be answered; that of neither has been answered fully." Lincoln shifts the emphasis from asking divine assistance to the subject about which those praying had been asking. What follows is a complex blending of theology and the reality of a war about to end. "The Almighty has His own purposes. 'Woe unto the world because of offences! for it must needs be that offences come; but woe to that man by whom the offence cometh'!" (8:333). This is an exact quotation from Jesus' words reported in Matt 18:7 (see also Luke 17:1–2), where the word translated as "offence" is the Greek *skandalon*. It refers to anything that would cause one of Jesus' disciples ("these little ones") who believed in him to lose faith and sin (Matt 18:6). The world of Jesus' words, which has no relevancy to that of Lincoln, for whom the context was the war between the states that is ending, and the offence that caused it was American Slavery. The fact that elsewhere Lincoln quotes much more familiar biblical passages imprecisely suggests that he went to the Bible to find the one on the offence and quotes it precisely, including the punctuation.

If Lincoln took great care in the preparation of his speeches, as White (*Greatest Speech,* 48–50) maintains, he apparently did not take the same care to observe the context of Matt 18:6–7. There the penalty for the offender is death by a millstone around his neck and being drowned in the sea. Would Lincoln ever have thought of such a severe penalty even for the worst slave owner? Did Lincoln assume that no one in the audience would be aware of that penalty? By not even hinting at a penalty Lincoln makes the quotation relevant for those of both North and South who accept the institution of slavery. And he leaves "this terrible war" as the woe caused by people collectively in both regions, not just the slave holders. For White's thoughtful treatment of this passage see the *Greatest Speech,* 144–46.

White's statement later, "Lincoln suggested that the war was a means of purging the nation of its sin" (157), is too strong, because Lincoln used the word sin a total of only two times. Of the members of the Temperance Society in Springfield he says that they deny the Christian "doctrine of the unpardonable sin" in their forgiving the drunkards (1:276). In the first debate with Douglas, Lincoln jests with him: "The judge is woefully at fault about his early friend Lincoln being 'a grocery keeper.'" Lincoln doesn't know if it would be "a great sin" if he had been a "grocery keeper" (3:16). Neither of these passages has pejorative implications on Lincoln's part. Although Lincoln thought slavery was immoral, he never would have used sin for the offense of slavery on the part of either the South or the North, because it would have hindered his message of healing and recovery.

Lincoln's statement that "one of those offences, which, in the providence of God, must needs come, but which, having continued through His appointed time," and what Lincoln continues to say is another way of saying that "the Almighty has His own purposes." This emphasizes that God is responsible for the war. Yet, paradoxically, Lincoln says that slavery, for which humans are responsible, is one of the offenses by which the war came.

Many scholars believe that these and other references to God in the Address are the capstone and ultimate proof of Lincoln's belief in a personal God. I cannot say that this is not true. However, it seems to me that Lincoln's faith was paradoxical. He believed in the existence of Providence (God) and that events *might* be controlled by such a deity, but he did not believe in a personal God as one he worshiped. This is why he does not include himself among "the believers in a Living God."

The discussion that follows further confirms the conviction that in the Second Inaugural, as usual, Lincoln refers to God and the Bible to win support for his political ambitions, this time his agenda for the postwar Union. This is true in spite of the fact that his language was greatly influenced by that of the Bible. For Lincoln's "appointed time" see Job 7:1; 14:14; and Hab 2:3, where "appointed time," though, is used of man's time, not God's. See, for example, Job 7:1: "Is there not an appointed time to man upon earth?"

With respect to "this terrible war, as the woe due to those by whom the offence came," Lincoln asks: "Shall we discern therein any departure from those divine attributes which the believers in a Living God always ascribe to Him?" By saying "the believers," not "we who believe" or "we believers," Lincoln is consistent in not identifying himself with any denomination of the Christian religion or Christian doctrine (for a different view, see White, *Greatest Speech*, 146–47).

Lincoln's words about believing in "a Living God," which he uses only here, do not occur precisely in the Bible, where the phrase is always "the living God." Perhaps Lincoln's phrase is closest to 1 Tim 4:10: "We trust in the living God" (see also Matt 16:16; 1 Sam 17:26; Josh 3:10; Hos 1:10; Jer 10:10; 23:36).). In the Bible the background for the expression is always pagan polytheism with its idolatrous practices (see the classic passages in Isa 40:19–20; 41:7; 44:9–20; 1 Cor 8:4–6).

Lincoln continues: "Fondly do we hope—fervently do we pray—that this mighty scourge of war may speedily pass away." For hope, see

Ps 33:22: "Let thy mercy, O Lord, be upon us, according as we hope in Thee." Perhaps Lincoln's thought was somewhat influenced by Rom 8:24–25: "We are saved by hope: but hope that is seen is not hope: for what a man seeth, why doth he yet hope for? But if we hope for what we see not, then do we with patience wait for it." The idea of praying fervently is emphatic in Jas 5:16: "The effectual fervent prayer of a righteous man availeth much." Yet if God wills [see "according to the will of God" in Rom 8:27] that it continue, until the wealth piled up by the bond-man's two hundred and fifty years of unrequited toil shall be sunk, and until every drop of blood drawn with the lash, shall be paid by another drawn with the sword, as was said three thousand years ago, so still it must be said, 'the judgments of the Lord, are true and righteous altogether'" (8:333). "Requited" is biblical, for example, "God hath requited me" (Judg 1:7; 1 Sam 25:21). "Bondman" is also biblical, a word in the KJV used for servant or slave, for example, "Thou wast a bondman in the land of Egypt" (Deut 15:15; see also Gen 44:33; Deut 16:12; 24:18, 22; Rev 6:15). See also "neither bond nor free" (Gal 3:28). The concept of the drawn sword for punishment occurs in Ezek 5:12, where the Lord says, with respect to the punishment of his people for their evils, that will scatter them abroad and "draw out a sword after them" (see also Ezek 12:14). The point is that God decides the punishment there is to be, if any.

The phrase "the mighty scourge of war" is a parallel with "this terrible war" used earlier. I agree with Professor White (*Greatest Speech*, 155) in the suggestion that "Lincoln's audience would have connected 'scourge' with Hebrews 12:6" (165): "For whom the Lord loveth he chasteneth, and scourgeth every son whom he receiveth."

As White says, the image perceived in the minds of his hearers is that of "the whipping a master inflicted upon a slave" and that it is God who scourges. However, there are two main differences between the text of Hebrews and that of Lincoln. In the Greek text of Hebrews "scourge" is in parallel with the word *paideuo*, which literally means "train a child" and then "discipline," "correct," "chastise." And the reason behind it is the Lord's chastisement because of love for the faithful as a father loves a son, whereas the reason behind Lincoln's words is God's chastisement by the war.

Considering these things and Lincoln's words "that this mighty scourge of war may speedily pass away," Isa 28:15–18 may be a more likely influence upon him than Heb 12:6. Isaiah proclaims the prophecy of the Lord's punishment of the wicked society in Jerusalem. "When the overflowing scourge shall pass through . . . Judgment also will I lay to the line, and righteousness to the plummet . . . when the overflowing scourge shall pass through, then ye shall be trodden down by it." This also ties in well with the vocabulary in Lincoln's quotation about the judgments of the Lord that follows.

The quotation about judgment is verbatim of Ps 19:9, except for his insertion of a comma. Again, he probably searched the Bible for a text he thought appropriate. He must also deliberately have calculated the date of the psalmist, in accordance with Ussher's view, because he first had four thousand and changed it to three thousand. That would be about the time of David (c. 1000 to 962 BC), who Lincoln thought wrote the Psalms.

Of all the designations for and attributes of the deity Lincoln used (Appendix 3), judge and judgment are not among them, although in the Bible God or the Lord is judge. Psalm 19 was originally two independent psalms. The first (verses 1–6) sings the praise of God's work of creation; the second (verses 7–14), describes the good life under the Law. For that reason the first verse of the psalm about the glory of God and his handiwork as indicative of "a great and good God" (*pace* White, 158–59) probably has nothing to do with the part of the psalm dealing with the Laws of God, of which the quotation is a part. It begins: "The law of the Lord is perfect, converting the soul" (Ps 19:7). The idea of judging is entirely lacking in the context of Ps 19:9. And "judgments" is synonymous with "ordinances," "precepts," "statutes" and "commandment" (verse 8), and "laws." For example: "these are the statutes, and judgments and laws" (Lev 26:46; see also Neh 9:13–14; Ezek 44:24; Dan 9:5). The first revision of the KJV, known in America as the American Standard Version (1901), for Ps 19:9 reads: "The ordinances of Jehovah are true, and righteous altogether." If the translators of the KJV had translated the Hebrew word with any of the words mentioned other than "judgments," Lincoln would not have had the quotation. Entirely oblivious of the context of the passage quoted, Lincoln chose the passage only to win support for his agenda for the critical future of the Union. The best way to do that was not to pass judgment himself but to let the case rest with the Lord. Lincoln's introduction of God is reminiscent of the *deus ex machina*, whereby a dummy of a god was brought into a Greek drama to miraculously resolve all the unresolved problems of the play.

After a careful introduction so as not to give offense to anyone, Lincoln constructed the body of his Second Inaugural with the use of the Bible in order to win both the North and South to his ambitions for a reunited Nation. The part of the address that begins, "Both read the same Bible" and ends with the quotation from the psalm (Bible) is really the body of the speech, dealing with both past and present. In rhetorical/literary criticism such a section is called an *inclusion* (Latin, *inclusio*, "closing off," "confinement"), whereby a phrase or an idea that begins a section is repeated, paraphrased, or otherwise mentioned at the end.

In the magnificently rhetorical conclusion to his Inaugural, Lincoln begins with the present moment and then exhorts his readers to action for the future, and again he may have been influenced by the Bible. With Lincoln's "to finish the work we are in" see John 4:34, where Jesus says that he is to do the will of God "and to finish his work." In Rom 9:27–28 Paul alludes to Isaiah who said a remnant would be saved "and finish the work . . ." With "a lasting peace, among ourselves" see "be at peace among yourselves" (1 Thess 5:13). King Nebuchadnezzar wrote "unto all peoples, nations . . . Peace be multiplied unto you" (Dan 4:1).

Lincoln's Second Inaugural Address has been called "the climactic expression of his biblical faith," a "Scripture-steeped masterpiece," and "the noblest political document known to history." "Surely, none was ever written under a stronger sense of the reality of God's government" (Wolf, 136 and 207 n. 8). Fornieri (*Political Faith*, 172) maintains that Lincoln's Second Inaugural was "the public expression of biblical faith." There is much to commend that view (but see here Appendix 3). I think, rather, its aim was to promote his ambitions for his post-war second term. He used the Bible as a means of persuasion to help him fulfill those ambitions without any indication of his personal faith. Indeed, he does not even include himself among those who are believers in the Living God.

With Lincoln's words, "With malice toward none; with charity for all," compare these biblical statements: "Let all your things be done with charity" (1 Cor 16:14) and "Laying aside all malice" (1 Pet 2:1). "Let all bitterness, and wrath, and anger . . . and evil speaking, be put away from you, with all malice" (Eph 4:31) and "Put off all these; anger, wrath, malice . . . And above all these things put on charity, which is the bond of perfectness" (Col 3:8, 14). No matter how much Lincoln may have been influenced by biblical language in the Address, it is significant that his words "With malice toward none; with charity for all," anticipated in earlier documents, are now emphatically affirmed.

As always, Lincoln's ambitions were morally motivated. With the war almost ended, and looking for the re-union of the states, in his Second Inaugural Address, as in his Cooper Union Address, he utters an exhortation, this time preceded with the words, "with firmness in the right, as God gives us to see the right" (8:333). In spite of invoking God's help to see the right, his hearers are exhorted to political faith grounded on moral action, not theological faith. Now he is sure of the right morally. He really does not need to invoke God's help, although it was a good ear catcher. In his masterful conclusion he exhorts his hearers to moral action: "Let us strive on to finish the work we are in; to bind up the nation's wounds; to care for him who shall have borne the battle, and for his widow, and his orphan—to do all which may achieve and cherish a just, and a lasting peace, among ourselves, and with all nations" (8:333). Soon after beginning his public career, in a handbill Lincoln defended the widow of Joseph Anderson and her son Richard vs James Adams, a political adversary (1:89–93, 95–106). With his words "to care . . . for his widow, and his orphan" Lincoln's public career ended as it had begun—with the concern for widows and orphans.

According to Benson (Lord Charnwood, 476–77), "Probably no other speech of a modern statesman uses so unreservedly the language of intense religious feeling. The occasion made it natural; neither the thought nor the words are in any way conventional; no sensible reader now could entertain a suspicion that the orator spoke to the heart of the people but did not speak from his own heart." Benson's book was first published in 1916, and many Lincoln scholars still accept that view. However, I believe that this study has tempered such strong opinions.

10

Conclusion: The First Precept
of Our Ancient Faith

LINCOLN USED THE KING James Version of the Bible, but we cannot be sure how and when he learned to read it. It is most likely that he eventually used the version in the Oxford Bible that Lucy Speed gave him about 1841. The traditions that he used the Family Bible and that he was seen reading it in the White House are myths. That Bible remained in the possession of the Johnston family until sixty years after Lincoln's death.

Contrary to traditions that Lincoln memorized many whole chapters of the Bible, quoted by chapter and verse precisely as stated, and that he frequently corrected misquotations are not substantiated in the Lincoln documents, which lead to quite opposite conclusions. The same is true for the myth that he would welcome public debate on the Bible and that he usually carried a copy with him. He once said the Bible says somewhere that man is selfish, although there is nothing about selfishness in the Bible. When Douglas challenged him about quoting scripture, he became befuddled and made an inept reply.

Lincoln's use of the Bible is paradoxical in that his language is replete with biblical words and phrases, allusions to it, and some exact quotations, but his knowledge of its content is neither deep nor profound. It is one thing to know the language of the Bible—what it says. It is another thing to know the context of what it says and to understand its meaning. Evidence indicates that Lincoln had a better knowledge of Euclid and Shakespeare than of the Bible.

In Lincoln's first public communication, in which he mentions the Bible as Scripture, we learn about his political ambition and his moral sensitivity. At first Lincoln was indifferent toward the institution of slavery. He shared the view of Henry Clay that slaves should be deported en masse to Africa where they could enjoy all the benefits of freedom.

Although he never opposed slavery where it already existed, he was against its spread into free territories. Finally, he became convinced that slavery was morally wrong and that in order to save the Union slaves had to be freed.

In his Lyceum Address (1838), Lincoln spoke on the perpetuation of our political institutions so conducive to civil and religious liberty. Paraphrasing the conclusion to the Declaration of Independence, he challenged every American to pledge his life, property, and sacred honor, as did the patriots of seventy-six, "to the support of the Declaration of Independence, so to the support of the Constitution and Laws." Motivated by the statements in the Declaration that all men are created equal and endowed with certain unalienable rights, Lincoln came to believe that Negroes had the right to eat the bread earned with their own hands without asking permission from anyone else.

Lincoln believed the disregard for equality would lead to the spread of slavery into free territories and further division of the Union. As a lawyer, he had been trained that the aim of a lawyer is to persuade by means of evidence. Along with the Declaration of Independence and the Constitution, Lincoln used the Bible as a means for persuading his hearers to support his political ambitions and to accept his moral ideals for opposing slavery. He found biblical evidence for the view that slavery was morally wrong in God's words to Adam that he would earn his bread by the sweat of his face. Because all men are created equal, Lincoln believed it was immoral for a man to earn his bread by the sweat of another man's face.

Understanding how Lincoln knew and used the Bible, I have been able to suggest some novel conclusions. For example, biblical allusions and quotations lead to the conclusion that the Washington mentioned in the Lyceum Address refers to the Government in the city of Washington, not to George Washington.

In the First Inaugural Address, Lincoln devotes most of the time expressing political faith in the documents of the founding fathers. The faith of the thirteen states made sure that the Declaration of Independence should be perpetual. One of the objects of the Constitution was "*to form a more perfect union.*" Because that perpetuity is now lost, "the Union is *less* perfect than before the Constitution" (4:265). That statement anticipates the intention of Lincoln in the Address to restore the Union to its perfect state.

Speaking comforting words to a pious Quaker woman, using innumerable titles for the deity to fit the circumstances, almost to being trite, and quoting the Bible occasionally do not confirm biblical faith. Both the devil and Douglas could quote scripture. Evidence in the documents indicates that Lincoln was concerned mostly with political, not religious, faith and that he was not motivated by his knowledge of the Bible or organized religion. Rather, his faith was motivated by the Declaration of Independence and the Constitution.

After Lincoln achieved his ambition of becoming president, he used the Bible less often and mostly in private communications. Then his ambitions were to end the war, free the slaves, and restore the Union. After his reelection as president, Congress passed the Thirteenth Amendment to the Constitution on January 31, 1865, and the war was almost over. Now his ambitions centered on the welfare of a restored Union and a lasting peace, so in his Second Inaugural Address he used the Bible again to help him achieve his ambitions.

Phrases and thoughts from several earlier documents anticipated some of those in the Address. Those documents dealt with the question of God's responsibility for the war, about which Lincoln was rather ambivalent until his election to a second term. In the Address he introduces God, not as an object of faith, but as the one who was ultimately responsible for the conflict. Thus, Lincoln absolves the slave holders of both the South and the North of responsibility for it. "The judgments of the Lord, are true and righteous altogether" (Ps 19:9). The case now rests with God.

Contrary to the usual views, Lincoln never thought of the Church as a universal institution, and he did not attend church services regularly. Although Lincoln used the Bible to help him achieve his ambitions, he never regarded it as sacred or authoritative, as did the Bible readers of his time. Instead of citing it by chapter and verse, he used words such as precept or maxim, the same words he used to introduce a popular saying or quotation from other literature. Moreover, in thinking of faith based on the Bible, it seems only natural to assume that there would be some evidence of belief or belief system such as Judaism or Christianity associated with it. Lincoln shows little knowledge of the Christian religion, and when he mentions it, he disassociates himself from it. In contrast, he calls the Declaration of Independence "the first precept of our ancient faith" and a "sacred instrument." He refers to the walls of the building where the Declaration and Constitution originated as "consecrated walls." Lincoln never hints of anything like that with respect to the Bible. In fact, the word faith is not a prominent part of Lincoln's vocabulary, and when he uses it apart from human relationships, it is always associated with politics.

There is nothing in the documents to support the alleged friendships of Lincoln with the Reverends Smith and Gurley. Nor is there evidence to support the view that they influenced Lincoln's thoughts about the Bible and religion. Evidence indicates that such friendships were no stronger than many of Lincoln's friendships with other men.

Lincoln never emphatically denied the charges of infidelity, nor did he reply by saying he believed in a deity or that he was a member of any religion. He replied only that he never denied the truth of the Scriptures and that he never spoke in disrespect of religion in general.

Lincoln's numerous titles for and attributes of the deity coincide with Max Mueller's definition of religion later, all of which precludes any attempt to determine Lincoln's personal view of the deity and his faith.

Herndon discusses Lincoln's religious beliefs, pro and con, at some length and sources for them. He thinks that Lincoln believed in God, immortality, and possibly a life beyond the grave, and he ought not to be condemned if at any time in his life he was skeptical of the Bible (Wilson and Davis, 265–69). Although Herndon is not always consistent in writing about Lincoln, this study has presented evidence that supports one of his views quoted by Glen E. Thurow: "Lincoln was very politic, and a very shrewd man in some particulars. When he was talking to a Christian . . . he adapted himself to the Christian . . . he was at moments, as it were, a Christian, through politeness, courtesy, or good breeding toward the delicate, tender-nerved man, the Christian, and in two minutes after, in the absence of such men, and among his own kind, the same old unbeliever."[13]

The Apostle Paul addressed his letters to pagans, believers, nonbelievers, Jews, and Gentiles. He often quoted or alluded to the Hebrew or Greek scriptures in the hope of winning converts to his own faith. In order to do so, he confesses to the Corinthians: "For though I be free from all men, yet have I made myself servant unto all, that I might gain the more. And unto the Jews I became as a Jew, that I might gain the Jews; to them that are under the law, as under the law, that I might gain them that are under the law; To them that are without law, as without law, (being not without law to God, but under the law to Christ,) that I might gain them that are without law. To the weak became I as weak, that I might gain the weak: I am made all things to all men, that I might by all means save some" (1 Cor 9:19–22).

Although Lincoln was surely not consciously imitating Paul, the two men were alike in that they both quoted scripture to support their respective objectives. And both sincerely believed that in saying and doing the things they did they were doing nothing wrong. Why? Because their goals were right. As the result, Paul spread incipient Christianity from Jews to Gentiles, and Abraham Lincoln emancipated the slaves in America.

Notes

1. "Historic Lincoln Bibles," in "Lincoln Lore," in the *Bulletin of the Lincoln National Life Foundation* 567 (Feb 19, 1940), edited by Louis A. Warren (Fort Wayne, IN, the Lincoln National Life Insurance Company, 1940), no page numbers.

2. This Bible is housed at 2995 Lincoln Farm Road, Hodgenville, Kentucky, 42748. Thanks to Jennifer Jones and Debbie Davendonis for this information (December 4, 2007). When I visited the site, the Bible was away for treatment. I am also indebted to the National Park Service, Lincoln Boyhood National Monument, 2916 E. South Street, Lincoln City, Indiana 17552, for the information about Christopher Bush, father of Sarah Bush, given later.

3. Park Service personnel give credit for this information to *Lincoln Lore*, vol. 49, The Lincoln Museum, Fort Wayne, Indiana.

4. I say this with some confidence, having studied ancient manuscripts while in Graduate School at Harvard University in 1946–1948. However, I make no claim to certainty.

5. Information verified by a member of the staff at the Library of Congress by telephone on December 9, 2002.

6. Information verified by Clark Evans, a member of the Library staff, on June 3, 2008.

7. Louis A. Warren, "Lincoln Lore" 567 (Feb 19, 1940). The best listing of "Lincoln Bibles" known to me is that of Robert S. Barton, "How Many 'Lincoln Bibles'?" (Published by the author, at G75 Granite St., Foxboro, Mass, August 1951). A copy of Barton's monograph of 12 pages was given me by Cindy VanHorn of the Lincoln Museum, Fort Wayne, IN.

8. See, for example, the works by Anderson, Burt, Thomas F. Schwartz, and Fornieri, *Language,* listed in the Bibliography.

9. From hymn 88 in Book 1, Isaac Watts, *Hymns and Spiritual Songs* (1707).

10. Speech in United States House of Representatives: The War with Mexico, January 12, 1848 (1:431–42).

11.   Lincoln's reference here is probably to the *Encyclopedia Americana*, for which the first English editions appeared in America from 1829–1833.

12.   See the Annotation in 7:542–43.

13.   Glen E. Thurow, "Abraham Lincoln," in *The Historian's Lincoln*, 129.

Appendix 1

Lincoln and the Church and Churches

L INCOLN FIRST MENTIONS *CHURCH* in a letter to Mary S. Owens, May
7, 1837 (1:78–79). About a year after Ann Rutledge died, some of the
older women in New Salem urged him to find a wife, and Miss Owens
became a likable prospect. Lincoln laments to her that he is as lonesome
in Springfield as he has been anywhere in his life. Only one woman spoke
to him since he came there, and he "should not have been seen by her, if
she could have avoided it." He confides to Miss Owens: "I've never been
to church yet, nor probably shall not be soon [Lincoln's double negative].
I stay away because I am conscious I should not know how to behave
myself" (1:78).

Lincoln's words about never being to church yet are ambiguous.
Does "never" mean that he has not ever gone to church, or not yet in
Springfield? At any rate, if he had gone to church regularly, he should have
known how to behave there. And *church* is an individual congregation,
not a universal institution.

In his temperance address, Lincoln says that it is easy to ascribe motives
to men of different classes. "The *preacher*, it is said, advocates temperance
because he is a fanatic, and desires a union of Church and State" (1:272).
Here *Church* is a universal institution, but Lincoln says that of the opinion
of the "the *preacher*," not of himself. On the other hand, people cannot say
of the former alcoholic, "a redeemed specimen of long lost humanity . . .
that *he* desires a union of church and state, for he is not a church member"
(1:272). Lincoln uses the phrase "church and state" with respect to others,
without any inference about himself or his view.

To the man who thinks that in the temperance movement "*moral
influence* is not that powerful engine contended for," Lincoln uses parody
effectively: of "the influence of *fashion*" among those who attend church:

What compensation he will accept to go to church some Sunday, and sit during the sermon with his wife's' bonnet upon his head? Not a trifle, I'll venture. And why not? There would be nothing irreligious in it: nothing immoral, nothing uncomfortable. Then why not? Is it not because there would be something egregiously unfashionable in it? Then it is the influence of *fashion*; and what is the influence of fashion, but the influence that *other* people's actions have [on our own ?] actions , the strong inclination each of us feels to do as we see all our neighbors do? (1:277)

Lincoln uses an exhortation as an appeal: "Let us make it as unfashionable to withhold our names from the temperance pledge as for husbands to wear their wives [*sic*] bonnets to church, and instances will be just as rare in the one case as in the other" (1:277). In every instance *church* is an individual congregation, not the institutional church.

Lincoln lost the election for representative to the state legislature in 1832, and he was disappointed because the people of his own county had deserted him, whereas the Whigs in Menard County had supported him. Years later (March 26, 1843) he wrote to Martin S. Morris, a delegate from Menard County, reflecting upon his loss (1:319–21). Lincoln says that among other things, "There was too the strangest combination of church influence against me." Baker, a Campbellite, got almost all of that church. Although Lincoln's wife had some relatives in the Presbyterian and Episcopal churches, he "was set down as either the one or the other, whilst it was every where contended that no ch[r]istian ought to go for me, because I belonged to no church, was suspected of being a deist, and had talked about fighting a duel." Baker, of course, had nothing to do with these things, and "as to his own church going for him, I think that was right enough" (1:320). In a second letter to Morris on the same issue, April 14, 1843 (1:321–22), Lincoln says that Baker "would not do the like," that is, violate party rules. Lincoln would as soon put his "head in the fire" as violate instructions to his advantage. Later, in his reply to the charges of infidelity, Lincoln admits that he is not "a member of any Christian Church" (1:382).

In his speech at New Haven, Connecticut, March 6, 1860 (4:13–30), Lincoln argues that the slave owner regards his slaves as property and that it influences his mind to believe that slavery is right. Then in a concocted story about the two ministers, a "dissenting minister" argued with one of "the established church." Here church is a theoretical orthodox congregation, as the words "the orthodox minister" later show, in contrast to a more liberal congregation of the dissenting minister. Thus, Lincoln thinks of *church* as a local congregation, not a universal church.

Lincoln stresses his position concerning individual churches and church members in a letter to Edwin M. Stanton, September 29, 1862 (5:445). He suspects that different religious denominations might have "some collision in their ministering among the colored people about Port-Royal, and perhaps elsewhere." Then he states his position: "Each church should minister according to its own rules, without interference by others differing from them; and if there still be difficulties about *places* of worship, a real christian charity, and forbearance on the part of all might obviate it" (5:445). Lincoln later writes essentially the same thing to Stanton (7:178–80) and in a Memorandum about Churches (7:223).

The following incidents in dealing with the churches in the South during the Civil War, about which Lincoln writes to his generals, support the view that he is concerned with individual churches and not the church as a universal institution. He writes to General Curtis, January 2, 1863 (6:33–34): "The U. S. Government must not, as by this order, undertake to run the churches. When an individual, in a church or out of it, becomes dangerous to the public interest, he must be checked; but let the churches, as such take care of themselves. It will not do for the U. S. to appoint Trustees, Supervisors, or other agents for the churches."

Here key words are "in a church" and "the churches." Fornieri (*Political Faith*, 98–99) quotes the passage from the letter to Curtis to support the argument that Lincoln "clearly subordinated the secular realm to the spiritual realm when describing the church as a 'greater institution' than the state. Lincoln's recognition of a higher spiritual authority shows that he acknowledged a sacred sphere beyond the reach of the federal government."

The point of the letter to Curtis is not just "a policy of noninterference with rebel churches." Rather, the dangerous person "in a church or out of it" must be equally checked. A dangerous church member is not to be excused because he belongs to "a higher spiritual authority" or is a member of "the church as a 'greater institution' than the state" (*pace* Fornieri).

The letter to Curtis is not an isolated case of Lincoln's dealing with individual church members and churches. In a Memorandum about Churches, March 4, 1864 (7:223), Lincoln repeats his view expressed to

Curtis: "The United States Government must not undertake to run the churches."

Lincoln received a petition signed by over three dozen citizens and three supporting letters requesting him to restore the Rev. Dr. Samuel B. McPheeters of Vine Street Church in St. Louis "to all his ecclesiastical rights." Lincoln responds in a letter to Oliver Filley, one of the letter writers, on December 22, 1863 (7:85–86). He has "no intimation as to what ecclesiastical rights are withheld." A Mr. Coalter had written: "Is it not a strange illustration of the condition of things that the question of who shall be allowed to preach in a church in St. Louis, shall be decided by the *President of the United states?*" (7:85).

Lincoln sees a contradiction in the information given him and says, "All this sounds very strangely; and withal, a little as if you gentlemen making the application, do not understand the case alike." Then he says that he had written to General Curtis on his position. Lincoln has never thought of "interfering as to who shall or shall not preach in any church." If the members are asking him to restore McPheeters to his position "over the heads of a majority of his own congregation, that too, will be declined." He "will not have control of any church on any side" (7:86).

In an endorsement concerning McPheeters (7:86), Lincoln reiterated his decision and says, "I directed, a long time ago, that Dr. McPheeters was to be arrested, or remain at large, upon the same rule as any one else . . . as to who should, or should not preach in any church" (7:86). Lincoln might have made the same decision on any non-legal matter concerning a member of any organization, as with the Young Men's Lyceum, for example. Finally, Lincoln says that the assumption he is "keeping McPheeters from preaching in his church is monstrous."

Lincoln's emphasis on church and churches instead of *the Church* as a universal institution is especially strong in his response to a committee of Methodists who presented him with a speech that was given at the General Conference of the Methodist Episcopal Church. The speech expressed to Lincoln their loyalty to the Union, support for his administration, and prayers for the preservation of the country. Lincoln responds that the government has been sustained by "all the churches," among which the Methodists have excelled. "God bless the Methodist Church—bless all the churches—and blessed be God, Who, in this our great trial, giveth us the churches" May 18, 1864 (7:350–51).

Those words of Lincoln provide the clue for understanding his view of *church* in his response to a delegation of Baptists, May 30, 1864 (7:368; recall discussion in text). He rebukes those holy men who are defending slavery and take the word of God to mean earn their bread by the sweat of other men's faces. "In the semblance of prayer and devotion, and, in the name of Him who said" the words about doing unto others, and profess to follow those words have "contemned and insulted God and His Church." Obviously, Lincoln is riled, and he is rebuking an extremely conservative group of men, who undoubtedly thought of the Church as a universal institution. What better response could he more expedient in order to shock them into seeing how wrong their position was? Unlike them, Lincoln may have thought of "His Church" as the Baptist Church as a whole or of the Baptist congregation of his visitors, but not a universal institution.

Lincoln's view about church and churches is clear in a letter to the Rev. William Nast, October 31, 1864 (8:83). Members of the Central German Conference of the Methodist Episcopal Church had passed resolutions supporting the President. Lincoln expresses his gratitude for the anticipated "definite and unequivocal statement of the continued loyalty and devotion of the Church you represent, to the free institutions of the country of your adoption" (8:83). This harks back to the "the perpetuation of our political institutions," the subject of Lincoln's Lyceum address.

There is no conclusive evidence that Lincoln thought of the church as a universal institution as generally understood among Christians and stated in some creeds: "one holy catholic and apostolic church" (Nicene Creed) and "the holy catholic church" (Apostles Creed). The evidence presented here supports my view that Lincoln's words about the church as an institution and the quotation from Matt 16.18 in his Lyceum Address were an afterthought to attract church members to support his political campaign. It might be that Lincoln never joined an established church in order to avoid further dissension among church groups and political parties, which would result in a loss of votes by all concerned.

Appendix 2

Lincoln's Attendance at Sunday Church Services

RECALL THE SUMMARY OF Lincoln's attendance at churches in the body of the text. The following records of his church attendance are based on the Lincoln Log, a chronology of Lincoln's daily life compiled by the Sesquicentennial Commission, the Abraham Lincoln Association, and other institutions concerned with Lincoln. All dates are Sundays, except where noted. My comments are enclosed by asterisks.

1859, August 14—Lincoln attends First Presbyterian Church services in Concert Hall *[Council Bluffs, IA]*. . . . He dines at the home of Mr. and Mrs. Thomas Officer, former Springfield residents. *Council Bluffs Nonpareil,* 14 August 1921 *For the speech see *CW,* 3:396–97.* His speech on Saturday evening "was in the character of an exhortation to the Republican party, but was in reality as good a speech as could have been made for the interest of the Democracy" (3:396). *It was politically expedient for Lincoln to attend church services with his hosts.*

1859, October 2—*Janesville, WI.* Lincoln remains at home of Mr. and Mrs. W. H. Tallman . . . and accompanies his host and hostess to Congregational Church. *Wisconsin Magazine,* January 1924—February 1924. *Lincoln had made political speeches at Milwaukee, Beloit, and Janesville.*

1860, February 26—Lincoln attends church with Henry C. Bowen *(New York business man and "pillar" in Beecher's Plymouth Church in Brooklyn).* *Abraham Lincoln to Simon Cameron,* 26 February 1860, *CW,* 3:521.

1860, March 4—Lincoln spends day with Robert and his classmates *[at Harvard].* He attends Phillips church. Percy C. Eggleston, *Lincoln in New*

England (New York: Seward, Warren & Co., 1922), 8, *Bulletin of Phillips Exeter Academy*, XII, No.3, 9.

1860, March 11—Lincoln and James A. Briggs *[New York politician still not supporting Lincoln]* hear Beecher preach at Plymouth Church in Brooklyn . . . James A. Briggs to S. P. Chase, 17 March1860, Simon P. Chase Papers, Library of Congress, Washington, DC.

1860, August 26—Lincoln attends church *[in Springfield],* where J. Henry Brown sees him. *Brown was probably John Henry Brown, a portrait painter, who said that he agreed with Lincoln* "in all things but his politics . . . In FtwL-Brown Journal, Photocopy.

1860, November 25—Mr. Lincoln attended St. James Church *[Chicago]* . . . with Hon. Isaac N. Arnold, and in the afternoon, by invitation, was present at the Mission Sabbath School and made a short address to the children. *Chicago Journal*, 26 November 1860. *It would be interesting to know what Lincoln said then.*

1861, January 6—Mr. and Mrs. Lincoln and Gov. Chase of Ohio attend church service. Harry E. Pratt, *Concerning Mr. Lincoln, in which Abraham Lincoln is Pictured as He Appeared to Letter Writers of his Time* (Springfield, IL: 1944), 35.

1861, February 17—Former President Fillmore calls for Lincoln at 10 A.M. with carriage and takes him to Unitarian Church *[Buffalo, N. Y.]* to hear Rev. George W. Hosmer. *In the evening* Lincoln attends service by Indian preacher, Father John Beason. *Villard, Eve of '61, 90; N. Y. Times*, 18 February 1861.

1861, February 24—Lincoln attends St. John's Episcopal Church, opposite Executive Mansion, with Sen. Seward (N. Y.) and after service spends two hours at Seward's home. *Washington National Republican*, 25 February 1861.

1861, March 10—Family attends New York Avenue Presbyterian Church, their church preference while in Washington. Dr. Phineas D. Gurley is pastor. Barton, *Life of Lincoln*, 2:42.

1861, March 17—Lincoln attends morning church service with Gen. Scott. *N. Y. Herald*, 18 March 1861. *No specific church is given.*

1861, April 14—President attends New York Avenue Presbyterian Church and meets Pastor, Dr. Gurley. David R. Barbee, 'President Lincoln and Doctor Gurley,' *Abraham Lincoln Quarterly* 5 (March 1948) 5. *This meeting with Gurley hardly tallies with Barton's statement above. Would Lincoln not have met Gurley on March 10?*

1861, May 19—Lincoln attends church service. *Washington, DC, but name of church not given.* *William O. Stoddard, Lincoln's Third Secretary. The Memoirs of William O. Stoddard,* ed. by William O. Stoddard, Jr. (New York: Exposition Press, 1955), 84.

1861, Saturday, June 1—Lincoln family reserves pew in New York Avenue Presbyterian Church. *Baltimore Sun,* 6 June 1861.

1861, June 9—President does not accompany Mrs. Lincoln to church today. *N. Y. Times,* 11 June 1861. *What does this imply about Lincoln's habit of going to church regularly?*

1861, July 21—President attends church service *[in Washington?].* Benjamin P. Thomas, *Abraham Lincoln: A Biography* (New York: Knopf, 1952), 271. *That account is ambiguous. Gen. McDowell's army:* "a heterogeneous array-Zouaves in red fezzes. . . . Wisconsin boys in homespun gray, Massachusetts boys in blue" *marched south of Washington. After recounting some maneuvers of several armies, Thomas writes*: "Lincoln went to church, as had been his custom since he came to Washington. Returning to the White House, he asked for news" (page 271). *Where had Lincoln gone to church that day before he returned to the White House? Our evidence does not support the view that Lincoln's going to Gurley's church was customary.*

1861, July 28—President and Mrs. Lincoln attend Presbyterian church services. Meet Sen. Browning (Ill.), who accepts invitation to dinner at Executive Mansion. Browning, *Diary.* *Was this meeting prearranged for political purposes?*

1861, August 25—President with Secs. Seward and Welles attend divine service at Camp of 2nd New Hampshire Regement attached to Gen. Joseph Hooker's brigade. *N. Y. Times,* 26 August 1861.

1861, October 13—President and Sec. Seward attend divine service during visits to camps in Virginia. *N. Y. Times*, 14 October 1861.

1861, December 22—Lincolns attend New York Avenue Presbyterian Church and drive Sen. Browning (Ill.) home. Browning, *Diary*.

1861, December 29—Sen. Browning (Ill.) with Lincoln at White House from 5 P.M. until church time. *Apparently, Lincoln did not go to church with Browning, because he*spends early part of evening with Cong. Alfred Ely (N. Y.). . . . *N. Y. Tribune*, 30 December 1861.

1862, November 30—President and Mrs. Lincoln attend services at New York Avenue Presbyterian Church. "Castine" [Noah Brooks], Washington, December 4, 1862, in Sacramento Union, December 30, 1862.

1863, January 4—Lincoln attends New York Avenue Presbyterian Church and drives Sen. Browning (Ill.) home. Browning, *Diary*.

1863, January 18—President attends morning service at Foundry M. E. Church . . . and becomes 'Life Director of the Parent Society' in return for contribution of $150. *Washington Chronicle*, 19 January 1863.

1863, Thursday, August 6—President attends church services, having proclaimed August 6, 1863, day of Thanksgiving. Hay, *Letters* and *Diary*.

1865, March 5—In morning President and Mrs. Lincoln attend religious service at Capitol and hear sermon by Bishop *[Matthew]* Simpson *[of Methodist Church].* *Washington Star*, 6 March 1865.

Scholars continue to transmit the tradition that Lincoln and Gurley were close personal friends. Lincoln did not make a special effort to get to his church and occasionally attended other churches in Washington on Sundays. I have found no evidence to support Wolf's statement: "Occasionally Lincoln went to the midweek prayer meeting" (126). Undoubtedly, Phineas D. Gurley belonged to the "Old School Presbyterian Theology" (White, *Greatest Speech*, 131), whose views Fornieri (*Political Faith*, 57–58, 172) accepts. However, how often Lincoln listened to Gurley's preaching is questionable. The undocumented statements of White (131–32) that "from the spring of 1861 to the spring of 1865, he

[Gurley] preached to Abraham Lincoln" must be reconsidered. From January 6, 1861, until March 15, 1865, there is record of Lincoln attending New York Avenue Presbyterian Church no more than eight times. How much Lincoln was influenced by Gurley is also questionable.

Sometimes Lincoln refused to participate in Christian activities when asked to do so. For example, when invited by the Rev. Alexander Reed, General Superintendent of the U. S. Christian Commission, to preside over their meeting in the Hall of the House of Representatives in Washington on February 22, 1863, simultaneously a Sunday and Washington's birthday, Lincoln responded: "While, for reasons which I deem sufficient, I must decline to preside, I can not withhold my approval of the meeting, and its worthy objects" (6:114).

Lincoln's declination of that invitation raises another question about his regular church attendance. The latest I know is by Burton (114): "In his youth Lincoln attended church with his dour and devout Baptist father, though the Holy Spirit seems rather to have passed him by on these occasions." That may be the reason Lincoln did not attend church regularly.

Although the Lincolns reserved a pew in New York Avenue Presbyterian Church, there is no record that he ever joined that or any other church. Whenever Lincoln did go to church, the media were sure to report the fact. As a matter of fact, Lincoln rarely went to church. Throughout his career there is a record of his attendance at church services of some sort only twenty-six times, a number far from confirming the tradition of his regular or customary church attendance.

There is no documentary evidence for Lincoln's attendance at church for the years 1830, when the family moved to Illinois, until August 14, 1859. During those years Lincoln's Sundays were occupied chiefly with letters of a personal and/or a political nature, travel, and sometimes legislative sessions. While in Congress, Lincoln wrote to Mary his wife on Sunday, April 16, 1848 (1:465–66), and complained about "attending to business; but now, having nothing but business—no variety—it has become exceedingly tasteless" to him. Apparently, he was not going to church to add variety to his life.

The tradition that the death of Willie on February 20, 1862, changed Lincoln's attitude toward formal religion and even his church attendance is widely accepted, but there is insufficient evidence to support that tradition. The year 1862 was an especially busy one for Lincoln. During the month of January he performed his usual tasks for twenty-nine days;

for February, twenty-seven days; for March, twenty-eight days. Lincoln's Sundays were generally occupied with personal affairs, receiving visitors, and matters of State, as collaborated by the Lincoln Log and the *CW.* For example, on Sunday, January 11, 1863 (6:53), Lincoln wrote to Jacob Collamer, Senator from Vermont: "If not going to church please call & see me at once; & if to church, please call as soon after, as convenient."

The fact that there is no additional record of Lincoln's church attendance in the New Entries in the Lincoln Log provides further evidence supporting the data given above.

Lincoln wrote to his "esteemed friend," Eliza P. Gurney, on Sunday, September 4, 1864 (7:535): "I have not forgotten—probably never shall forget—the very impressive occasion when yourself and friends visited me on a Sabbath forenoon two years ago." On the lighter side, a Dr. F. W. Forsha had been told on Sunday, September 28, 1862 (5:444–45), that Lincoln was too busy to see him. Forsha had said that if the President would give him a ward in a hospital to treat soldiers with his "medisen up and on the wounded Soldiers for three Months" their wounds would be healed, and they would be fit for duty within a month. On the next day Lincoln wrote to William A. Hammond, Surgeon General, to allow him to try his "Balm." Hammond met with the "doctor" and wrote to Lincoln that he was "satisfied that he is an ignorant quack."

Most of the occasions for Lincoln's church going were in the year 1861, his first in the presidency, and often his attendance at church was in the company of some politician whose support he sought. Especially important among such persons was Orville H. Browning. Although the two men were personal and political friends, sometimes they were political adversaries. Moreover, Browning continued to criticize Lincoln on any matter he differed from him. As Lincoln began his presidency, he needed Browning's support in order to help consolidate his own position. What better way could he maintain that support than by going to church with Browning, who attended it regularly? Other persons with whom Lincoln attended church were also being courted for political advantage. In such cases his church going was also a matter of expediency rather than custom. And while visiting army camps, the most practical occasions for Lincoln to greet soldiers, as he always wanted to do, were church services.

As with the case of the death of Eddie on February 1, 1850, there is no substantial evidence that the death of Willie on February 20, 1862, motivated Lincoln to attend church more regularly. According to the

Lincoln Log and the *CW*, Lincoln did not attend the Cabinet meeting on February 21, but he did hold conferences with Secretary Seward and with General Butler. On Sunday, February 23, Lincoln held a conference at the War Department before the viewing of Willie's body later in the day. On Monday, after the funeral, Lincoln went along to the cemetery, but there is no record that he attended church before November 30, 1862. And after that there are records of his attendance at services of worship only on January 4 and 18, 1863, and on March 5, 1865.

We cannot doubt Lincoln's intense, sincere grief at the loss of his beloved son Willie. Nevertheless, evidence indicates that he continued his work as president, seemingly unhindered, and that he attended church even less often than before.

Appendix 3

Lincoln's Titles for and Attributes of the Deity

I HAVE SUGGESTED THAT although the word Creator occurs in the Bible, Lincoln probably got that designation for the deity from the Declaration of Independence. It ends with an appeal by the founding fathers "for the support of this Declaration, with a firm reliance on the Protection of Divine Providence, we mutually pledge to each other our Lives, our Fortunes, and our sacred Honor." Since the word providence does not appear in the Bible, I believe that a case could be made for the Declaration as the origin of Lincoln's use of it. As with the words God and Almighty, Lincoln uses providence too often and in so many ways that it borders on triteness and insincerity. Consider, for example, Lincoln's remark about Judge Douglas being confident that Providence was responsible for the death of President Taylor: "I suspect that confidence is not more firmly fixed with the Judge than it was with the old woman, whose horse ran away with her in a buggy. She said she trusted in Providence till the britchen broke, and then she didn't know what on airth to do" (2:150–51). In this quip, Providence seems to be deity, but it is the object of the woman's faith, not that of Lincoln. Indeed, the quip implies the lack of confidence in Providence on the part of Lincoln, whatever he means by it. As with the words God and Almighty, Providence is just one of many ways he refers to the deity, for which I make no claim of completeness.

I have also included the designations that are more likely those of William H. Seward (hereafter, Seward). Designations likely to be influenced by the Bible are indicated by references to it.

According to Wolf (179–80), "One of the elements of perennial newness in Lincoln's statements about God is the abundant wealth of his titles and attributes in describing the Creator. They can all be summarized under a phrase in his Second Inaugural, 'believers in a Living God.'" An investigation of the documents results in a somewhat different conclusion. I have corrected and expanded Wolf's list, and sometimes include suggestions about why Lincoln used a specific title.

Almighty. Lincoln uses the designation absolutely about twenty-eight times and about sixty-seven times with attributes, which are, at the same, titles, as the following examples indicate. The designation occurs also in formal documents conveying sympathy, condolence, or congratulations, and in proclamations, all probably written by Seward and signed by Lincoln. The designation occurs absolutely in the Bible some forty times in the Old Testament, most often in Job, but not once in the New Testament.

Almighty Architect (1:178, his first use of the word almighty).

Almighty arm (4:191). Occurs in the C Version of Lincoln's Farewell Address at Springfield, of which there are three versions. Some words are Lincoln's and others are those of his secretary, John Nicolay, so the origin of the words is uncertain.

Almighty Being (4:190). Occurs in the B Version of the Farewell Address, but the title does not appear anywhere else in the *CW*, so its authenticity is uncertain.

Almighty Father and the power of His Hand (6:332, Seward).

Almighty God (1:269; 2:310; 4:241; 6:319, 320, (496 Seward); 7:35, 333, 334; 8:101 (136, Seward). See Gen 17:1; Ezra 10:5; Rev 19:15.

Almighty Hand (6:496, Seward).

Almighty Power (6:245). First certain original source is in Edward McPherson, *The Political History of the United* States (1865), so Lincoln's use of the title is uncertain.

Almighty and Merciful Ruler of the Universe (7:432, Seward).

Almighty God the beneficent Creator and Ruler of the Universe (8:55, Seward).

Almighty Ruler (8:326-7). Although this designation appears in an autographed copy of Lincoln's speech upon his nomination for a second term as President, there has been much difference of opinion about it.

The Almighty, the Maker of the Universe (4:226).

The Almighty Ruler of nations (4:270).

Author of man (3:479-80).

Creator of His Creatures (2:546).

Great Disposer of events (8:56, Seward).

Divine Being (4:190). Occurs in the A Version of Lincoln's Farewell Address, but in the words of Nicolay. Lincoln uses "the Divine Being who determines the destinies of nations" (5:213).

Divine actions and attitudes. Lincoln has a propensity for the word divine; sometimes it may not be authentic. Divine is used with all of the following: assistance (5:279, in editor's words), aid (3:354), attributes (8:333, in Second Inaugural), guidance (5:213, 186, Seward, 279, editor's words), protection (7:533), interposition (6:244, authenticity uncertain), gift (3:359), arm (5:279, editor's words), rule (3:350, 554; 4:30), judgments (5:422), authority (6:227), favor (7:533), law (1:473; 2:4), ordinance (3:445), image and likeness (2:546), purposes (6:499, Seward), wisdom (2:89; 4:191, may not be authentic), and sustenance (4:234).

Although the precise words for most of these expressions do not occur in the Bible, the ideas behind them are certainly biblical. I have already discussed most of them. The "arm of the Lord" (Isa 51:9; 55:1; John 12:38) or arm of God was a symbol of the deity's help, comfort, protection, and victory. Of many examples, see the words of the Lord to the Israelites about their bondage in Egypt: "I will rid you out of their bondage, and I will redeem you with a stretched out arm" (Exod 6:6; see also Deut 4:34; 5:15; 7:19; 11:2; 2 Kgs 17:36; Isa 51:59). "Thou hast with thine arm redeemed my people" (Ps 77:15). "Thou hast scattered thine enemies with thy strong arm . . . Thou hast a mighty arm" (Ps 89:10, 13; see also Acts 13:17; Ps 98:1; Isa 62:8; Jer 27:5; 32:17; Ezek 20:33, 34; Luke 1:51; John 12:33).

Divine Power (4:207). In 2 Pet 1:3 the author writes of God and "his divine power" that has given all things to the believers in the author's community.

Divine Will (5:403, 420, 497). Elsewhere Lincoln uses the biblical "Will of God" (3:204, 3 times; 5:403, twice). "Will of God" occurs twenty-three times in the Old Testament, but not once in the New Testament. Lincoln also uses the biblical "God wills" (3:204; 5:404; 8:333, 367). See "God wilt" (2 Chr 20:12; Ezek 9:8; 11:13).

Divine Majesty (6:332, Seward).

Providence (1:275). Lincoln uses the word for the first time in his Temperance Address. He says that when something becomes so widespread as the use of alcohol the new temperance movement upsets many people. Such a widespread feeling on any subject is not easily subdued. "The success of the argument in favor of the existence of an over-ruling Providence, mainly depends upon that sense" (1:275). Here he uses the designation for deity. Afterwards, he uses the word about sixty-six times in various ways, as the following examples show.

Divine Providence (2:132; 4:52, 190, 234; 5:421; 7:48, 534, may not be authentic).

Providence of God (2:132; 5:223; 8:333).

Hand of Providence (2:136, 150).

Interference of Providence (2:150).

Will of Providence (5:420).

Providence wrought by means (5:422).

Dispensations of his (God's) *Providence* (2:310, Seward).

Reliance on Providence (5:53).

An all-wise Providence (5:215).

The Providence of the Great Spirit (6:152).

The ever watchful providence of Almighty God (6:496, Seward).

The mission entrusted to you by Providence (7:165, Seward).

Under the blessing of Providence (7:532).

Which are appointed by Providence (8:141).

Under the blessing of Divine Providence (7:48).

Appointed by Providence to repair the ravages of internal war (8:141).

The signal success that Divine Providence has recently vouchsafed (7:533, may not be authentic).

Imploring the assistance of Divine Providence (4:52; see also 4:190-1, 234; 5:421; 7:48, 533).

God (1:260). Lincoln uses the word God for the first time in the questionable *Copybook Verses* in a frivolous way: "but God knows When" (1:1). He uses a similar expression, though, in writing to Herndon: "and the Lord knows what" (1:477). God occurs in the quotation from Robert Browning, "God tempers the wind" in his letter to Mary Speed (1:260). Elsewhere Lincoln uses the designation about 310 times, mostly in the absolute sense as here, but also in various other ways, as the following phrases indicate. All are in Lincoln's words from vol. 1 of the *CW*, although I do not use quotation marks or *Italics*. God forbid (1:165); Would to God (1:268); the noblest work of God—an honest man (1:269). To the Almighty God we commend him (1:269); God grant it may be (1:270); which is God's decree (1:273); God be praised for that (1:282); God made me one of the instruments (1:289); God bless you (1:328); God knows who all (1:394); May God preserve us (1:395); and God grant he may be able (1:442).

The following are from volume 2 of the *CW*. Leave the consequences to God; through the help of God; the God of battles; the providence of God; God speed it; as opposite as God an mammon; God made man; God did not place good and evil before man; responsible to God alone; it has pleased Almighty God; May God in his mercy; so sure as God lives; God is with us; thank God; so surely as God reigns over you; God made us separate; in God's name; and in all God's creation.

Father. It occurs with various attributes as titles, as the examples that follow show.

The common God and Father of all men (5:128, Seward).

Our Heavenly Father (5:478; 8:117; 5:186—8:55, Seward).

The Almighty Father (6:332, Seward).

Our beneficent Father who dwelleth in the Heavens (6:497, Seward).

Our good father in Heaven (2:222). See "Our Father which art in heaven" (Matt 6:9; Luke 11:2).

Your Father in Heaven (2:501). Lincoln uses it three times in a quotation of Matt 5:48 (recall earlier discussion).

High Heaven (1:178).

God in Heaven (3:488).

As with biblical writers, Lincoln thinks of heaven as the dwelling place of God. See Lincoln's "As there is a just and righteous God in Heaven" (3:488) and Deut 4:39; Josh 2:11; 2 Chr 20:6; Dan 2:28; Matt 22:30. Lincoln's words are both a title and attributes. He uses heaven also as a metonym for deity (1:314, 439; 3:239, 541; 6:156, 166; 7:351, 500—6:156, Seward). The kingdom of God in Mark (sixteen times) and Luke (thirty-two times) becomes mostly the kingdom of heaven in Matthew (thirty-two times; kingdom of God, four times). Lincoln does not use either of those designations.

The Father of Mercies (7:533). In 2 Cor 1:3-4 Paul writes: "Blessed be God . . . the Father of mercies, and the God of all comfort; Who comforteth us in all our tribulation." Lincoln's linking of blessing and comfort with the woes of the nation at war coincides with the language and thought of Paul. This may be the best application of a biblical phrase to a context of Lincoln. With Paul's words compare Isa 51:12; 66:13; especially Wis 9:1: "Lord of mercy."

The great Father of us all (6:152).

The God of our Fathers (4:191) C Version of Farewell Address.

God disposes (7:301).

G-d knows (3:509). Orthodox Jews often wrote the name of the deity Yahweh that way in English to signify the omission of the word in speaking because it was too sacred to be pronounced. Lincoln used that designation only in his letter to Norman B. Judd, who may have been Jewish.

Just and righteous God in Heaven (3:488). Here attributes are part of a title.

Supreme Being (4:220-221).

The Great god who made him (5:373).

A Just God (8:333).

The justice and goodness of God (7:282), attributes as part of a title.

The Great Spirit (6:152). This and the title listed next are synonymous in the same sentence of Lincoln spoken to some Indian chiefs who came to Washington to meet with him. He greets them with words from their language. He mentions "wigwams" and calls white people "this pale-faced people" and mentions the differences between them and "their red brethren." The chief reason for the difference is that the former are "numerous and prosperous because they cultivate the earth, produce bread, and depend upon the products of the earth rather than wild game for a subsistence." Again, Lincoln mentions the national situation as another difference: "Although we are now engaged in a great war between one another, we are not, as a race, so much disposed to fight and kill one another as our red brethren." Lincoln is not able to give them advice, and then in terms familiar to them he says: "whether, in the providence of the Great Spirit, who is the great Father of us all," it is best for them "to maintain the habits and customs" of their race or "adopt a new mode of life" (6:152). This is an excellent example of showing how adept Lincoln was at adapting titles of the deity to specific circumstances.

The great Father of us all (6:152).

God of hosts. I cannot find this title in the *CW* (*pace* Wolf, page 180). It occurs forty times in the Old Testament. Lincoln also does not use "Lord of hosts, which occurs 245 times in the Old Testament, but neither title occurs in the New Testament. It is surprising that Lincoln does not use either of those, especially when dealing with military matters.

God of Right (Wolf). It occurs as "the God of the right" in a letter to Charles D. Gilfillan (2:395), an eminent Republican in St. Paul, Minnesota. Lincoln declines an invitation to speak there to assist in the Republican cause during the coming political contests. He concludes the letter: "May the God of the right, give you the victory *now*, as He surely will in the end" (2:395). Lincoln has invented a designation of the deity to express his belief that the Republican cause was the morally right one.

The God of Nations (6:40). Occurs in a communication to Caleb Russell and Sallie A. Fenton, secretaries, written by John Hay and signed by Lincoln.

The Most High (5:498). Occurs four times in the Old Testament and five times in the New Testament. See Num 24:16; Deut 32:8: Pss 50:14; 73:11; 91:1; Acts 7:48.

The Most High God (6:496, Seward). See Gen 14:20; Ps 78:56; Dan 5:18; Mark 5:7; Acts 16:17; Heb 7:1.

Holy Spirit. Does not occur in Lincoln's words, but see His Holy Spirit (6:332, Seward).

A living God (8:333). Occurs in Lincoln's Second Inaugural Address (discussed earlier).

Great and Merciful Maker. It appears as "our great, and good, and merciful Maker" in Lincoln's letter to his step brother, John D. Johnston (2:97; see earlier discussion).

Lord. Lincoln uses this designation many fewer times than he uses God. He writes to Speed, "I say, enough, dear Lord" (1:282), and his text now is a quotation from Exod 14:13: 'Stand still and see the salvation of the Lord' (1:289); whom the Lord made on purpose for such business (1:335); and the Lord knows what (1:477). Lincoln uses Lord in a quotation from Exod 15:1 (2:441), and he calls the quotation from Matt 5:48 'one of the admonitions of the Lord' (2:501). In the first quotation the Lord is God and in the second, Jesus. Lord occurs frequently of God in the Old Testament and of God and Jesus in the New Testament.

Lincoln accuses Douglas of taking any decision of the court as a "Thus saith the Lord" (3:28), and he uses this ubiquitous biblical quotation simply as an ear catcher. During the election campaign of 1860, he wrote to Lyman Trumbull that he remembered "Peter denied his Lord with an oath" after he said he would not. Lincoln says he would not swear that he would not make any commitments, but he thinks he would not. Lincoln uses Lord in the quotation from the Psalms in his Second Inaugural Address (8:33), and he repeats it later (8:367).

Maker (1:382; 2:10, 89, 97; 3:359; 7:334, all in the absolute sense). See Ps 95:6; Prov 14:31; 17:5; 22:2; Isa 17:7; 45:9, 11, 13; 51:13; 54:5; Jer 33:2; Hos 8:14; Heb 11:10. Lincoln uses Maker where Creator might be expected, for example: "when Adam first came from the hand of his Maker" (2:10). But see Gen 2:7: "The Lord God formed man of the dust of the ground" and Gen 2:18: "I will make him an help meet for him."

Supreme ruler of the Universe (7:165, Seward).

Overall, Lincoln's use of deity is comparable to that in certain individual documents, especially his letter to John Johnston about his dying father; the series of letters to Joshua Speed, a nonbeliever; concerning his love affair with Fanny; and later to Eliza Gurley; his remarks to the Indians and to the "Loyal Colored People of Baltimore." From those documents, as from his other documents, we cannot be certain about his personal view of deity.

So what can we conclude from Lincoln's use of innumerable titles, attributes, and actions of the deity? (1) The usage is so frequent and occurs in so many varied contexts that sometimes one or the other borders on frivolity, triteness, and perhaps insincerity. (2) The list, therefore, provides no sure insight into Lincoln's concept of deity or of his religious faith, because what he says occurs most often in political contexts. (3) The origin of Lincoln's faith was political and the basis for it was the documents of the founding fathers, especially the Declaration of Independence and the Constitution. (4) Consequently, Lincoln was motivated by the oath of office he took when he became president and is affirmed in the First Inaugural Address, March 4, 1861 (4:262–71). From the documents, we can learn only about Lincoln's political faith.

(5) However, in spite of all that we have observed, a divine being was surely on Lincoln's mind, and there have been endless discussions of his religion and of his belief in a deity. I do not have the answer, so all I do is suggest one. The multiplicity and variety of titles for and attributes of the deity may well reflect Lincoln's own struggle to comprehend the nature of the deity and its involvement in human affairs. At the same time, that multiplicity and variety seem to indicate that he had not come to a final

conclusion on the subject. If that be true, all attempts to determine his personal belief in a deity are futile.

In his *Introduction to the Science of Religion*, Max Mueller defined religion: "Religion is a mental faculty or disposition, which independent of, nay in spite of, sense and reason, enables man to apprehend the Infinite under different names and under varying guises." Although not published until 1873, it seems to me that Lincoln's understanding of the deity and of religion might be aptly described by that definition.

Appendix 4

Lincoln's Understanding of the Bible

I N HIS COMMUNICATION TO the people of Sangamon County, Illinois, Lincoln regarded *Education*, not *the scriptures*, as the "means" of certain values (1:8). He does not understand the Bible as scripture(s) in the sense of being sacred and authoritative. For that reason he rarely used the words compared with his frequent use of the word Bible. Even in his two lectures on discoveries and inventions, he never uses the word scripture(s), although he cites chapter and verse, which he never does elsewhere.

Lincoln used the word scriptures again in his handbill replying to the charges of infidelity. He admits that he is not a member of any Christian church but that he has "never denied the truth of the Scriptures" (1:382). We must take those words about *never* denying the truth of the scriptures in light of his earlier statement to Mary Speed that he did not doubt that the Bible could be "the best cure for the 'Blues' could one but take it according to the truth" (1:261). Recall Lincoln's befuddlement when he says to Douglas in their last debate that the Bible says somewhere we are desperately selfish but that we would have discovered that fact without the Bible (3:310).

That Lincoln thought of the Bible as literature is confirmed in his use of the word in his Lyceum speech. With his mind on the Declaration of Independence and the Constitution and Laws (1:112), in speaking on the perpetuation of our political institutions, he hopes that "the scenes of the revolution" will be "recounted, so long as the bible shall be read" (1:115). In his Eulogy on Henry Clay (1:121–32), Lincoln says that the abolitionists would "even burn the last copy of the Bible, rather than slavery should continue a single hour." He is aware that in some Bibles there is a text not in his and that the abolitionists "have made more use of it, than of any passage in the Bible." The words that follow are crucial for understanding his use of the Bible in comparison with his view of the Declaration and the Constitution. "As I trace it, from Saint Voltaire, and was baptized by Thomas Jefferson, and since almost universally, regarded as canonical authority '*All men are born free and equal*'" (2:130–31). The documents of our government are "canonical authority," not the Bible.

In a speech at Chicago (2:484–502), Lincoln remarks that his friend the Judge has said he is a poor hand to quote Scripture, the word he uses only because Douglas had used it. He replies by quoting "one of the admonitions of the Lord" about being perfect as the Father in Heaven, which he uses three times, and then mentions the Savior, all of which imply piety. His seeming piety is almost frivolous. The Bible is really not primary in Lincoln's thinking, because he relates the biblical principle of moral perfection to the argument against Douglas that all men are created equal, the admonition to be as nearly reached as possible. The Declaration is primary in his thinking, as his reference to the Constitution a bit later in the speech shows (2:501). Those are what is sacred and authoritative, not the Bible.

The same thing is true in a speech at Springfield (2:504–20), where Lincoln also uses the word scripture because the Judge had said he has "a proneness for quoting scripture." Then he uses a conglomeration of phrases from the parable of the lost sheep, which he says the savior applies to rejoicing in heaven over one sinner who repents more than over ninety-nine just persons who need no repentance (from Luke). Lincoln accused the Judge of taking more credit for the defeat of the Lecompton Constitution than anyone else. If the Judge benefits from the parable, "let him repent." Then instead of returning to the scripture, Lincoln says that repentance before forgiveness "is a provision of the Christian system." Politics, not the scripture, is his concern: "On that condition alone will the Republicans grant his forgiveness" (2:511). Lincoln uses the scripture to ridicule the Judge.

In the Fragment on Pro-slavery Theology (2:222–23), Lincoln says that the Almighty gives no answer to the question if it is the will of God that a slave remain a slave or be set free, "and his revelation—the Bible—gives none—or, at most, none but such as admits of a squabble, as to its meaning" (3:204). Lincoln gives no authoritative answer from the Bible as God's revelation, nor does he imply a special sanctity of the Bible, as Dr. Ross had. This is comparable to his statement that we could have discovered the fact of human selfishness without the Bible.

In his lectures on discoveries and inventions (2:437–42; 3:356–63), although the Bible is the basis for what he says, there is nothing in them to indicate that he thought of it as being especially sacred or authoritative. In fact, in the second lecture, he says about the origin of speech and Adam naming the animals, "it would appear that speech was not an invention of man, but rather the direct gift of his Creator. But whether Divine gift, or invention, it is still plain that if a mode of communication had been left to invention," it must have been an adaptation of the organs of speech (3:359). Later in the lecture, Lincoln lists the Bible with history, science, government, commerce, and about all social communication as the things that would be gone if phonetic writing were taken away (3:361). Here he also thought of the Bible as literature, without implying sanctity (for other examples of the same kind, see 3:438–62; 4:13–30; 5:419–25).

I have suggested that Lincoln used the speech of the one who presented the Bible to him from the "loyal colored people of Baltimore" (7:542–43) as a rough outline for his impromptu acceptance speech. It is interesting, and perhaps informative, to observe that the presenter used the designations "Bible" and "Holy Scriptures" and that Lincoln did not use either in his reply. Instead, he really laid it on for his special audience with his praise and terminology for the Bible he never uses elsewhere. Here we should compare Lincoln's not knowing right from wrong without the Bible with his comments to Douglas that we would have learned the fact we are desperately selfish without the Bible.

Terminology Lincoln uses to introduce language from the Bible provides an important clue to his understanding of it. He uses several common designations with respect to other literature and to the Bible without implications of sanctity. The following are examples.

With respect to the U. S. invasion of Mexico, Lincoln asks John M. Peck, a prominent Baptist clergyman, "Is the precept 'Whatsoever ye would that men should do to you, do ye even so to them'" obsolete and not applicable? (1:473).

In a speech at Peoria, Lincoln appeals to all his fellow countrymen not to let slavery, "the one retrograde institution in America," destroy "the noblest political system in the world." He asks if there is no danger "to liberty itself, in discarding the earliest practice, and the *first precept of our ancient faith*." He leaves no doubt that he has in mind the Declaration of Independence by appealing to the audience "to turn slavery from its claims of 'moral right,' back upon its existing legal rights, and the argument of 'necessity.' Let us return it to the position our fathers gave it; and then let it rest in peace. Let us re-adopt the Declaration of Independence, and with it, the practices, and policy, which harmonize with it" (2:276). Who could hear or read the fine rhetoric and not realize that the Declaration has a sanctity and authority greater than the passage he had cited from the Bible as a precept?

Lincoln makes the same appeal to the audience in his Cooper Union speech. He speaks about the times of Washington and "our fathers who framed the Government under which we live." With the same kind of emphatic rhetoric, Lincoln says: "If you would have the peace of the old times, readopt *the precepts and policies* of the old times." In the conclusion to his speech, he cites a saying of Jesus as *"the divine rule,"* but immediately afterward he leaves all thought of the Bible and returns to politics. Lincoln used the same ear catching phrase to introduce the same quotation of Jesus in the conclusion to his speeches at Dover, New Hampshire (3:554) and at New Haven, Connecticut (4:30). Recall the discussion of *"one of the admonitions of the Lord"* to introduce a quotation from Matt 5:48.

Lincoln's favorite word for introducing sayings of various kinds, including some from the Bible, is maxim, which he uses for the first time in his communication to the people of Sangamon County. Near the end he says he holds it "a sound maxim, that it is better to be only sometimes right, than at all times wrong" (1:8). Regarded as a famous saying, it originated with Lincoln. Hereafter, he uses the same word about twenty-four times with various subjects. You will find interesting and informative examples of how Lincoln uses a maxim, which he sometimes coined to fit the occasion, in the *CW*: 1:64, 273, 280; 2:318, 352, 406; 3:17, 92, 98, 111, 122–23, 130, 481; 4:142, 149; and 5:65.

Lincoln's use of maxim in various circumstances and applications provides insight into his use of the word with reference to the Bible. When speaking about the character of political candidates at the end of a speech at Cincinnati, Lincoln says: "The good old maxims of the Bible are applicable, and truly applicable to human affairs" (3:462). Here the word maxim is no more authoritative because he uses it with reference to the Bible than any of the other times he uses it.

There is no conclusive evidence that Lincoln believed the Bible was sacred and authoritative with respect to the issue of slavery. On the other hand, there is conclusive evidence that he believed the Declaration of Independence and the Constitution were sacred and authoritative documents of enduring value for determining the immorality of slavery. He also shows influence from those documents unlike anything he says about the Bible.

In the Lyceum Address, Lincoln warns against mob violence that threatens Government. In order to guard against it: "As the patriots of seventy-six did to the support of the Declaration of Independence, so to the support of the Constitution and Laws, let every American pledge his life, his liberty, and his sacred honor . . . Let reverence for the Laws . . . let it become the *political religion* of the nation." Among the means of its communication, it is to be preached from the pulpit (1:112). Consider also Lincoln's question about a sub-treasury: "Was the sacred name of Democracy, ever before made to endorse such an enormity against the rights of the people?" (1:162).

Speaking in the U.S. House of Representatives, Lincoln criticizes President Polk for the war against Mexico and says that any people "has the *right*" to overthrow the present government and form a new government that suits them. "This is a most valuable,—a most sacred right—a right, which we hope and believe, is to liberate the world" (1:438).

At the invitation of the Mayor Alexander Henry of Philadelphia, on February 21, 1861, Lincoln said he would join him "to listen to those breathings rising within the consecrated walls where the Constitution of the United States, and . . . the Declaration of Independence was originally formed" (4:239). Lincoln thought even the walls of the building were sacred. These statements reveal a sense of sacredness and authority unlike anything Lincoln ever says about the Bible.

The evidence presented in this appendix leads to the conclusion that Lincoln did not think of material from the Bible as any more sacred than passages from other literature, which he introduced in the same way as those from the Bible. For Lincoln the Declaration of Independence and the United States Constitution were sacred and authoritative documents. Nevertheless, he soon learned that the Bible was an effective means to winning support for his political ambitions and for achieving his goals established in his Second Inaugural Address for the reconstruction, reconciliation, and re-union of the divided Nation, and peace among all people, without revenge against any.

Appendix 5

Lincoln's Relationships with The Reverends James Smith and Phineas Densmore Gurley

THERE IS EVIDENCE FOR questioning the tradition, still widely accepted, that the Rev. James Smith, pastor of First Baptist Church in Springfield and later in Washington, DC, and the Rev. Phineas D. Gurley, pastor of New York Avenue Presbyterian Church, Washington, DC, were special friends of Lincoln who had great influence in shaping his biblical faith. The tradition about Smith is fully accepted by White (*Greatest Speech*, 129–32), Carwardine (36–38), and Fornieri (*Political Faith*, 56–57, 140) and ignored by Thomas, Donald, and Burton. Guelzo (*Abraham Lincoln*, 149–52, 157, 188, 323) accepts the tradition and says that Lincoln "also handed diplomatic posts to politically friendly clergymen, including James Smith" (323). But how diplomatic was Lincoln in his consideration of his "friend" Smith for such a post? In the *CW* there is no record of any communication between only Lincoln and Smith. In a communication from thirty-nine men to James Smith, January 24, 1853 (2:188), expressing their "great satisfaction" on his "discourse on the subject of temperance," Lincoln's signature is the last on the list of "Your friends." We should hardly think of Lincoln as a better friend of Smith than the other men.

There is one instance that may indicate a friendship of the two men. According to the *Lincoln Log*, June 11, 1861, "Lincoln's former pastor, Dr. James A. Smith of Springfield, is visiting at Executive Mansion. *Baltimore Sun*, 12 June 1861." This probably indicates nothing more than a casual, friendly visit among men who respected each other. If it means more than that, it is difficult to explain what follows.

Lincoln had been informed that Dr. James Smith was removed from the position of acting consul at Dundee, Scotland, and that his son Hugh was appointed to that office in 1861 (6:51–52), but because of illness he turned over duties of the office to his father. In a note to William H. Seward, January 9, 1863 (6:51–52), Lincoln nominated "Dr. Smith . . . an intimate personal friend of mine" for the position. Then Lincoln adds: "and I have unconsciously superseded him, if at all. Sec. of State please inform me how it is." Is it not a bit strange that Lincoln would supersede such a close personal friend consciously or unconsciously? In a later communication to Seward, January 14, 1863 (6:58), an intimate personal friendship between Lincoln and Smith is even less certain. Apparently, Lincoln had nominated a Mr. Hall for the consulship, but he did not accept it. Learning that, Lincoln writes to Seward: "and as I was unconscious, in appointing Mr. Hall, (if I did it) that I was interfering with my old friend, Dr. Smith. I will be obliged if the Sec. of State will send me a nomination for Rev. James Smith, of Ills. for that Consulate" (6:58). On February 18, 1863, the Senate confirmed the nomination for the consulship.

If James Smith was a "conservative Democrat" (Guelzo, *Redeemer President*, 151), did that have a bearing on Lincoln's strange actions about Smith's appointment to Dundee? And should that matter if the two men were such personal intimate friends?

In all of this, we learn nothing substantive about the personal relationship between Lincoln and Smith. And all of this took place almost a year after the death of Lincoln's son Willie on February 20, 1862, after which Lincoln and Smith are said to have become such good personal friends. Moreover, Lincoln had a propensity for adding superlatives to the names of his "friends." He refers to a "Geo. C. Beilor" as "my intimate personal friend" (5:82). We cannot identify the person referred to or even the correct name and spelling (5:82). Other designations are "my personal friend" (2:43, 47; often), "my good personal and political friend" (2:38), "my esteemed friend" (2:48), "my good friend (4:51, often), "my especial friend" (7:27), "our gallant and brave friend" (7:88). Should not Lincoln's glowing expressions of friendships raise some doubt about the validity of the tradition of his special friendship with the Rev. James Smith, whom he calls "an intimate personal friend"?

There is a similar difficulty with the tradition of a deep special friendship between Lincoln and the Rev. Phineas Densmore Gurley and his influence on the religious thought of Lincoln, especially after the death of Willie. This tradition is generally accepted by scholars, for example, Wolf (pages 126, 128, and note 20, page 209), White (*Greatest Speech*, 131–33, 138–40, 147, 154), Fornieri (*Political Faith*, 57–58, 172),

Carwardine (223–24), Thomas (478–79), Trueblood (74, 101, 115–16), Donald (337, 599), and Current (54, 64, 72). They and other scholars are greatly influenced in what they say about Lincoln and Gurley based on the dubious assumption that Lincoln regularly attended Gurley's church.

First, there is conflicting evidence about when Lincoln first met Gurley. According to Barton (2, 42), on Sunday, March 10, 1861, the Lincoln family attended church at New York Avenue Presbyterian Church, where Gurley was pastor. Presumably, Lincoln would have met Gurley then. However, according to another account (see Appendix 2), the President attended the same church on April 14, 1861, "and meets Pastor, Dr. Gurley," a typical contradiction in the lore. According to the *Lincoln Log*, on October 5, 1861, "Lincoln receives a request from Dr. Gurley to send Rev. Henry Hopkins of Massachusetts as chaplain to Alexandria, Va.," the kind of request Lincoln received many times.

On February 24, 1862, Gurley conducted the funeral service for Willie at the White House (*National Intelligencer*, 25 February 1862). That service and Gurley's ministering to the family at the time are ministerial duties one would expect of any pastor ministering to his parishioners. The formal communications that follow more than a year later indicate nothing about a special personal relationship between the two men. On August 10, 1863, Gurley wrote a letter to Lincoln "on behalf of the Rev. Peyton Harrison, an excellent and venerable minister of the Old School Pres. Church who is now under arrest." Lincoln wrote a note to Robert C. Schenck, c. August 10, 1863 (6:378), "the officer in command in Baltimore," to take no further action toward Harrison until ordered to do so. Again, this is typical of requests Lincoln received, considered, and finalized. For another note of the same kind by Gurley see 8:291. There is no record that Lincoln ever responded to Gurley personally.

Contrast the terminology Lincoln uses when writing to persons known as personal friends: "Dear Mack [John McNamar]. . . . your friend" (1:60); "Dear Fell [Jesse W. Fell]. . . . Your friend" (1:120); "Dear Stuart [John T. Stuart]. . . . Your friend" (1:143); "Dear Butler [William Butler]. . . . Your friend in spite of your ill-nature" (1:140); "Dear Butler . . .Your friend as ever" (1:141); "Dear Row [John Rowan Herndon]. . . .Your friend, as ever" (1:150); "Dear Speed [Joshua F. Speed]. . . . Yours forever" (1:257); "Dear William [William H. Herndon] . . . Yours as ever" (2:118–19). These observations must be considered in any further discussion of Lincoln and his friends the Reverends Smith and Gurley.

Finally, there is no record that Lincoln ever spoke about Smith or Gurley in such affectionate terms of friendship as he does to known friends. Here are some examples.

To Robert Allen: "never break the tie of personal friendship between us" (1:49).

To Joshua F. Speed: "Ever your friend" (1:306) and "a friendship such as ours . . . As ever, Yours" (1:391).

To William H. Herndon: "suspect nothing but sincere friendship. . . . Your friend, as ever" (497–98).

To Joseph Gillespie: "The better part of one's life consists of his friendships; and, of those, mine with Mr. Edwards was one of the most cherished . . . To lose his friendship . . . would oppress me very much . . . my uniform and strong friendship for him . . . Your friend, as ever" (2:57–59).

To William Kellogg: "I believe you will not doubt the sincerity of my friendship for you. Yours very truly" (3:507).

To Robert C. Schenck: "I esteem Gov. Francis Thomas . . . He has given me evidence of sincere friendship" (6:239).

To Stephen A. Hurlbut: "my friendship and confidence for you remains unabated" (7:327).

To Nathaniel P. Banks: "I entertain no abatement of confidence, or friendship for you" (8:131).

We might think that if Smith and Gurley were such good friends of Lincoln some correspondence between him and them would have been preserved.

Based on the evidence of the *CW*, as with the case of the Rev. James Smith, there is not a single communication of Lincoln to Gurley. Edgar DeWitte Jones (37) reproduces some writings of Dr. Gurley, who refers to himself "as Mr. Lincoln's pastor and intimate friend." If a closer friendship developed after Willie's funeral, Lincoln did not make a special effort to get to Gurley's church and occasionally attended other churches in Washington on Sunday.

Undoubtedly, Phineas D. Gurley belonged to the "Old School Presbyterian Theology." However, how often Lincoln listened to Gurley's preaching is questionable. The undocumented statements of White (131–32) that "from the spring of 1861 to the spring of 1865, he [Gurley] preached to Abraham Lincoln" must be reconsidered. From January 6, 1861, until March 15, 1865, there is record of Lincoln attending New York Avenue Presbyterian Church no more than eight times, and he may have heard Gurley one or two other times. Whenever the Lincolns did attend church, it was sure to be in the news.

Bibliography

Abbot, Richard H. *Cotton and Capital: Boston Businessmen and Antislavery Reform, 1854–1868.* Amherst: University of Massachusetts Press, 1991.

Anastaplo, George. *Abraham Lincoln: A Constitutional Biography.* New York: Oxford University Press, 1999.

Anderson, Dwight G. et al. "Quest for Immortality: A Theory of Abraham Lincoln's Political Psychology." In *The Historian's Lincoln,* edited by Gabor S. Boritt and Norman O. Forness, 253–84. Urbana: University of Illinois Press, 1996.

Angle, Paul M., editor. *Herndon's Life of Lincoln.* New Introduction by Henry Steele Commager. New York: Da Capo, 1942.

———, and Earl Schenck Miers, editors. *The Living Lincoln.* New Brunswick, NJ: Rutgers University Press, 1955.

Arnold, Isaac Newton. *The Life of Abraham Lincoln.* 4th ed. Lincoln: University of Nebraska Press, 1994.

Attie, Jeanie. *Patriotic Toil: Northern Women and the American Civil War.* Ithaca, NY: Cornell University Press, 1998.

Babcock, Bernie. *The Soul of Abe Lincoln.* New York: Grosset & Dunlap, 1919.

Baker-Benfield, G. J. *The Honors of the Half-Known Life: Male Attitudes toward Women in Nineteenth Century America.* New York: Rutledge, 2000.

Banton, Blanton, and Lauren M. Cook. *They Fought Like Demons: Women in the Civil War.* Baton Rouge: Louisiana State University Press, 2002.

Barbee, David Rankin. "President Lincoln and Doctor Gurley." *The Abraham Lincoln Quarterly* 5 (1948) 3.

Barrett, Oliver R. *The Immortal Autograph Letters, Documents, Manuscripts, Portraits, Personal Relics, and Other Lincolniana.* New York: Parke-Berret, 1952.

Barton, William E. *Abraham Lincoln and His Books.* Chicago: Marshall Field, 1920.

———. *The Life of Abraham Lincoln.* 2 vols. London: Arrowsmith, 1925.

———. *The Soul of Abraham Lincoln.* New York: Doran, 1920.

Belz, Herman. *Reconstructing the Union: Theory and Policy during the Civil War.* Ithaca, NY: Cornell University Press, 1969.

———. *Abraham Lincoln, Constitutionalism, and Equal Rights in the Civil War Era.* New York: Fordham University Press, 1998.

Benson, Godfrey Rathbone. *Abraham Lincoln.* New York: Holt, 1917.

Beran, Michael Knox. *Forge of Empires, 1801–1871: The Revolutionary Statesmen and the World They Made.* New York: Free Press, 2007.

Boritt, Gabor S. *The Gettysburg Gospel: The Lincoln Speech That Nobody Knows.* New York: Simon & Schuster, 2005.

———. *Lincoln and The Economics of The American Dream.* Memphis University Press, 1978.

———, editor. *The Lincoln Enigma: The Changing Faces of an American Icon.* Oxford University Press, 2001.

Boritt, Gabor S., and Norman O. Forness, editors. *The Historian's Lincoln: Pseudohistory, Psychohistory, and History*. Urbana: University of Illinois Press, 1996.

Boritt, Gabor et al. *Of The People, By The People, For The People and Other Quotations from Abraham Lincoln*. New York: Columbia University Press, 1996.

Boylan, Anne M. *The Origins of Women's Activism: New York and Boston, 1797–1840*. Chapel Hill: University of North Carolina Press, 2002.

Briggs, John Channing. *Lincoln's Speeches Reconsidered*. Baltimore: Johns Hopkins University Press, 2005.

Brooks, Noah. "Personal Reminiscences of Lincoln." *Scribner's Monthly* 15 (1878) 561–69.

———. "Personal Reminiscences of Lincoln." *Scribner's Monthly* 15 (1878) 673–81.

———. "Recollections of Abraham Lincoln." *Harper's Magazine* 30 (1865) 229.

Browne, Francis Fisher. *The Everyday Life of Abraham Lincoln*. Lincoln: University of Nebraska Press, 1995.

Burlingame, Michael. *The Inner World of Abraham Lincoln*. Urbana: University of Illinois Press, 1994.

———. "New Light on the Bixby Letter." *Journal of the Abraham Lincoln Association* 16 (1955) 1–30.

———. *With Lincoln in the White House: Letters, Memoranda, and Other Writings of John G. Nocolay, 1860–1865*. Carbondale: Southern Illinois University Press, 2000.

———, editor. *Benjamin P. Thomas, "Lincoln's Humor" and Other Essays*. Urbana: University of Illinois Press, 2002.

Burlingame, Michael, and John R. Turner Ellinger. *Inside Lincolns' Whitehouse: The Complete Civil War Diary of John Hay*. Carbondale: Southern Illinois University Press, 1997.

Burt, John. "Lincoln's Address to the Young Men's Lyceum: A Speculative Essay." *Western Humanities Review* 51 (1997) 304–20.

Burton, Orville Vernon. *The Age of Lincoln*. New York: Farrar, Strauss & Giroux, 2007.

Carpenter, F. B. *Six Months at the White House*. New York: Hurd and Houghton, 1866.

Carwardine, Richard J. *Lincoln*. London: Pearson Longman, 2003.

———. *Lincoln: A Life of Purpose and Power*. New York: Knopf, 2006.

Chittenden, L. E. *Recollections of President Lincoln and His Administration*. New York: Harper & Brothers, 1891.

Clinton, Catherine. *Harriet Tubman: The Road to Freedom*. Boston: Little, Brown, 2004.

———. *The Other Civil War: American Women in the Nineteenth Century*. Rev. ed. New York: Hill and Wang, 1999.

———, and Nina Silber, editors. *Divided Houses: Gender and the Civil War*. New York: Oxford University Press, 1992.

Coleman, Charles H. *Abraham Lincoln and Coles County, Illinois*. Brunswick, NJ: Scarecrow, 1955.

Cott, Nancy F. *The Bonds of Womanhood: "Women's Sphere" in New England, 1780–1835*. New Haven: Yale University Press, 1997.

Current, Richard., editor. *The Political Thought of Abraham Lincoln*. Indianapolis: Bobbs-Merrill, 1967.

Curtis, William Elroy. *The True Abraham Lincoln*. Philadelphia: Lippincott, 1919.

Cutler, Barbara. *Domestic Devils, Battlefield Angels: The Radicalism of American Womanhood, 1830–1865*. Dekalb: Northern Illinois University Press, 2003.

Dillon, Merton L. *The Abolitionists: The Growth of a Dissenting Minority*. Dekalb: Northern Illinois University Press, 1974.

DiLorenzo, Thomas J. *The Real Lincoln: A New Look at Abraham Lincoln, His Agenda, and Unnecessary War*. Roseville, CA: Prema, 2003.

Donald, David Herbert. *Lincoln*. London: Cape, 1995.

———. *We Are Lincoln Men: Abraham Lincoln and His Friends*. New York: Simon & Schuster, 2003.

Douglas, Ann. *The Feminization of American Culture*. New York: Knopf, 1978.

Dubois, Ellen Carol. *Feminism and Suffrage: The Emergence of an Independent Women's Movement in America, 1848–1869*. Ithaca, NY: Cornell University Press, 1999.

Du Bois, W. E. B. *John Brown*. Edited by David R. Roediger. New York: Random House, 2001.

Endy, Melvin B. "Abraham Lincoln and American Civil Religion: A Reinterpretation." *Church History* 44 (1975) 229–41.

Fehenbacher, Don E. *Abraham Lincoln: Speeches and Writings, 1832–1865*. 2 vols. New York: Literary Classics of the United States, 1989.

———. *Prelude to Greatness: Lincoln in the 1850s*. Stanford: Stanford University Press, 1962.

Fehrenbacher, Virginia, and Mark E. Neely, editors. *Recollected Words of Abraham Lincoln*. Stanford: Stanford University Press, 1996.

Filler, Louis. *The Crusade Against Slavery: Friends, Foes, and Reforms*. Algonac, MI: Reference Publications, 1986.

Fletcher, George P. *Our Secret Constitution: How Lincoln Redefined American Democracy*. New York: Oxford University Press, 2001.

Foher, Philip S. *Frederick Douglas: A Biography*. New York: Citadel, 1964.

Foner, Eric. *Nothing But Freedom: Emancipation and Its Legacy*. Baton Rouge: Louisiana State University Press, 1989.

———. *Reconstruction: America's Unfinished Revolution, 1863–1877*. New York: Harper & Row, 1988.

Fornieri, Joseph R. *Abraham Lincoln's Political Faith*. DeKalb: Northern Illinois University Press, 2005.

———. *The Language of Liberty: The Political Speeches and Writings of Abraham Lincoln*. Washington, DC: Regnery, 2009.

Fredrickson, George M. *The Inner Civil War: Northern Intellectuals and the Crisis of the Union*. New York: Harper & Row, 1965.

———. "A Man but Not a Brother: Abraham Lincoln and Radical Equality." *Journal of Southern History* 41 (1975) 39–58.

———. "The Search for Order and Community." In *The Public and Private Lincoln: Contemporary Perspectives*, edited by Cullom Davis, et al., 86–98. Carbondale: Southern Illinois University Press, 1979.

Goodwin, Doris Kearns, *Rivals: The Political Genius of Abraham Lincoln*. New York: Simon & Schuster, 2005.

Guelzo, Allen C. *Abraham Lincoln: The Religion of a President and the Ideas of His Time*. Grand Rapids: Eerdmans, 1999.

———. *Abraham Lincoln: Redeemer President*. Grand Rapids: Eerdmans, 1999.

———. *Lincoln's Emancipation Proclamation: The End of Slavery in America*. New York: Simon & Schuster, 2004.

Hamlin, Hannibal. *The Soul of the Bible. being selections from the Old & New Testaments & the Apocrypha*, edited by Ulysses B. Pierce. Boston: Beacon, 1921.

Harris, William C. *With Charity for All: Lincoln and the Restoration of the Union.* Lexington: University Press of Kentucky, 1997.

———. *Lincoln's Rise to the Presidency.* Lawrence: University Press of Kansas, 2007.

Harrold, Stanley. *The Abolitionists and the South, 1831–1861.* Lexington: University Press of Kentucky, 1999.

———. *Subversives: Antislavery Community in Washington, D.C., 1828–1865.* Baton Rouge: Louisiana State University Press, 2003.

Hein, David. "Research on Lincoln's Religious Belief and Practices: A Bibliographical Essay." *Lincoln Herald* 86 (1984) 2–5.

Herndon, William H., and Jesse Weik. *Abraham Lincoln: The True Story of a Great Life.* 2 vols. New York: Appleton, 1893.

Hill, John Wesley. *Abraham Lincoln, Man of God.* New York: Putnam, 1920.

Hoffert, Silvia D. *When Hens Crow: The Women's Rights Movement in Antebellum America.* Bloomington: Indiana University Press, 1955.

Holland, Josiah Gilbert. *The Life of Abraham Lincoln.* Springfield, MA: Gurdon Bill, 1866.

Holzer, Harold. *Lincoln as I Knew Him: Gossip, Tributes, and Revelations from His Best Friends and Worst Enemies.* Chapel Hill: Algonquin Books of Chapel Hill, 1999.

———. *Lincoln at Cooper Union: The Speech That Made Abraham Lincoln President.* New York: Simon & Schuster, 2005.

———. *The Lincoln Image: Abraham Lincoln and the Popular Print.* New York: Scribner, 1984.

———. *Lincoln Seen and Heard.* Lawrence: University Press of Kansas, 2000.

Horner, Harlan Hoyt. *The Growth of Lincoln's Faith.* New York: Abingdon, 1939.

Houser, M. L. *Some Religious Influences Which Surrounded Lincoln.* Peoria, IL: Schriver, 1941.

Jackson, Samuel Trevena. *Lincoln's Use of the Bible.* New York: Abingdon, 1920.

Jaffa, Harry V. *The Conditions of Freedom: Essays in Political Philosophy.* Baltimore: Johns Hopkins University Press, 1975.

———. *A New Birth of Freedom: Abraham Lincoln and the Coming of the Civil War.* Lanham, MD: Rowman & Littlefield, 2000.

Jayne, Allen. *Lincoln and the American Manifesto.* Amherst, NY: Prometheus, 2007.

Johannsen, Robert W. *Lincoln: The South and Slavery: The Political Dimension.* Baton Rouge: Louisiana State University Press, 1991.

Johnson, William J. *Abraham Lincoln the Christian.* New York: Eaton & Mains, 1913.

Johnstone, William J. *How Lincoln Prayed.* New York: Abingdon, 1931.

Lamon, Ward Hill. *The Life of Abraham Lincoln from His Birth to His Inauguration.* Boston: Osgood, 1872.

Laurie, Bruce. *Beyond Garrison: Antislavery and Social Reform.* New York: Cambridge University Press, 2006.

Leonard, Elizabeth D. *Yankee Women: Gender Battles in the Civil War.* New York: Norton, 1997.

Levine, Bruce. *Half Slave and Half Free: The Roots of Civil War.* New York: Farrar, Straus & Giroux, 2005.

Lindstrom, Ralph G. *Lincoln Finds God.* New York: Longmans, Green, 1958.

Loewen, James W. *Lies My Teacher Told Me: Everything Your American History Textbook Got Wrong.* New York: Simon & Schuster, 2007.

McFreely, William S. *Frederick Douglas.* New York: Norton, 1995.

McPherson, James M. *Abraham Lincoln and the Second American Revolution*. New York: Oxford University Press, 1991.

———. *Battle Cry of Freedom: The Civil War Era*. New York: Oxford University Press, 2003.

———. *Drawn with the Sword: Reflections on the American Civil War*. New York: Oxford University Press, 1996.

———. *Ordeal by Fire: The Civil War and Reconstruction*. 3rd ed. New York: McGraw-Hill, 2000.

———. *"This Mighty Scourge": Perspectives on the Civil War*. New York: Oxford University Press, 2007.

———. *The Struggle for Equality: Abolitionists and the Negro in the Civil War and Reconstruction*. 2nd ed. Princeton: Princeton University Press, 1995.

Miers, Earl Schenck, editor. *Lincoln Day by Day: A Chronology, 1809–1865*. 3 vols. Washington, DC: Lincoln Sesquicentennial Commission, 1982.

Milgang, Herbert. *The Fiery Trial: A Life of Lincoln*. New York: Viking, 1974.

Miller, Randall et al., editors. *Religion and the American Civil War*. New York: Oxford University Press, 1998.

Miller, William Lee. *Lincoln's Virtues: An Ethical Biography*. New York: Knopf, 2002.

Moorhead, James H. *American Apocalypse: Yankee Protestants and the Civil War, 1860–1869*. New Haven: Yale University Press, 1978.

Morel, Lucas E. "Lincoln's Political Religion and Religious Politics." In *Lincoln Revisited: New Insights from the Lincoln Forum*, edited by John Y. Simon et al., 19–44. New York: Fordham University Press, 2007.

Neely, Mark E. *The Abraham Lincoln Encyclopedia*. New York: McGraw-Hill, 1984.

———. *The Fate of Liberty: Abraham Lincoln and Civil Liberties*. New York: Oxford University Press, 1991.

———. *The Last Best Hope of Earth: Abraham Lincoln and the Promise of America*. Cambridge: Harvard University Press, 1993.

Neilson, William. *Exercises on the Syntax of the Greek Language*. New York: Swords, Stanford, 1842.

Nevins, Allan. "Lincoln and His Writings." In *The Life and Writings of Abraham Lincoln*, edited by Philip Van Doran Stern, xii–xvii. New York: Random House, 1940.

Nicolay, John G., and John Hay, editors. *Complete Works of Abraham Lincoln*. 12 vols. New York: Tandy, 1905.

Noll, Mark A. *America's God: From Jonathan Edwards to Abraham Lincoln*. New York: Oxford University Press, 2002.

———. "The Bible and Slavery." In *Religion and the American Civil War*, edited by Randall M. Miller et al. New York: Oxford University Press, 1998.

———. "Both Pray to the Same God:" The Singularity of Lincoln's Faith in the Era of the Civil War." *Journal of the Abraham Lincoln Association* 18 (1997) 1–26.

———. *The Civil War as a Theological Crisis*. Chapel Hill: University of North Carolina Press, 2006.

Nye, Russell B. *William Garrison and the Humanitarian Reformers*. New York: Little, Brown, 1995.

Oates, Stephen B. *Abraham Lincoln: The Man Behind the Myths*. New York: Harper & Row, 1984.

———. *With Malice Toward None: The Life of Abraham Lincoln*. New York: HarperCollins, 1994.

Ostergard, Philip. *The Inspired Wisdom of Abraham Lincoln: How the Bible and Christianity Shaped an American President*. Carol Stream, IL: Tyndale, 2008.

Ostervald, J. F. *La Sainte Bible*. Paris: 58, rue de Clichy, 1794.

Packard, Jerold M. *The Lincolns in the White House: Four Years That Shattered a Family*. New York: St. Martins, 2005.

Paludan, Philip Shaw. *A People's Contest: The Union and the Civil War, 1861–1865*. New York: HarperCollins, 1989.

———. *The Presidency of Abraham Lincoln*. Lawrence: University Press of Kansas, 1994.

Parish, Peter J. *The American Civil War*. New York: Holmes & Meier, 1995.

Peterson, Merrill D. *Lincoln in American Memory*. New York: Oxford University Press, 1994.

Rable, George C. *Civil Wars: Women and the Crisis of Southern Nationalism*. Urbana: University of Illinois Press, 1989.

Randall, James G. *Civil War and Reconstruction*. Rev. ed. Edited by David H. Donald, et al. Lexington, ME: Heath, 1969.

———. *Constitutional Problems Under Lincoln*. Rev. ed. Urbana: University of Illinois Press, 1951.

———. *Mr. Lincoln*. Edited by Richard N. Current. New York: Dodd, Mead, 1957.

———, and Richard N. Current. *Lincoln the President: Last Full Measure*. New York: Dodd, Mead, 1955.

Rankin, Henry B. *Personal Recollections of Abraham Lincoln*. New York: Knickerbocker, 1916.

Reck, Emerson W. *Lincoln: His Last 24 Hours*. Jefferson, NC: McFarland, 1987.

Sandburg, Carl. *Abraham Lincoln: The Prairie Years*. 2 vols. New York: Harcourt, Brace, 1926.

———. *Abraham Lincoln: The War Years*. 4 vols. New York: Harcourt, Brace & World, 1939.

Schwartz, Barry. *Abraham Lincoln and the Forge of National Memory*. Chicago: University of Chicago Press, 2000.

Schwartz, Thomas F. "The Springfield Lyceums and Lincoln's 1838 Speech." *Illinois Historical Journal* 83 (1990) 45–49.

Scripps, John Locke. *Lincoln: The First Biography of Him*. 1860. Reprint, Detroit: Cranbrook, 1900.

Shenk, Joshua Wolf. *Lincoln's Melancholy: How Depression Challenged a President and Fueled His Greatness*. Boston: Houghton Mifflin, 2005.

Silber, Nina. *Daughters of the Union: Northern Women Fight the Civil War*. Cambridge: Harvard University Press, 2005.

Simon, John Y. et al., editors. *Lincoln Revisited: New Insights from the Lincoln Forum*. New York: Fordham University Press, 2007.

Simon, Paul. *Lincoln's Preparation for Greatness: The Legislative Years*. Urbana: University of Illinois Press, 1990.

Steers, Edward Jr. *Lincoln Legends, Myths, Hoaxes, and Confabulations Associated with Our Greatest President*. With an Introduction by Harold Holzer. Lexington: University Press of Kentucky, 2007.

Stoddard, William Osborn. *The Boy Lincoln*. New York: Appleton, 1905.

Stout, Harry S. *Upon the Altar of the Nation: A Moral History of the American Civil War*. New York: Viking, 2006.

Tarbell, Ida M. *The Life of Abraham Lincoln.* 2 vols. New York: Doubleday & McClure, 1900.

Thomas, Benjamin P. *Abraham Lincoln: A Biography.* New York: Modern Library, 1952.

Thomas, John L. *The Liberator, William Lloyd Garrison: A Biography.* Boston: Little, Brown, 1963.

Thompson, Kenneth W., editor. *Essays on Lincoln's Faith and Politics.* Lanham, MD: University Press of America, 1983.

Thurow, Glen E. *Abraham Lincoln and American Political Religion.* Albany: State University of New York Press, 1976.

———. "Abraham Lincoln and American Political Religion." In *The Historian's Lincoln,* edited by Gabor S. Boritt, and Norman O. Forness, 125–42. Urbana: University of Illinois Press, 1988.

Tripp, C. A. *The Intimate World of Abraham Lincoln.* Edited by Lewis Gannett. New York: Free Press, 2005.

Trueblood, Elton. *Abraham Lincoln: Theologian of American Anguish.* New York: Harper & Row, 1973.

Weik, Jesse. *The Real Lincoln.* New York: Houghton Mifflin, 1922.

White, Ronald C. Jr. *A. Lincoln: A Biography.* New York: Random House, 2009.

———. *The Eloquent President: A Portrait of Lincoln Through His Words.* New York: Random House, 2005.

———. *Liberty and Justice for All: Racial Reform and the Social Gospel.* Louisville: Westminster John Knox, 2002.

———. *Lincoln's Greatest Speech: The Second Inaugural.* New York: Simon & Schuster, 2002.

———. *The Social Gospel: Religious Reform in Changing America.* Philadelphia: Temple University Press, 1996.

Wieck, Carl F. *Lincoln's Quest for Equality: The Road to Gettysburg.* DeKalb: Northern Illinois University Press, 2002.

Wilson, Douglas L. *Honor's Voice: The Transformation of Abraham Lincoln.* New York: Knopf, 1998.

———. *Lincoln Before Washington: New Perspectives on the Illinois Years.* Urbana: University of Illinois Press, 1997.

———. *Lincoln's Sword: The Presidency and the Power of Words.* New York: Knopf, 2007.

———. "William H. Herndon and His Lincoln Informants." *Journal of the Abraham Lincoln Association* 14 (1993) 1–35.

Wilson, Douglas L., and Rodney O. Davis, editors. *Herndon's Informants: Letters, Interviews, and Statements about Abraham Lincoln.* Urbana and Chicago: University of Illinois Press, 1998.

Wilson, Rufus Rockwell. *What Lincoln Read.* Washington, DC: Pioneer, 1932.

Winger, Stewart Lance. *Lincoln, Religion, and Romantic Cultural Politics.* DeKalb: Northern Illinois University Press, 2003.

Wolf, William J. *The Almost Chosen People: A Study of the Religion of Abraham Lincoln.* Garden City, NY: Doubleday, 1959.

Zall, Paul M. *Lincoln on Lincoln.* Lexington: University Press of Kentucky, 1999.